LOGIC

Key Concepts in Philosophy

Key Concepts in Philosophy
Series Editors: John Mullarkey (University of Dundee) and Caroline Williams (Queen Mary, University of London)

Epistemology: Key Concepts in Philosophy, Christopher Norris
Ethics: Key Concepts in Philosophy, Dwight Furrow
Language: Key Concepts in Philosophy, José Medina
Mind: Key Concepts in Philosophy, Eric Matthews

Logic

Key Concepts in Philosophy

Laurence Goldstein, Andrew Brennan,
Max Deutsch, Joe Y. F. Lau

BLOOMSBURY
NEW DELHI • LONDON • OXFORD • NEW YORK • SYDNEY

First published in India 2017
First published 2005 by Continuum International Publishing Group
Reprinted 2007,2009, 2010

This edition published with permission from Bloomsbury Publishing Plc
50 Bedford Square, London WC1B 3DP

British Library Cataloguing-in-Publication Data
A catalogue record for this book is available from the British Library.

Library of Congress Cataloging-in-Publication Data
Logic / by Laurence Goldstein ... [et al.].
p. cm. — (Key concepts in philosophy)
Includes bibliographical references and index.
ISBN 0-8264-7408-X — ISBN 0-8264-7409-8 (pbk.)
1. Logic. I. Goldstein,Laurence,1947- II. Series.
BC101.L64 2005
160-dc22 2005045563

ISBN : 978 93 86250 76 6
10 9 8 7 6 5 4 3 2
For sale in the Indian subcontinent only

Bloomsbury Publishing India Pvt. Ltd
Second Floor, Building No. 4
DDA Complex LSC, Pocket C – 6 & 7
Vasant Kunj, New Delhi 110070
www.bloomsbury.com

Typeset by Servis Filmsetting Ltd, Manchester
Printed at Manipal Technologies Limited, Manipal

DEDICATION

During the course of writing this text, one of our authors (Andrew) got married. The rest of us were fortunate enough to be already happily wed, and we accordingly dedicate this text to four excellent women: Ann Baldoni, Carol Goldstein, Lusina Ho and Norva Y. S. Lo.

CONTENTS

INTRODUCTION

Here is a brief synopsis of the content of this book.

CHAPTER 1 – REASON AND UNREASON

Reasoning is one important activity that contributes to our complicated form of life. Most of us reason badly, at least some of the time. It is possible to describe our reasoning activity and identify some of the ways in which we go wrong. We sometimes go wrong in uninteresting ways, but certain other ways of going wrong, such as when we commit subtle fallacies, are worth studying. Another worthwhile enterprise, closely related to the first, is to devise systems of good reasoning. This enterprise is known as 'logic'. As one might expect, logic, unlike skipping or motorcycle maintenance, is not a simple pursuit and, in the nature of things, it gives rise to philosophical problems. Hence 'philosophy of logic', which is the investigation of such problems. What is remarkable about many of the problems in the philosophy of logic is that thinking about them leads straight to contradiction or to some outrageous or nauseating conclusion. Many of our discussions will be motivated by first illustrating how such paradoxes arise. This provides the impetus for tackling these problems. We may be able to show that the appearance of contradiction is an illusion, or to show that things are not as bad as they first seemed, thereby reducing the outrage or the nausea. Some of the questions arising in the philosophy of logic have a long history – they puzzled the ancient Greeks and the great mediaeval logicians; some are at the heart of classic works in Hindu and Buddhist literature.

CHAPTER 2 – HOW TO PROVE A POINT LOGICALLY

As noted in Chapter 1, there seem to be standards of good reasoning, and one of the functions of logic is to construct reasoning procedures that meet the highest standards. Aristotle was the first person to attempt this. He brought some order, or system, to a species of reasoning known as syllogistic. Aristotle's procedures were considerably refined over the years, and we now have pictorial and even tactile methods for dealing with syllogistic reasoning. One really useful device for making reasoning clear and transparent is the use of symbols – hence 'symbolic logic'. With a nice, clear notation, much reasoning can be set out as a proof in which a conclusion is shown to follow from the starting assumptions or premises. This is called proof by natural deduction. In this chapter, we introduce briefly the symbolism of first-order logic, and give some examples of natural deduction proofs. Next we raise some simple, but puzzling, questions about the rules for proof just introduced. For example, if a proof, in which a conclusion is deduced from some premises, is supposed to justify the drawing of that conclusion, how are the rules themselves justified? We look at a very simple rule – called *modus ponens* – which seems obviously valid. Yet we find a weird argument that seems to cast doubt on it. It turns out that if we don't already understand the words and concepts that formal logic symbolizes, then the rules of proof will not help us get a grasp of them. Other puzzles about the meanings of logical words like 'if', 'and', 'or' and 'not' are briefly discussed. It turns out that defining the meanings of these very fundamental words is not at all easy.

CHAPTER 3 – TRUTH

The notion of *truth* is so basic that we might be tempted to think that we have an intuitive understanding of what truth is. But what is it? Different considerations lead to two completely different types of answer. One line of thought takes as its starting point the fact that, on many occasions in which we use the phrase 'It is true that', that phrase can be eliminated practically without loss. Thus 'If it is true that there are black swans in Australia, I'll eat my hat' means pretty much the same as 'If there are black swans in Australia, I'll eat my hat'. If the word 'true' is used only for stylistic purposes, then it is not a philosophically deep notion, and truth is not a real property –

the word 'true' is more akin to some punctuation – like, perhaps, underlining or italicizing, as used for emphasis. For obvious reasons, this attitude towards the notion of truth is called 'deflationary'. The opposite attitude – that truth is something important – can be spawned by reflection on the fact that searching for truth is an honourable, demanding and uplifting occupation that can in no way be trivialized. Even in a simple case, for example, where we have the statement 'There are seven sheep in the field', we are inclined to say that the truth of this statement (if it is indeed true) resides in the fact that, in the relevant vicinity there are sheep, just seven of them, no more, no less and they are in a field, the very field to which the speaker is drawing attention. On this view, truth is a property of statements (or propositions or sentences or beliefs . . . the question of what are the bearers of truth and falsity is an interesting one in itself) and a statement is true when it corresponds to some state of affairs, in the way just illustrated. This, in outline, is the correspondence theory of truth, and it is one of a variety of *substantive* theories of truth that we shall consider in this chapter.

CHAPTER 4 – THE LOGIC OF PARTS OF SPEECH

A language consists of various types of words or phrases, such as names, connectives, quantifiers, predicates and descriptive phrases. Every such component poses its own puzzle or paradox, and some attempt will be made to resolve some of these in this chapter. Suppose that the role of a singular term (a name or a definite description or a singular demonstrative) is just to pick out some object. Then, in any sentence in which a singular term features, it should be possible, without changing the truth or meaning of the sentence, to substitute for that term an expression that picks out the same object. But it isn't always. So a perfectly natural supposition becomes contaminated by doubt. Is the supposition faulty or can the doubt be stilled? The problem dates back to antiquity. The ancient version can be reconstructed as follows: Suppose it's true to say 'That hooded man is not known to me'. Now, as a matter of fact – a fact of which I am unaware – that hooded man is my brother; in other words, 'that hooded man' and 'my brother' are expressions that pick out the very same person. But substituting 'my brother' for the subject term of the original statement produces the *false* statement 'My brother is not known to me'. A classic modern version of the problem occurs in Frege's paper 'On Sense and Reference'. In Frege's example, the sentence 'The Morning Star is the Evening Star' conveys information to someone who does not know that the same planet, Venus, is clearly visible both in the west at dusk and in the east at dawn. By contrast, 'The Morning Star is the Morning Star' apparently gives no useful information at all. A similar phenomenon seems to occur in many other contexts. For example 'Lois believes that Superman flies' is true, yet 'Lois believes that Clark Kent flies' is false, for Lois does not know that Clark Kent looks slicker, acts bolder and is altogether less earthbound when he dons the supersuit. The fun in this chapter is not restricted to problems with names. Equally fascinating puzzles about the other parts of speech that play important roles in our reasoning are explored along, of course, with ways of defusing them.

CHAPTER 5 – IS NECESSITY REALLY NECESSARY?

Science investigates how the world actually is. In the actual world, metals expand when heated. But we can easily conceive of a possible world in which things are very different, in which, for example, metals contract when heated, or even where the chemical elements are different from those in our universe. The scientific laws for that world would be very different from the scientific laws that describe our own world. So science tries to find the truth about what actually is, but which might have been different. Another way of putting this is to say that the truths of science are contingent truths. If science deals with the province of contingency it might be claimed that logic deals with the realm of necessity – that the laws of logic would be the same in any possible world. This chapter introduces the branch of logic that deals with necessity and possibility. In exploring this we come up against some disturbing questions: for example, is it more strange to say that Dick – being unmarried – is necessarily a bachelor, than to say that the statement 'All bachelors are unmarried' is a necessary truth? And what about water? Yes, water! Is it necessarily made up of molecules of H_2O or just contingently so? Why have some philosophers thought the notion that water is necessarily H_2O is weird, if not downright incoherent. And if what is necessary is what cannot be changed, then does the fact that a sentence about tomorrow was true yesterday mean that what happens tomorrow is destined to occur? We show how that question is connected to the question of whether the statement 'P or not P' expresses an undeniable, indeed necessary, truth.

CHAPTER 6 – ENTAILMENT

If someone draws a conclusion that you think is wrongly drawn, you might say 'That conclusion does not follow'. The notion of a conclusion logically following from some premises is, putting things the other way round, the same as that of the premises *entailing* the conclusion. But what is *entailment*? The 'classical' answer – in terms of the logic introduced in earlier chapters – is that premises entail a conclusion if it is never the case that the premises are true when the conclusion is false. One problem with this answer is that there are many cases where we have good reason to suppose that premises fail to entail a conclusion yet which, according to the classical criterion, are genuine entailments. Various attempts have been made to improve, to 'strengthen' the classical criterion, and we ponder a few of these. It transpires that the issue of entailment is closely connected with a range of problems about necessity, logical consequence and – not surprisingly – with puzzles over conditional statements (ones like 'If Laurence tells a joke, we'll laugh'). Some of the ambiguities of conditional statements in natural language are explored, and the conclusion is that logic only provides precision and partial insight into things that we already grasp. It would be a mistake, so we conclude, to regard the precise codifications of formal logic as an ideal against which natural language, and its own very rich logic, fall short.

CHAPTER 7 – CRITIQUES OF LOGIC

To call someone 'logical' is often a compliment, and having a logical mind is widely regarded as valuable. Yet the very enterprise of logic itself has come under criticism from some quarters. This chapter looks at three sources which have generated critiques of logic. The first criticism is that logical reasoning is too rigid, and this might be detrimental to creativity. The second criticism is that logic cannot accommodate certain religious insights which somehow seem to transcend logic. For example, is the charge of contradiction not an appropriate criticism for certain religious doctrines, or even something to be actively embraced in the search for enlightenment? A third criticism of logic comes from the work of certain writers on feminism and cultural history. It has been suggested by some authors that formal logic has been an instrument of oppression and male domination, and that accordingly logic should be discarded or perhaps radically reformed. We ask whether formal logic is especially 'male friendly', or has a significant role to play in supporting the oppressive political values of patriarchal societies. We shall argue that the wholesale rejection of logic is unwarranted. Although logic does not have all the answers to the problems we face, abandoning it would not improve our ability to tackle them.

CHAPTER 1

REASON, UNREASON AND LOGIC

1.1 INTRODUCTION: GRACE, DICK AND BERT

Grace is walking along the street with Dick, and points out to him a house, partially concealed by trees, with a large pond in the front garden. She says to him 'The man who lives in that house must be heterosexual'. Bewildered, Dick asks how she knows that. 'Well', says Grace, 'if that house has a big pond, then the house has a large frontage. If the house has a large frontage, then it must have many rooms. But all the houses in this part of town have one kitchen and at most two bathrooms, so that particular house has many bedrooms. If the house has many bedrooms, then there must be a lot of children living there. Therefore the man who lives in that house must have fathered a lot of children, so he must be heterosexual.' Dick is impressed by this chain of reasoning. Next day he goes for a walk with Bert, and points out to him a different house, the front garden of which is hidden by a hedge. 'The man who lives in that house can't be straight', says Dick. 'Why?' asks Bert. Beckoning Bert to peer with him through the hedge, Dick replies: 'No pond'.

What is amusing about this (old) joke is that Dick, as his name implies, is a logical moron, and stupidity of that magnitude is funny. It is true that Grace's chain of reasoning has some weak links, but it is not wildly implausible. She first seeks to establish, in the manner of Sherlock Holmes, the conditional proposition: 'If that house has a large pond in the front garden, then a heterosexual man lives there.' Call this 'Claim 1'. Add to that proposition the observation 'That house does have a large pond in the front garden' (Claim 2) and we can validly infer the conclusion 'A heterosexual man lives in that house'.

BOX 1: Validity and soundness

A *valid* argument is one the conclusion of which follows logically from the premises. A *sound* argument is one that is both valid and has true premises. For example, the argument: 'All geese are camels; all camels are animals; therefore (conclusion) all geese are animals' is valid, but not sound. A valid argument cannot take you from true premises to a false conclusion. So the conclusion of a sound argument must be true. A valid argument with at least one false premise may have a false conclusion, but notice that (as in the example just given) a valid argument can have a false premise but a true conclusion. A valid argument can even have premises all of which are false, yet have a true conclusion. For example: 'Einstein lived for more than 100 years; anyone who lived for more than 100 years was a genius. Therefore Einstein was a genius.' The conclusion follows logically from the premises, or equivalently, the premises entail the conclusion.[1] (You know roughly what 'logically follows from' means. The important question of what it means *exactly* is discussed in Chapter 5.)

So the culmination of Grace's reasoning, her final argument, the *coup de grâce*, can be represented like this:

1. If tra-la-la, then triddly-dee-dee (the conditional)
2. Tra-la-la

Therefore 3. Triddly-dee-dee

Logicians would call this the *form* of Grace's final argument, because it does not contain the sentences that Grace used, yet Grace's actual argument can be retrieved by making appropriate substitutions (substitute 'That house has a large pond in the front garden' for 'tra-la-la' on both occasions that the latter occurs, and, similarly, substitute 'A heterosexual man lives in that house' for each occurrence of 'triddly-dee-dee').

Logicians prefer 'p's and 'q's to 'tra-la-la's and 'triddly-dee-dee's, so, if we adopt their notation, we can render the form of Grace's final argument very economically as

1. If p then q
2. p

Therefore 3. q

BOX 2 : Formalization

The first step is to take a sentence, e.g. 'If any house has a large pond in the front garden, then a heterosexual man lives there' and spell it out as a gory half-English-half-logic hybrid, as follows: 'For all x, if x is a house then, if x has a large pond in the front garden then there is a y such that y is a man and is heterosexual and y lives in x'. The final step is to paraphrase this by using logical symbols. The result is the rather nice-looking well-formed formula

$$(x)(Hx \supset (Fx \supset (\exists y)(My \;\&\; Sy \;\&\; Lyx))$$

'For all . . .' is known as the universal quantifier, and, as shown, we symbolize 'For all x' as '(x)'. 'There is a . . .' is the existential quantifier and is symbolised by '∃' Here we have used the letter 'H' to stand in the position of the one-place predicate '. . . is a house', 'F' for 'has a large pond in the front garden', 'M' for '. . . is a man' 'S' for '. . . is heterosexual' (or '. . . is straight'), and 'L' abbreviates the two-place predicate '. . . lives in. . .'. The horseshoe sign '⊃' is often used to represent the English 'if . . . then', and the ampersand '&' to represent the English 'and'. Both '⊃' and '&' are known as logical connectives, as are '~' ('not'), 'v' ('or'), '≡' ('if and only if'). These connectives connect sentences together to produce longer sentences. The logical connectives are truth-functional. What this means is that the truth-value (truth or falsity) of any complex sentence formed by the use of logical connectives can be calculated if the truth-values of the component sentences are known. A simple example: Let 'R' abbreviate 'The current Olympic 100m champion can run 100m in less than 5 seconds'. If we know whether this is true or false, then, simply in virtue of knowing the meaning of 'It is not the case that', we know whether '~R' is true or false. So '~' is truth-functional. By contrast, although we know the meaning of 'hopes', and know the truth value of R, this knowledge alone is insufficient to allow us to work out whether 'The current Olympic 100m champion hopes that R' is true or false – we'd need to ask or to psychoanalyse him.

This form of valid argument is so basic that we have a name for it. That name is *Modus Ponendo Ponens*, or *Modus Ponens* for short, or MP for shorter. Now compare the wordiness of Grace's final argument with its form as we have just rendered it. Simple, austere beauty has been achieved by the use of symbols, and it is because logicians are symbol-manipulators that the subject is often called 'symbolic logic'. (It is also often called 'formal logic' because, as in the case we have been discussing, we don't spend long dirtying our hands with the argument expressed in natural language, but study, instead, its form – its skeleton or structure – which is elegantly revealed by the use of symbols.)

Back to Dick and the house (I forgot to mention that its name is 'Green Gables') that he showed to Bert. Like us, Dick was impressed by Grace's reasoning and tried to capitalize on it. Grace derived a conclusion (Claim 1) about a particular house, but really what she established was the general point: 'If any house has a large pond in the front garden, then a heterosexual man lives there.' It is not particularly easy to translate this sentence into the language of logic (see Box 2), but, even without a logical proof, we can easily see that it is a general statement about all houses, so one of the things it entails is 'If Green Gables has a large pond in the front garden, then a heterosexual man lives at Green Gables'. Dick accepts this proposition – let's call it 'Dick's Claim 1'. But, as he and Bert observe when they peer through the bushes, Green Gables does not have a large pond. So, Dick's Claim 2 is 'It is not the case that Green Gables has a large pond'. Now, the conclusion that Dick draws from these two claims is that it is not the case that a heterosexual man lives in Green Gables. So (writing 'not-' instead of the cumbersome 'it is not the case that'), we can render the form of Dick's argument as:

1. If p then q
2. Not-p

Therefore 3. Not-q

But Dick's conclusion (3) certainly does not follow from his premises. His premises could be true and his conclusion false (a sure sign of invalidity). The conditional premise 'If Green Gables has a large pond in the front garden, then a heterosexual man lives at Green Gables' tells us what is the case if Green Gables has a large pond, but it tells us nothing about what is the case if, as premise 2 assures us, it is not the case that Green Gables has a large pond – perhaps a heterosexual man lives there and has either fathered no children, or has fathered some but has not provided them with much space. The invalidity of Dick's argument is so blatant that it makes you laugh.[2] His argument is fallacious, and the particular fallacy he commits is called *denying the antecedent*.

What is interesting about fallacies is that, in many circumstances, we commit them without realizing it. We laugh immediately we hear the punch-line of the 'pond' joke, so we spontaneously recognize the *invalidity* of Dick's argument. But an argument may contain lots of premises, or some premises that are quite complex. With such complicated arguments, we usually cannot tell, just like that, whether they are good or bad, and it is here that the methods of logic come into their own.

1.2 LOGIC AND REASONING

The story of Grace, Dick and Bert introduces us, rather surprisingly, to all the issues of this chapter. We listened in on two dialogues, in one of which Grace was engaging in what seemed to be some reasonably good reasoning, whereas in the other, Dick's reasoning was apparently seriously flawed. Reasoning is what humans do during a large part of their waking hours. Mostly it is done without verbal accompaniment – if we are trying to decide whether to have a shave, there will be many considerations that come into play, such as when we last shaved, whether we have any important meetings that day and who is likely to attend them, and would they prefer to see us shaved, and do we care about that, and whether, even if shaving is likely to create a good impression, that benefit outweighs the benefit of saving ten minutes by not shaving and so on – but typically we don't give voice to such considerations or to the further deliberations that culminate in the decision to shave or not. But, of course, when we *give* reasons, this is normally done vocally or in writing. Sometimes we extend the mind by using, as aids to reasoning, auxiliaries such as writing, diagrams and other artefacts, and even our fingers.[3]

There are deep questions to be asked about this process of reasoning. As we saw, in a typical stretch of reasoning, even about so mundane a matter as to whether or not to shave, we bring to bear certain considerations, but how are these selected? How is each assigned a weighting when we come to consider the extent to which they should influence us? How do these assignments feed into the decision-making process? What is the connection between a burst of reasoning and the string of sentences we use when giving expression to this reasoning? And so on. These problems need to be solved by a combination of empirical research and philosophical sophistication.[4] However, as philosophers of logic, our concerns are with different issues such as 'What distinguishes good reasoning from bad?', 'Can we identify paradigm examples of bad reasoning (e.g. Dick's) and say why they are bad?', 'Can we establish a code of how we ought to reason (as opposed to a catalogue of how we do reason, for the latter would make rather depressing reading, given that people often reason badly)?' In our discussion of the pond joke, we moved towards establishing such a code. We started to use symbols to illustrate the form of an argument, and indicated that certain argument forms were OK – or 'valid' to use the technical term – while others were not. This is the beginning of logic.

Logic is sometimes said to be the science of reasoning, but that assertion is somewhat misleading. Logic is not the empirical investigation of people's reasoning processes or the products of such processes. If it can be called a science at all, it is a *normative* science – it tells us what we *ought* to do, not what we do do. If Dick adds 17 to 19 and comes up with the answer 45, then we can patiently go through some arithmetic with him to show that the *right* answer is 36. Similarly, if someone reasons badly then, in certain cases, we may be able to go through a bit of logic with him and show that his reasoning was wrong. That's what 'normative' means. Logic lays down norms – standards of correctness[5] – for right reasoning, so we can say that someone is wrong who flouts them; we can say that he or she ought to do otherwise. Gottlob Frege, widely acclaimed as the father of modern logic, put it like this: 'the laws of logic are . . . the most general laws, which prescribe universally the way in which one ought to think if one is to think at all' (Frege 1964, p. 12).

It may seem that there is a certain *arrogance* about this claim that logic is a normative discipline. Physics investigates how things are in the physical world, and physicists come up with explanations and laws. The physicist tries to tell us how things are. But the logician does not try to tell us how things are – he does not try to tell us how people actually reason – but how they *ought* to reason. How does the logician earn the right to do that? Suppose that a logician nominates what he takes to be the most fundamental principles of how we ought to reason. We may ask him to justify that choice of principles. But he seems logically debarred from doing so! Because to justify a principle appears to require producing a good argument in favour of that principle. If that argument incorporates any of the logician's favoured set of fundamental principles, then his argument relies on principles the acceptability of which the argument is supposed to be establishing! That's no good – the argument goes round in a circle, simply begging the question at issue. But the argument cannot rely on more fundamental principles because, *ex hypothesi*, the logician has listed the most fundamental principles. This is a nice conundrum to which we shall return. But in the meanwhile, ask yourself the question 'Can a logical principle be justified only by giving a logical argument in support of it?'

1.3 MAD AND BAD REASONING

There is a lot of irrationality about but, in a certain sense, no speaker can be entirely irrational.[6] Imagine someone who accepted

K: All pigs are animals

and accepted also

L: Porky is a pig

but simply could not see that this committed him to accepting

Z: Porky is an animal.

One way you would NOT succeed in getting him to accept the inference would be to tell him

M: If 'K' is true and 'L' is true then 'Z' must be true

For this crazy person would most likely reply that he accepts 'K', 'L' and 'M' but could not see that this committed him to accepting 'Z'. Frustrated, you tell him

N: If 'K' is true and 'L' is true and 'M' is true, then 'Z' must be true

But he just replies that he accepts 'N' too, but still doesn't see that this commits him . . .

BOX 3 : A note on notation

It is important to distinguish between letters used as abbreviations, letters used for variables (schematic letters) and letters used for metavariables. The letters we have used here – 'K', 'L' etc. – are abbreviations for particular sentences. We earlier used lowercase letters 'p', 'q' as variables – these are to be thought of as letters for which simple sentences can be substituted, but they are not themselves any particular simple sentences or the abbreviations of any such. Complex well-formed formulae (wffs) are constructed from simple ones by the employment of logical connectives and other signs. So, for example 'p ~(q & r)' is a complex wff. We use metavariables, conventionally upper case 'A', 'B', 'C' etc. from the beginning of the alphabet, as occupying positions that can be filled by wffs, simple or complex. So the most general way of stating *Modus Ponens* is: From 'A ⊃ B' and 'A', infer 'B'. Often, we don't bother with the quote marks when no confusion is liable to ensue.

As you can see, the process of persuasion would go on *ad infinitum* with not a hope of success.[7] There is no way of rationally convincing this person, and we are right to say that, if he really cannot infer that 'Z' must be true if 'K' and 'L' are, then he simply does not understand what 'all' or 'must' mean, or does not know what a lot of the words in those sentences mean. If a person does not know the meanings of such words as 'and', 'or', 'if' and 'not', that person can hardly be called a speaker of the language. And to have grasped the meaning of 'and' is, at least, to have enough reasoning power to infer 'A' from 'A and B'. Thus, someone who has even a rudimentary grasp of language cannot be totally irrational.

If Bert is able to perform the inference of (Z) from (K) and (L), but also, when he sees himself in the mirror, infers that he is Napoleon, then he is mad as a hatter, but is not *totally* irrational. It's just that some, or many, of his inferences are seriously mistaken. Errors of reasoning range from the numbingly gross to those that are so subtle that over two thousand years of searching has failed to locate their roots. The logician's Holy Grail is a notation for formulating thoughts clearly and unambiguously, and an inference machine that is guaranteed to reason unerringly. This was Leibniz' vision: a *characteristica universalis* and a *calculus ratiocinator*.[8]

Let's begin with the numbingly gross. This is the realm of the crass cognitive illusion. As an example, a significant number of Filipinas who, out of economic necessity, work abroad as maids, are duped by unscrupulous con artists who become their boyfriends and pretend to be rich businessmen. A newspaper recently ran a story on the latest victim whom, to preserve her anonymity, we shall call 'Imelda'. Given that the same thing had happened to a number of her friends, Imelda really should have known better. Available to her were numerous premises of the form 'Man X has duped my friend Y'. Typically, X says that he loves Y, talks of marriage, spends time with her and then asks for some money to help fund a business project; Y parts with her life savings; X runs off with the money never to be seen again. X has become her ex, and Y is left wondering why. Given all the evidence that was available to her about such duplicity and infidelity, Imelda's probabilistic reasoning went badly wrong. She concluded that, highly probably, her businessman friend would marry her and remain with her until they were parted by death. A strict Bayesian calculation,[9] or even something less sophisticated (for example, common sense), should have persuaded her that he wouldn't. What deflected her from the path of reason may have been avarice, but it may have been pity and kindness. There may have been an element of self-deception or of wishful thinking. It would clearly be mistaken to suppose that there is a unique type of psychological deficit, underlying *all* instances of erroneous reasoning.

A less blatant error in probabilistic reasoning is known as the base-rate fallacy. Casscells *et al.* (1978) posed the following problem to a group of subjects consisting of teachers and fourth-year students at the Harvard Medical School:

> If a test to detect a disease whose prevalence is 1/1000 has a false positive rate of 5 per cent, what is the chance that a person found to have a positive result actually has the disease, assuming that you know nothing about the person's symptoms or signs? —— per cent

The correct answer is 2 per cent, but less than one fifth of the Harvard subjects gave an answer close to that. Most subjects answered 95 per cent. They reasoned that if 5 per cent of the positives are false, the remaining 95 per cent must be true – i.e. that 95 per cent of those testing positive must really have the disease. One way to see that this is wrong is to picture *yourself* on the streets administering this test. If you test 1000 people, you know that almost all of them (say 999) will not have the disease. But 5 per cent of them (i.e. around 50) will test positive whereas typically only 1 person will actually have the disease. Therefore only about one in every 50 people who test positive actually has the disease. The typical Harvard medic is out by a factor of around 47.

Obviously it would be wrong to conclude that those Harvard people who got the wrong answer were just as irrational as Imelda. Although they were medical people and the problem was about a medical procedure, the problem is posed in quite technical statistical terms and this may have somehow inhibited their reasoning. When the question is posed in a more user-friendly fashion, most well-educated people get the answer right (Cosmides and Tooby, 1996; Koehler, 1996). So we should beware of heaping scorn on the Harvard Medical School. To err is human, and that we sometimes commit fallacies does not convict us of rampant unreason.

Copi and Cohen (1998, p.690) define a fallacy as 'a type of argument that may seem to be correct, but that proves, on examination, not to be so'. There are many sorts of fallacy. The one committed by Dick (*Denying the Antecedent*) is an example of a logical fallacy, so-called because it exemplifies an invalid form of argument that can be illustrated (as we did) with symbols. Informal fallacies are more difficult to characterize but they seem to occur either when the premises of an argument are not quite relevant to its conclusion or when we fall prey to a bewitchment by language. The most obvious case of the latter is when we fail to notice that a word is being used in an argument in two quite different senses. Thus, if someone were to claim that the end of life is the bringing of happiness to others, and to add that death is the end of life, then, if that person were to conclude that death is bringing happiness to others, we could readily identify his mistake – he has committed the Fallacy of Equivocation, for, in the first part of his argument, the word 'end' is being used in the sense of 'purpose', in the second part, in the sense of 'terminus'.

This example is, of course, childish and contrived, but the Fallacy of Equivocation is sometimes committed even in serious philosophical writing. It is possible for a human being to be of the female sex. I am human. But it does not follow logically that it is possible that I (the male author who is writing this section) am of the female sex. According to G. E. Moore, there is an equivocation on 'possible' here and it is the same equivocation that infects the argument of a philosophical sceptic who comes to the conclusion that it is possible (for example) that he does not have two parents.[10]

There is a huge number of types of fallacy and we sometimes commit them through lack of perspicuity or sometimes deliberately, for the purpose of intellectual subversion.[11] But they can be detected with greater or lesser ease. By contrast, there are errors of argument that are extremely difficult to unravel – so difficult, in fact, that some of them have defied the best efforts of very clever people for hundreds of years to identify just where the reasoning goes astray. Such errors occur in what are called 'paradoxes'. Mediaeval authors called them 'insolubles'. As you can see in the next few boxes, in one version of the Sorites Paradox, apparently impeccable reasoning leads to the conclusion that blue is green; in the Liar Paradox, to the conclusion that some statements are both true and false; in the Surprise Examination Paradox, to the conclusion that no such examination can be given, and so on. Clearly errors of reasoning occur in all these cases yet there is no agreement to date as to the location of their source.

BOX 4 : The Sorites Paradox

Take a large pot of blue paint and paint a card with it. The card is blue. Add a smidgen of yellow paint to the blue pot, stir well in and paint a second card. The colour of that card is indistinguishable from that of the first, so the second card is blue too. Add another smidgen of yellow to the pot, stir well in and paint a third card; that card is visually indistinguishable from the second so the third card is blue too. You can see where this is leading: each card is visually indistinguishable from the one before, so you cannot logically say that they have different colours. By the time you have added the thousandth drop of yellow and painted a card with it, the reasoning tells you that it is the same colour as the 999th, which is the same colour as the 998th. . . . Which is the same colour as the first, namely blue. But, of course, by this time the colour of the paint in the pot is green! So the 1000th card is green, but logic tells us that it must be blue!!??

BOX 5 : The Liar Paradox

Consider the statement 'This statement is false'. If it's true, then what it says is true – namely, that it is false. If it is false, then, since that is exactly what it claims itself to be, it is true. So if it is either true or false, it is both true and false!

BOX 6 : The Surprise Examination Paradox

The teacher on Friday says 'There will be a surprise examination one day next week'. Since the school week ends on Friday, Friday cannot be the day of the surprise examination (since, as the pupils can see right now, if no examination has been given by Thursday evening, Friday would be the only day left for the examination, so it would be expected – not a surprise). But, with Friday ruled out, Thursday becomes the last possible day for the examination, so, by similar reasoning, Thursday is ruled out too – you can see right now that if no exam has taken place by Wednesday evening then, with Friday already eliminated as a possible day for the exam, Thursday would be the only day available, and hence would be expected and not a surprise. By similar reasoning, Wednesday, Tuesday and Monday are ruled out in turn. In other words, no surprise examination can be given on any day next week. Come next week, the teacher waltzes in on (say) Tuesday and hands out the examination papers. Surprise!

1.4 THE CLAIM THAT LOGIC IS NOT RELATED TO REASONING

We have looked at some of the ways in which error is liable to creep into reasoning. Yet correct reasoning is highly desirable. Innocent people could be found guilty as a result of poor legal reasoning. Sloppy scientific reasoning can lead to the propagation of false theories. It would therefore be of value to have some system of reasoning that was mathematically precise. What is widely regarded as the first great treatise of modern logic, Frege's *Begriffschrift* (1879), stakes out this rationale very clearly. The first thing that is needed, according to Frege, is a language in which none of the constituent symbols is ambiguous, and a syntax (grammar) so constructed that sentences are not open to multiple interpretations (unlike the sentences of ordinary language – compare 'Do you think that Woody's a plant?', 'I have done nothing to deserve a meeting with President Bush', 'What is this thing called love?', etc.). Next, one requires a set of simple rules for permissible deductions. For example, given a premise A, we should be permitted to infer the negation of the negation of A. In symbols: From A infer ~~A – the Rule of Double Negation. *Modus ponens*, that we have already encountered, is another such elementary rule of inference. The package consisting of vocabulary, grammar and rules of inference is called a *formal system of logic*. It would seem that, armed with such a system, we could perform deductive reasoning to our heart's content, safe in the knowledge that we have so constructed our deductive apparatus that, if we start with true premises, we shall, so long as we stick to the rules, be able to infer only true conclusions. On this conception, logic is, at root, a tool for reasoning and for maintaining consistency.

Given what has just been said, it may seem odd that a philosopher, Gilbert Harman, has claimed that 'there is no clearly significant way in which logic is specially relevant to reasoning' (Harman 1986a, p. 20). Harman's main point is that reasoning is the psychological process of revising one's beliefs, perhaps modifying some, augmenting some, relinquishing others, whereas logic merely tells us about inferring propositions on the basis of a set of rules. Harman seems incorrectly to identify logic with a certain system of logic – so-called classical logic – and not fully to appreciate that one of the tasks of a logician is to devise systems of logic that are faithful to best reasoning practice. But he is right to emphasize that the psychological process of reasoning is different from performing proofs within a formal system of logic. In order to see this, consider an alleged counterexample to *modus ponens* devised by Vann McGee:

> Opinion polls taken just before the 1980 election showed the Republican Ronald Reagan decisively ahead of the Democrat Jimmy Carter, with the other Republican in the race, John Anderson, a distant third. Those apprised of the poll results believed, with good reason:
>
> (1) If a Republican wins the election, then if it's not Reagan who wins it will be Anderson.
>
> (2) A Republican will win the election.
>
> Yet they did not have reason to believe
>
> (3) If it's not Reagan who wins, it will be Anderson.

Since, in this example, there are only two Republican candidates, we can read the sentence 'A Republican will win the election' as 'Reagan will win or Anderson will win'. Then premise (1) is seen to be truistic, and premise (2), which is an acceptable premise, has the same truth-conditions as the conclusion (3). So here we have a classically valid argument – if you look carefully, it is another instance of *modus ponens* – substitute 'A Republican will win the election' for 'A' and 'If it is not Reagan who wins the election, it will be Anderson' for 'B'. Yet clearly it would be foolhardy to believe the conclusion that, if it's not Reagan who wins, it will be Anderson, on the basis of one's belief in the truth of the premises.

David Over (1987) has pointed out that McGee's example is not really a counterexample to *modus ponens*, for *modus ponens* is a rule which allows us to infer a conclusion from certain *assumptions*, and in fact (3) does validly follow, given that we assume (1) and (2). But McGee speaks not of what we assume, but of what we should *believe*. So the fallacy that McGee's example highlights is a fallacy of *reasoning*, where reasoning is the psychological process we have been talking about which can result in our beliefs getting modified. As we have pointed out, although there is a close connection between the two, logic must be distinguished from reasoning.

Modern logic is commonly understood to include deduction (the study of what conclusions can be extracted from premises[12]), induction (the study of drawing conclusions that, strictly speaking, go beyond the premises), model theory (where the elements of logical formulae are associated with objects in make-believe worlds), metatheory (proofs about proofs), etc.; this is the kind of material found in standard logic texts. Reasoning is what humans do when they engage in the process of figuring out, revising or reinforcing their beliefs. It is quite clear that the rules of logic are not co-extensive with the principles of reasoning (the principles of how we ought to reason). For, importantly, beliefs, unlike statements, have degrees of strength, and when we revise a belief it is normally against the background of other relevant beliefs. A belief may strengthen or weaken when new evidence comes to light. A set of principles governing belief will determine the readjustment of the strength-values for resident beliefs when new evidence (observation, recognition of a bias, confrontation with a powerful consideration, etc.) becomes available to an agent.

Fallacies are departures from good reasoning, so, once we have understood a particular fallacy, we can attempt to say what principle has been breached. Dick's 'pond' mistake was a simple error of logic, but, in the case of McGee's example, the relevant principle is:

> We should not believe a conclusion to be true if the strength of our belief in one of the premises on which that conclusion rests is less than the strength of our belief in a competing proposition.

This is a principle of reasoning. Two propositions are competing (for an agent) if they are genuinely different answers to a question and that agent favours one over the other – would dispense with one in favour of the other. (The notion of a 'genuinely different answer' may be difficult to spell out exactly, but, intuitively, the sort of suggestion we want to exclude is that 'Reagan will win the election or $2+2=4$' genuinely competes with 'Reagan will win the election' as an answer to the question 'Who will win the election?') Reasonable people apprised of the poll would have believed

(4) Reagan will win or Carter will win

more strongly than they would have believed (2) – if asked to choose between them, they would pick (4) – so, according to our principle, they ought not to believe (3). Two claims, both acceptable, may be in competition. Claim (2) is acceptable to somebody who is convinced that Reagan will win – both Carter and Anderson are out of the picture, so far as he is concerned. But if forced to be more circumspect, say, by being offered the same odds for a bet on (2) as on (4), we know where he would put his money.[13]

The example we have been considering concerns *theoretical* reason – reasoning about what to believe. That there is a close connection between logic and the psychological process of *theoretical* reasoning is hardly surprising if logic is the attempt to represent, systematize and elucidate the norms for such reasoning. The psychologistic counterpart to the logical principle *modus ponens* is: rational people who believe A and also believe (If A then B) are committed to the belief B. But, in the realm of *practical* reasoning, where we are trying to figure out not what to believe but what to *do,* this tight connection does not seem to hold. As John Searle points out, a person who desires A and believes that (If A then B) is not committed to desiring B. Searle's example: '[T]here is nothing *logically* wrong with a couple who want to have sexual intercourse and who believe that, if they do, she will get pregnant, but who do not want her to get pregnant' (Searle 2001, pp.254–5). Practical reasoning involves values, and (often conflicting) desires. We might conclude, as Searle does, that there can be no deductive logic of practical reason. Or, less drastically, we might conclude that we can make deductions about whether or not to shave today, whether to have sex, or about what means to adopt in order to achieve certain ends, but that the underlying logic must accommodate inconsistent *desires*.[14]

1.5 JUSTIFYING LOGICAL PRINCIPLES

Although, as we have seen, there are rules for reasoning that are different, indeed, are of a different kind, from the rules of logic, we have been unwilling to endorse Harman's view that logic is not specially relevant to reasoning. The special relevance is that theoretical reasoning in which one infers a conclusion from certain beliefs is often reflected in a logical proof that shows that a conclusion is implied by certain premises. Further, a good system of logic provides us with a code of how we ought to reason, at least within a certain restricted area of discourse. But which system of logic to use? We said that logical proofs within the system should not always mimic our everyday reasoning for, as earlier indicated, our reasoning is frequently erroneous and infected with fallacy. We said that our chosen system of logic should be faithful to best reasoning practices. But there seems to be a bit of a chicken-and-egg situation here, since our best reasoning practices are presumably those that are logical.

This was a problem we encountered at the end of Section 1 – how are we to justify the adoption of a particular logical system? Within deductive logic, for example, there are several competing systems on the market. You might think that the answer is simple: we know what logical connectives such as 'not', 'or' and 'if . . . then' mean, so we should simply accept as the rules for right reasoning those rules that faithfully encapsulate these meanings. For example, we should accept the rule that from 'A', we may validly infer 'A or B'. (If it is true that Dick is in the doghouse, it logically follows that Dick is in the doghouse or Grace is in the garden.) The trouble with that suggestion is that it presupposes that we know the meaning of a connective antecedent to knowledge of the rules for its use. But you can start to teach the meaning of 'tree' to an infant by pointing at trees and saying 'tree'. You cannot, however, point to an or. It seems, then, that the meaning of 'or' is learnt not through being shown some object associated with that word but by acquiring the rules for its use – there is no knowing the meaning prior to knowing those rules. More chicken-and-egg.[15]

You might think that the rules for the use of a logical connective such as 'or' are so obvious that it is a waste of time bothering to justify them. But just consider these two apparently obvious rules:

(i) A entails (A or B)

That is the rule we were just discussing. There is no possible state of affairs in which the premise A could be true while the conclusion (A or B) is simultaneously false, so the standard criterion for entailment (for a conclusion following logically from premises) is satisfied.

(ii) The premises (A or B), (It is not the case that A) entail B

This is a rule governing the logical connectives 'or' and 'not'. Again, this seems an entirely acceptable rule. But now take the premise 'Lance Armstrong was the only cyclist to win the Tour de France after recovering from testicular cancer'. By Rule (i), that premise entails 'Lance Armstrong was the only cyclist to win the Tour de France after recovering from testicular cancer or Shakespeare wrote the song *Jailhouse Rock*'. Now, that last sentence, taken together with a new premise 'It is not the case that Lance Armstrong was the only cyclist to win the Tour de France after recovering from testicular cancer' entails, by Rule (ii), 'Shakespeare wrote the song *Jailhouse Rock*'. So a simple chain of reasoning, involving only rules (i) and (ii) leads us from two premises about Lance Armstrong (one the negation of the other) to the conclusion that Shakespeare wrote the song *Jailhouse Rock*! Generalizing (since we could have used quite different sample sentences in the above argument) the rule seems to emerge that from any proposition and its negation, *any conclusion whatsoever* logically follows! This is very hard to swallow, so the lesson seems to be that we need to go back to basics and examine whether our rules (i) and (ii) can be properly justified.[16] It may turn out, on close examination, that the rules to which the behaviour of some of our logical connectives conform are not as simple as we may have first thought.

There has been quite a lot written, in recent times, about this problem of justifying deduction and justifying the choice of a particular system of deductive logic (Pinto 2001) but a good start was made by Aristotle some 2350 years ago. The fundamental rule that Aristotle was concerned to justify was the Law of Non-Contradiction (LNC), that it is not possible for a proposition and its negation both to be true at the same time. This can be regarded as a prohibitive rule: from A one cannot validly infer not-A. Aristotle was aware of the conundrum noted earlier: that normal methods for defending a principle, for example giving a demonstration or a proof, cannot apply here, for we should find ourselves in the invidious position of defending a *basic* principle by appealing to less basic ones. Aristotle's solution was that, although one cannot prove LNC, one can establish that someone who fails to embrace the principle is someone who can't speak properly (note the connection with the Lewis Carroll argument mentioned earlier), for to speak one has to have terms to pick out objects, so one has to understand boundaries – the boundary, say, between a particular apple and the non-apple surroundings; to talk about apples one must know that nothing can simultaneously be apple and not-apple. A person who is unable to do that, Aristotle hints, is no better than a vegetable (Aristotle, *Metaphysics*, 1008b11).

Wittgenstein likewise thinks that we can give no *explanation* of the unacceptability of contradictions and, correlatively, of the acceptability of LNC. It is obviously no explanation to say that we exclude mutually contradictory conclusions *because* they are contradictory (Wittgenstein 1980, Vol.1, §1132); in Wittgenstein's view, no justification for excluding them can go beyond saying that we just have no use for them (1980, Vol.1, §44; Vol.2, §290). But, while it is perfectly true that justification must come to an end somewhere, is the point at which Wittgenstein draws the line the right one? Possibly not. Why should the claim that we do not accept contradictions because of what the word 'not' means not be a perfectly reasonable explanation? (The meaning of the word 'and' should also feature in the explanation, but, for now, let's concentrate on 'not'.)

The very fact that we can recognize cases where a word is being used abnormally – as Wittgenstein acknowledges we can (1953, §§141, 142) – indicates that there is a *normal* use for that word. If we can say what the normal use for 'not' is, then we should be able to see why, unless special conditions prevail, we cannot assert (acknowledge as true) a contradiction. A fruitful way of establishing what the normal use of 'not' is is to ask why we have that word in ordinary language – what is the word *for*, what is its function? When the word is serving that function, then it is being used normally.

Aristotle again provides a useful starting point. In a parenthetical remark at *Categories* 12b5–12b15, he argues that there are oppositions in nature that precede, in the order of being, our statements which reflect them:

> Nor is what underlies an affirmation or negation itself an affirmation or negation. For an affirmation is an affirmative statement and a negation a negative statement, whereas none of the things underlying an affirmation or negation is a statement. These are, however, said to be opposed to one another as affirmation and negation are, for in these cases too, the manner of opposition is the same. For in the way an affirmation is opposed to a negation, for example 'he is sitting' – 'he is not sitting', so are opposed the actual things underlying each, his sitting – his not sitting.

(There is further elaboration in the *Metaphysics* (1004a31–1004b10, 1018a20–1018a38, 1051a5–1051a13, 1061a7–1061a14).)

Aristotle is here contrasting the world of things (*ta onta*) with the world of words (*ta legomena*). But there is a level intermediate between these two. The *recognition* of an opposition in nature is prelinguistic. Accepting one of two options perceived to be opposed involves recognizing that the other must be rejected. Accepting and rejecting are also ontologically more fundamental than statement-making. Statements are used as a means of expressing, indicating or conveying our acceptances or rejections. As Huw Price (1990) explains, there is a primitive awareness of incompatibility; it is this that gives us the occasion for rejection and hence, with the development of language, for the use of the word 'not'. He writes:

> To signal significantly, one needs to be capable of discrimination. One needs to signal in some circumstances and to remain silent in others. One needs a sense that these are mutually exclusive possibilities . . . [A]t . . . times nature offers us an opportunity, and our choice is simply to accept or to decline. To have a sense that there is a decision to be made in such a case seems already to have a sense of the incompatibility of the options. Once language comes to be associated with the activity of agents, there

is thus a need for negation in formulating, offering and expressing choices.

Using language is one of the activities of normal human agents. Only by a process of abstraction can language be *dissociated* from agents, from the language-involving activities (Wittgenstein calls these 'language-games') that are its natural habitat. As Price shows, agents need to make choices, often choices between mutually excluding options. We recognize the incompatibility between such options, and use the word 'not' as a linguistic marker of this recognition. Socrates' sitting excludes his not sitting; my acceptance that he is sitting excludes my rejection of the same proposition, so I cannot assert both that he is sitting and that he isn't. We cannot assert a contradiction because acceptance excludes rejection, and the use of the word 'not' registers this basic fact.[17] We thus arrive at the prohibition against inferring ~A from A. A prohibition is a rule about what not to do, but we can easily convert this one into a permission, a rule about what to do. It is simply 'From A infer that it is not the case that ~A'. This reads like an instruction to a person, but we can put it in a de-personalized way: A ⊦ ~~A. Please note that we have not shown that the inference in the opposite direction is a valid one. It would be a matter for further discussion whether ~~A ⊦ A is a rule of logic.

Another basic act that humans and other animals perform is putting together bits of information. The lion pounces on its prey only when a *conjunction* of circumstances give it a good chance of a kill – that deer is weak *and* it has become detached from the herd *and* . . . The linguistic counterpart to compiling bits of information is conjoining sentences so, again, it is natural for human agents to have a word for conjunction, and the most common word in English that we use for conjoining sentences is 'and'. If two sentences are true, then the conjunction of them is true too, but if either or both of the original sentences are false, then the conjunction is false. The rule of inference that reflects this logical behaviour of 'and' is: from premise A and premise B one may validly infer the conclusion (A & B). Deductive validity is a matter of *truth-preservation* – if the premises of a deductive argument are true, then the argument is valid only if the conclusion is true. Notice that our rule of inference for 'and' meets this criterion: if either A or B is false, then the conclusion (A & B) is false, but that's fine, because we go wrong in deductive reasoning, i.e. we argue *invalidly*, when we start with *true* premises and end up with a false conclusion. (It is a good question, and one that we shall address in Chapter 5, whether arguments are invalid *only if* they fail the test of it not being possible for the premises to be true while the conclusion is false. In the Lance Armstrong argument above it was not possible for the premises to be true simply because the premises contradicted each other. So the Lance argument passes that test. Yet many of us have a strong disinclination to call that argument valid.)

The stalking lion's pouncing was described in terms of its being triggered by a conjunction of the right circumstances. In other words, *if* those circumstances prevail, *then* the lion pounces. So, once again, we find ourselves using a logical connective ('if . . . then') in the description of a very common kind of circumstance – the triggering of an action or an event. That little word 'if' has proved an extremely tricky one for logicians, and several books have been written about it. We have already encountered a rule illustrating the logical behaviour of 'if', namely *modus ponens*: from premise (If A then B) and premise A, infer B. De-personalized and smartened up, this becomes: $A \supset B, A \vdash B$. Another rule, this time involving both '$\supset$' and '$\sim$' is *modus tollendo tollens*: $A \supset B, \sim B \vdash \sim A$. Most logicians agree that these two principles really do reflect how 'if . . . then' works (despite Van McGee's apparent counterexample to MP). But the question of what *other* rules accurately display the logical behaviour of 'if . . . then' is a hugely contentious one.

1.6 SUMMARY

Some logicians take the view that the subject has developed in such a way that it now has nothing in particular to do with human reasoning but is, more or less, a branch of pure mathematics. No doubt part of modern logic can be viewed in just that way. But Aristotle, the father of the subject, regarded logic not as concerned with deriving truths but with eliciting principles of correct reasoning, and it is the relation between logic and reasoning that we have been stressing here. In a piece of reasoning, we make a transition, working our way from some starting point to a conclusion, and we have here taken logic to be concerned with the rules for the valid transitions from propositions to propositions.[18]

We confronted a conundrum. People habitually reason badly, so the rules of logic cannot just record our transitions from propositions to propositions, they must supply some standards of correctness. These rules are supposed to guide us as to the logical behaviour of such words as 'not', 'and', 'or', 'if . . . then'. But these are words of ordinary language, and each does not have a single sense, and there are disagreements about what they mean, and meanings change over time. So how can we possibly discern the rules for the *correct* use of these words? We have attempted to get out of this tangle by trying to discover naturalistic explanations for at least the core meanings of some of these words by trying to see what central purposes such words serve, and so to elicit (and hence justify) some of the rules for their logical behaviour.

SUGGESTIONS FOR FURTHER READING

In this chapter, we have tried to say what logic is by looking at the relationship between logic and reasoning and you may now wish to pursue these matters further with Engel (1991, chaps. 12, 13). We mentioned that Gilbert Harman's book *Change in View* (Harman 1986) examines this relationship and concludes that logic has no special relevance to reasoning. Although we argued that Harman was wrong about this, we would not wish to say that learning logic provides a safe immunization against bad reasoning or a guarantee of good reasoning. But it helps, as does the development of a philosophical nose for detecting argumentative error. A classic discussion of experiments on errors in human reasoning is Kahneman, Slovic and Tversky (1982). A Monty Python sketch on the nature of argument and other useful material can be found at http://www.geocities.com/sheherazahde/Sociology/Argument.html and there is a discussion of fallacies and their detection at http://www.jfk-online.com/ exploring.html. An excellent book that explores the question of what it is that makes one system of cognitive processes better than another (p. 74) and which intersects with this chapter at various points is Stich (1990).

CHAPTER 2

HOW TO PROVE A POINT LOGICALLY

2.1 BEGINNINGS

Modern systems of logic are based on two breakthroughs made in ancient Greece four centuries before the birth of Christ. One group of thinkers, the Stoics, were captained by an eccentric type – Zeno of Citium (born around 336 BCE) – with the brilliant Chrysippus as his second-in-command. Chrysippus was apparently a close observer of dogs, arguing that if you watch a dog following a scent along a path, the animal's behaviour reveals its grasp of elementary logic. Suppose the path it is following diverges into three: the dog will sniff along one of the trails and if the scent dies out it will return to the junction. It will then sniff along the second path, and if the scent dies out there too, it will return to the junction and set out on the third path *without even bothering to sniff at the ground*! This observation showed – so Chrysippus argued – that dogs follow the principle:

Either the First, the Second or the Third
Not the First
Not the Second
Therefore the Third

The Stoics' use of 'the First', 'the Second', etc. is an early example of an attempt at symbolism – obtaining the same effect we nowadays achieve by using 'p's and 'q's. There was an even earlier school of logic – the Megarians – who were the inspiration for the Stoics and it is to these schools that we owe a primitive version of the notation and principles of *truth-functional logic*.

BOX 1: Truth-functions

When complex sentences or formulas are built out of simpler ones using 'not', 'and', 'or' and 'if . . .', the truth or falsity of the complex sentence is determined by the truth or falsity of its components. Consider 'p & q' for the case where 'p' is true and 'q' is true. In that case 'p & q' is true too. Now consider what to say if either or both of 'p', 'q' were false. In these cases, the complex 'p & q' is false. When the truth or falsity of a complex formula or sentence is determined by the truth or falsity of its components, the connectives out of which it is constructed are called 'truth-functional'. 'Because', 'until', 'it's idiotic to say that . . .' are not truth-functional connectives. Textbooks often use truth-tables to summarize the facts about truth functionality:

p	**~p**
T	**F**
F	**T**

The truth-table for 'not' shows that denying or negating 'p' simply reverses its truth-value. Given that 'p' is true, its negation is false, and given that it's false, its negation is true.

p	q	**p & q**
T	T	**T**
F	T	**F**
T	F	**F**
F	F	**F**

This truth table specifies the condition under which an 'and' sentence (a conjunction) is true or false. When both of the conjuncts are true, the whole thing is true, but the 'and' formula or statement is false in all other cases.

p	q	**p v q**
T	T	**T**
F	T	**T**
T	F	**T**
F	F	**F**

Statements built up using 'or' are true when either of the components is true, and false only when both components are false. If this *inclusive* reading of 'or' (the disjunction operator) seems a bit strange to you, think of the operator as representing the phrase 'either/or', and it will probably make a lot more sense. In some languages, there is an exclusive disjunction word, that is, these languages have a word that means 'either . . . or . . . , but not both'. This sense of 'or' is easily captured by writing '(p v q) & ~(p & q)' when required.

p	q	**p ⊃ q**
T	T	**T**
F	T	**T**
T	F	**F**
F	F	**T**

The hook operator, '⊃', representing 'if . . ., then . . .' is highly convenient while being at the same time the source of many problems. Conditional ('if . . ., then . . .') sentences are not usually put forward in everyday speech unless their 'if. . . .' clauses (their *antecedents*) are thought to be true. The logician, however, has to consider all possibilities. The puzzles associated with the case where the antecedent is false and the whole formula or sentence is true are discussed in the main text.

p	q	**p ≡ q**
T	T	**T**
F	T	**F**
T	F	**F**
F	F	**T**

The biconditional connective, '≡', is often represented in English as 'iff', short for 'if and only if'. It expresses the equivalence in truth value of the formulas on either side of the expression. When two statements are equivalent in truth-value, the truth of either is sometimes said to be *necessary and sufficient* for the truth of the other.

One thinker who was on the scene even earlier than Zeno is nowadays given credit as the founder of formal logic. His name is Aristotle (born 384 BCE) and his influence from that time to now can be gauged to an extent by the honorific under which he was widely known in medieval Europe: 'The Philosopher'. His theory of syllogisms pioneered the first abstract notation for representing what is now known as the *logic of quantifiers*. When truth-functional logic is combined with the logic of quantifiers, the resulting formal system is known as first-order logic. We already saw examples in Chapter 1 of first-order formulas, using quantifiers, variables and connectives.

While Aristotle and the Stoics provided the foundations for first-order logic, it took more than two thousand years before any system of first-order logic was formulated in a comprehensive way. Over these two millennia, many puzzling questions were discussed in sophisticated ways by brilliant thinkers in Europe, India and China. But as far as thinkers based in Europe – and under the sway for the most part of the Roman Catholic Church – were concerned, Aristotle's syllogistic was their best formal technique for representing arguments. Only after the work of George Boole, Gottlob Frege and Charles Sanders Peirce in the nineteenth century were the first fully fledged languages of first-order logic actually presented, and not until 1928 – with the publication of David Hilbert's lectures[1] – did systematic versions of first-order logic become available in a form that could be learnt by students and general readers.

The search for formal systematization of the 'laws of thought' or 'principles of right reasoning' may have some risks attached. As we saw in Chapter 1, Harvard medical students were likely to get the wrong answer in a statistics question when it was put to them in a technical, abstract form. When phrased in less abstract terms, though, they were more likely to get the right answer. As Chrysippus might perhaps have pointed out, dogs would not be helped by being taught truth-functional logic, for they already reason quite well without it. Indeed, in ancient China, it seems that abstract reasoning was deliberately avoided in mathematical works like the Han classic *The Nine Chapters on Mathematical Procedures* and in the later third-century CE commentary on it by Liu Hui. Some writers nowadays argue that the mathematical classics focused on practical problems in everyday settings in order to protect readers from confusion that might be induced by symbolic abstraction. As Karine Chemla has argued, the ancient Chinese mathematicians were well aware that one problem could 'stand for' a range of problems, but they deliberately avoided abstracting the common core from a range of problems, preferring to treat each particular problem individually.[2]

No similar qualms about abstract generalizations seem to have affected the ancient Greeks, nor those who developed the systems of logic put forward during the nineteenth and twentieth centuries. Instead, a variety of codes, or micro-languages, were invented according to apparently clear and simple rules. At the core of these languages are special symbols, some of which do similar tasks to those carried out by the words of natural language. Each of these symbols was one thing that stood for many. While the truth-functional connectives (sometimes called *logical constants*), like 'and', 'not', 'if . . ., then . . .', join up shorter expressions that make sense into longer ones that also make sense, other logical symbols stand for, represent, or refer to things that lie outside the language itself – objects, truth, falsity, properties, sets of things, or whatnot. One appeal of logical languages is that they seem to provide extremely clear examples of how complex expressions can be built by simple rules out of elementary parts. Might they not then provide insight into how the meaning or truth of whole sentences is a function of the meanings or truth of their parts? Like x-rays, logical forms seem to show us the deep structure – the bare bones – of language. Yet their very simplicity and clarity pose, in the starkest way, problems that take us to the very limits of thought itself, problems whose simple formulation belies the mind-boggling bafflement they can induce in us.

2.2 CONSEQUENCE

The ancient Greeks were interested in the fundamental question of good reasoning: what follows logically from what? An argument – in the logician's sense – is a series of sentences, statements or propositions[3] in which one of the sentences is put forward as following logically from the others. When I say 'The sun is bright today' and then, a moment later, I sigh and say, 'Bert has my sunglasses', my second statement has followed the first. But it has not followed *from* the first in any logical sense. No doubt there was some association of ideas that made my thoughts move from the brightness of the sun to wondering where my sunglasses are, and then remembering leaving them perched on Bert's nose. But the statement that Bert has my sunglasses is not a logical consequence of the sun's being bright today. Why not? Because logical consequence has to carry truth from what is said to what follows logically from it. That the sun is bright today does not necessitate that Bert has my sunglasses. By contrast, the proposition that Bert has my sunglasses does necessitate that Bert has something of mine, which – in turn – necessitates that someone has something of mine. Put the other way around, the point is this: that someone has something of mine is a logical consequence of the proposition that Bert has my sunglasses.

Although, as we see in Chapter 6, the concept of *following logically from* is itself ambiguous, we are now in a position to make a first attempt to define 'following logically from', or 'logical consequence'. Let's use Greek letters in honour of the ancient pioneers of abstract symbolism and say that a sentence, ϕ, follows logically from, or is a logical consequence of, a set of sentences Γ, when and only when the following condition holds: if all of the sentences in Γ are true, then ϕ is true as well. Notice that there can be as many or as few sentences in Γ as you like, even none at all! In the special case where Γ is empty, then ϕ has the self-guaranteeing feature of being a logical truth (like 'either McGee is right or McGee's not right', 'if p then p', and so on). We return to logical truth and other special cases later in the chapter.

Aristotle's syllogisms standardly consisted of two premises from which the conclusion followed logically, for example:

> All humans can count to a hundred. All Spaniards are humans.
> So all Spaniards can count to a hundred.

In this case, Γ contains the first two sentences as its members, and the conclusion, that all Spaniards can count to a hundred, follows logically from them. Of course, not all humans really can count to a hundred, but that doesn't matter. The point about logical consequence is that *if* it is true that all humans can count to a hundred, and true that all Spaniards are humans, then it is also true that all Spaniards can count to a hundred. More abstractly, the pattern of the above argument is

> All Fs are Gs. All Ks are Fs. So all Ks are Gs

and this was recognized as one of the basic patterns of valid argument – valid in that, for whatever three nouns we choose to replace 'F', 'G' and 'K', the resulting argument will never be one that leads from true premises to a false conclusion. Another basic pattern of valid syllogistic argument is No Fs are G. Some Ks are Gs. So some Ks are not Fs. More complex arguments, with more than two premises, could be handled by the theory of the syllogism, provided, that is, they could be represented as a chain of arguments, each link of which has two premises from which a conclusion could be derived using the basic syllogism patterns. That conclusion would then become a premise for the next link in the chain, and so on until the final conclusion was reached. Since all complex arguments were supposed to reduce to arguments that matched the basic patterns, the theory of syllogistic reasoning, developed in detail by mediaeval logicians, was for some time the best available example of a system of logic.

The Stoics also looked for patterns that would never fail to deliver conclusions that are logical consequences of their premises. They became fascinated by the patterns that were the result of combining sentences with each other using the truth-functional words like 'if', 'and', 'or' and 'not' as the glue. Consider

> If the arrow is in flight, then it is in motion. The arrow is not in motion.
> So the arrow is not in flight.

The Stoics claimed that the pattern exemplified by the above argument would never lead from true premises to a false conclusion. Using their own special notation to lay bare the sentence structure, they symbolized the general form for which the above argument stood as a particular case as:

> If the First, then the Second. Not the Second.
> So not the First.

which is usually called *modus tollendo tollens*, or just *modus tollens* for short. The Stoics' 'first' and 'second' notation seems to be an attempt at introducing variables. We would write the same argument form as

> $p \supset q, \sim q$. Therefore $\sim p$.

Our variables don't represent any English sentences in particular, so the same formal pattern could equally well have the following argument corresponding to it:

> If the door was locked, Grace used her key to open it. She did not use her key to open it.
> So the door was not locked.

Variables are always used according to a rule for consistency: whatever sentence is first plugged into the place held by the variable 'p', for example, the very same sentence should be used to replace 'p' wherever else 'p' occurs in the formula or argument.

By minding only the 'p's and 'q's we can specify argument forms which reveal the bare bones on which valid inferences depend. Using the metalogical variables introduced in Chapter 1, Box 3, we can formalize *modus ponens* and *modus tollens* like this:

(MP) A ⊃ B, A. So B.
(MT) A ⊃ B, ~ B. So ~ A.

Remember, though, that symbolizing rules in this way does not mean that we will have a perfect fit between our symbols and their English 'equivalents'. The sign '⊃' does not capture exactly the meaning of 'if . . ., then . . .' in English, any more than the sign '&' exactly captures the meaning of 'and'. In logical systems, the conjunction 'A & B ' is true provided both 'A' and 'B ' are true. Nothing else matters. But in English, the order of sentences, including those joined by 'and', often indicates chronology. Think of the fact that Charles Darwin married Emma Wedgwood, and he and Emma together had ten children. English speakers usually regard the previous sentence as indicating that the marriage occurred before the birth of the children (as if 'and' can be read as 'and then'). From the point of view of logic, this sentence says nothing different from what would be said if we had stated that Charles Darwin and Emma Wedgwood together had ten children and he married her.

Can we fix the meaning of '&' at least for logical purposes? This is trickier than it seems at first: questions about the meanings of connectives are really hard to settle as we will see later in the chapter. For the time being, we just take the truth tables (see BOX 1, this chapter) as fixing how we will use the connectives for the purposes of defining logical consequence. According to the tables, 'A ⊃ B' follows logically from '~A v B', and '~A v B' follows logically from 'A ⊃ B'. Why? Because each of these formulas is true or false under exactly the same conditions. Take 'A ⊃ B', and suppose, for example, that 'A' is false. According to the table for '⊃', 'A ⊃ B' will be true in this case. Now think about '~A v B' for the same case (where 'A' is false). Now, '~A' will be true (negation reverses truth-value) and so '~A v B' will be true as well (check the table if you don't believe it).

You can work out the other cases for yourself. The way we have defined the connectives neatly ensures that '~A v B' is a logical consequence of 'A ⊃ B', and also vice versa. Likewise, given our definition of the conditions under which '&' formulas are true or false, 'B' is a logical consequence of 'A & B' in the sense that the truth of the latter guarantees the truth of the former.

Anyone who refused to accept that one of the conjuncts is true after accepting a conjunction as true would be speaking a very abnormal version of English and be using 'and' in a very odd way. Of course people sometimes use 'and' to mean 'and then'. When they do this they add something extra to the logical understanding of 'and'. They are not in any way doubting the fact that from 'A & B' it follows both that 'A' is true and that 'B' is true. To see the problem of querying the bare logical understanding of conjunction, imagine Dick tries to put forward the revolutionary view that the truth of the conjunction does not guarantee the truth of each of the conjuncts. How is this new view to be phrased? Dick argues: 'when "A & B" is true it does not follow logically that both "A" and "B" are separately true'. This won't do at all. Dick has just used 'and' in stating his supposedly revolutionary view, and the version of 'and' he used is the truth-functional one!

Never easily deterred, Dick tries again. This time he says: 'What I mean is that it's possible for "A & B" to be true while "A" is false.' This only looks like a smarter move until we ask what 'while' means. In normal situations if you are told that Samantha waited while John shopped, this means that Samantha waited, and that John shopped, and – moreover – that the waiting occurred at the same time as the shopping. Phrases like 'while' and 'at the same time' are often used in contexts where there is no possibility of referring to time at all. Mathematical objects, for example, have no causal or temporal relations with anything. Numbers don't wait around while their partners shop. Yet the teacher might tell the class: 'Two is an even number and at the same time it's also a prime number' where the use of 'at the same time' is meant to convey surprise about the conjunction of the two facts – that two is both even and prime. Even in this case there is no getting away from 'and' in its conjunctive sense. So it appears that logic doesn't teach the learner the meaning or content of words like 'and', 'if', 'or' and 'not' in other, independently definable, terms. Rather, it looks as if the the learner already has to understand the meaning of 'and', *etc.* in order to do logic at all![4]

2.3 DEDUCTIONS

One of the ambitions of systems of first-order logic is to find rules or patterns whose repeated use will enable the derivation of one logical formula from one or more other formulas, and derive these in turn from yet others, and so on. In each case, the derived or deduced formula must be a logical consequence of the formulas from which it is derived. This is an easy thing to do. Think again about:

(MP) A ⊃ B, A ⊢ B

using '⊢' as a symbol to show that any formula placed to its right follows from any formula or formulas to its left. The MP rule permits us – given 'p ⊃ q', and also given 'p' – to deduce 'q'. Or, given '(r & p) ⊃ (s v q)', and 'r & p' to deduce 's v q'. Now, by repeated use of the MP rule, it is easy to prove

r ⊃ s, s ⊃ t, r ⊢ t

Let's try to lay the proof out in a systematic fashion. First, we list the assumptions in the order given in the argument:

(1) r ⊃ s
(2) s ⊃ t
(3) r

Actually, since the intention of a proof system is to write down only what is permitted by the rules of the system, we should have a rule saying that we can make an assumption whenever we want. In its most liberal form, such a rule might say: *assume any well-formulated formula at any time you like in a proof.* We are given the premises of an argument, so we can 'assume' them, and we might need to make some additional assumptions in order to deduce a conclusion. That's perfectly fine, so long as we keep track of any such assumptions so that, at the end of a proof, we are able to see just what propositions were needed in order to deduce the conclusion. If we call the rule of assumptions 'A', then we can employ this rule and annotate the premise-assumptions as follows:

(1) $r \supset s$ A
(2) $s \supset t$ A
(3) r A

What next? From lines (1) and (3) we can deduce – using the rule of MP – something, namely ‘s’. So let us write that down next:

(1) $r \supset s$ A
(2) $s \supset t$ A
(3) r A
(4) s 1,3 MP

In writing this down, we have simply noted, on the right hand side, that we are taking the formulas already entered on lines (1) and (3) as instances of the premises required to be input to the MP rule, in order to derive ‘s’ as output. But now we have ‘$s \supset t$’ at line (2) and ‘s’ itself at line (4), so we can repeat the use of MP, this time taking these different premises as input to the rule.

(1) $r \supset s$ A
(2) $s \supset t$ A
(3) r A
(4) s 1,3 MP
(5) t 2,4 MP

And now this is almost a proof of ‘t’ from the initial premises entered on lines (1) and (2). Why almost? In a simple case like this, it is obvious that MP has just been applied twice over to get from the premises to the conclusions. In more complex cases, as we mentioned, it is essential to have a procedure for tracking the assumptions that are in use at any given stage of a proof. That way, the reader can easily check what each line of a proof proves, that is, what is said to be deduced from what. In a fully notated system of proof, then, a method of tracking assumptions has to be devised: this will, from a logical point of view, be more significant than the notes made on the right hand side, which are usually dispensed with once the rules of the system have been learnt.

One standard convention is to write to the left of the line number the number of any assumptions on which the formula at that line itself depends. If the formula at that line is an assumption, then it will be shown as depending only on itself. Here is the same proof with the assumption numbers inserted in bold:

1	(1)	$r \supset s$	A
2	(2)	$s \supset t$	A
3	(3)	r	A
1,3	(4)	s	1,3 MP
1,2,3	(5)	t	2,4 MP

Each of the first three formulas is shown to depend only on itself. The formula written at line (4) is derived from the formulas on lines (1) and (3) by the MP rule, so the dependencies at that line are shown as the formulas at (1) and at (3). Finally, the formula at line (5) is derived by rule from the formulas at lines (2) and (4). Since the formula at line (4) itself depends on the formulas at lines (1) and (3), then the formula at line (5) depends on the formulas at lines (1), (2) and (3) – notably, the three premises from which the conclusion was to be proved.

A proof in this kind of natural deduction system is a sequence of formulas, in which each later formula follows by rule from earlier ones. More precisely, a proof of a formula ϕ from a number of assumptions A_1, A_2, A_3, . . . and so on, is a finite sequence of formulas where ϕ is the last item of that sequence, and each item in the sequence is either an assumption or follows from earlier items in the sequence by means of one of the natural deduction rules. Consider line (4) of the proof above:

1,3 (4) s 1,3 MP

This states that 's' is derivable from the formulas at lines (1) and (3). On the right, we show that the rule in question is MP, but this piece of housekeeping is logically dispensable. Since 's' does follow from the formulas at lines (1) and (3) by the rule of MP, this is a case where we have a proof of 's' by the definition just given. Proofs consist of proofs: writing out a proof means starting from a proof and then building on to it to make a further proof, and on that to make a further proof, until the desired result is achieved.

Now suppose ϕ is a single formula which is a logical consequence of the formulas A_1, A_2, A_3, . . . Is there a simple set of rules so that by repeatedly applying them we can prove ϕ from A_1, A_2, A_3, . . .?

The answer is 'Yes'. All the standard systems of natural deduction actually do specify a small set of basic rules that have this remarkable feature: in all cases where a formula is a logical consequence of some (possibly empty) group of formulas, there is a proof of that formula from the group, using only rules from the basic set in the system. It is easy to see why this feature is called *completeness*. When we prove that a system of logic is complete in this sense, we are proving something *about* a logical system and hence we are doing *metalogic*.

It can also be established by a metalogical proof that the *only* formulas that can be proved by the basic rules in standard systems of natural deduction are those that are logical consequences of the assumptions from which they are deduced. This second result – the consistency of natural deduction systems – when combined with the completeness result gives a very satisfying prize. Whenever any formula ϕ is provable by the rules of a natural deduction system from a bunch of formulas $A_1, A_2, A_3, \ldots$, then ϕ is a logical consequence of $A_1, A_2, A_3, \ldots$ and conversely.

2.4 DOES MP PROVE ANYTHING AT ALL?

No sooner have we found a neat system of proof than we run up against a problem which is a bit like the one about the content of 'and'. It seems that logical rules do not give us independent grasp of the meaning of rules of inference like MP: instead, you already need to be disposed to accept the validity of certain inferences that are cases of MP before you can be said to grasp the MP rule itself. Put more dramatically, the MP rule is not just a convention about inference, one over which different reasoners might legitimately disagree. Rather, it formalizes our existing grasp of logical consequence.

To see this, ask yourself whether it would be possible to convince a doubter to accept MP. The nicest exploration of this question was carried out at the end of the nineteenth century by Lewis Carroll and has already been mentioned in Chapter 1.[5] Carroll imagines a conversation between Achilles and the tortoise – two characters from one of Zeno's paradoxes.[6] The tortoise begins by quoting just two steps from Euclid's reasoning in the first proposition of *Elements of Geometry*:

(*A*) Things that are equal to the same are equal to each other.
(*B*) The two sides of this Triangle are things that are equal to the same.
(*Z*) The two sides of this Triangle are equal to each other.

'Readers of Euclid will grant', the tortoise says, 'that *Z* follows logically from *A* and *B*, so that any one who accepts *A* and *B* as true, *must* accept *Z* as true.' Achilles agrees. Next the tortoise slyly points out that some people might say they accept that *Z* follows from *A* and *B*, but have some doubts about accepting *A* and *B* themselves. Further, some people – ones who are not very good at logical or mathematical reasoning – might accept *A* and *B* as true, but be doubtful about the transition from *A* and *B* as premises to *Z* as a conclusion.

The second case is the tricky one, and by not querying it the poor warrior falls into the tortoise's trap. According to the tortoise, someone might accept *A* and *B*, but not

(C) If *A* and *B* are true then *Z* must be true.

Achilles at this point is puzzled as to why statement (*Z*) is not just labelled as '(*D*)'. 'If you accept *A* and *B* and *C*,' he exclaims, 'you *must* accept *Z*!' But the tortoise hesitates: 'If *A* and *B* and *C* are true, *Z must* be true,' he murmurs thoughtfully. 'That's *another* hypothetical, isn't it?' he asks. 'And, if I failed to see its truth, I might accept *A* and *B* and *C*, and *still* not accept *Z*, mightn't I?' In the face of this obtuseness, what is Achilles to say? He grants that the tortoise could hesitate in this way, hence he has to add another premise to the argument, namely:

(*D*) If *A* and *B* and *C* are true, then *Z* must be true.

Achilles is not so very bright, and what is probably now obvious to you seems not to dawn immediately on him, namely that we have started an infinite regress. Moreover, in this regress, a version of MP is going to keep appearing over and over again. If there are people who really don't grasp MP, and are not disposed to reason in accordance with it, no amount of repeating the rule will explain the validity of an MP inference to them.[7]

We can now provide a way out of the regress generated by Carroll's puzzle. The tortoise gets Achilles to write down:

(*C*) If *A* and *B* are true then *Z* must be true.

as if this will strengthen the argument from *A* and *B* to *Z*. By doing this, the tortoise is making it look as if the original argument had a missing premise – namely *C*. If he's right, then the argument from *A*, *B* and *C* to *Z* will be better than the argument from *A* and *B* alone to the conclusion *Z*. So we can now ask whether adding *C* would give a logically competent person a good reason to believe *Z*, given that the person in question already believed *A* and *B*. Once we put the question, it's easy to see that the tortoise is not adding anything extra at all.[8] For the existing premises already give any logically competent subject good reasons for believing *Z* on the basis of belief in *A* and *B*. Adding *C* does not give logically competent people any better reason for belief in *Z*. The tortoise's trick was to make the rule of inference itself appear to be a further reason for accepting the conclusion, and once Achilles misses that sleight of hand he is doomed to go on adding infinitely more 'premises' of the same kind to the argument.

We saw already in the case of McGee's argument in Chapter 1 that there can be fallacies of reason*ing* even in the presence of perfectly valid arguments. What the tortoise has done is trick Achilles into not being able to defend a perfectly good inference, by insisting that some people would not be able to reason from (that is, make the inference from) the premises to the conclusion. Of course, there will be such people and they will be people who are not logically competent in the first place. That people who lack logical competence will not regard believing the premises of a valid argument as giving good reason for believing the conclusion is hardly a surprise. The tortoise has not cast doubt on the validity of the original inference, but has shown something else instead: that some level of logical competence is necessary before we start formalizing inference. Studying logic may, of course, improve someone's initial competence, but it can do nothing for those who are logically incompetent in the first place.[9]

Logical competence as just defined does not get around all problems. It does not, for example, help us see our way out of McGee's puzzling argument that was discussed in Chapter 1. His argument went like this:

(1) If a Republican wins the election, then if it's not Reagan who wins it will be Anderson.
(2) A Republican will win the election.
(3) If it's not Reagan who wins, it will be Anderson.

This looks as if it has the form

$R \supset (\sim G \supset A), R \vdash \sim G \supset A$

Formalized this way, the extra information that gave rise to the puzzle was hidden: Reagan was ahead of both Carter and Anderson, and Anderson was so far out of the race that if Reagan had not won, then Carter, not Anderson would have won. But Reagan and Anderson were Republican candidates, while Carter was a Democrat. Filling in some of this missing information – as was done in Chapter 1 – the argument goes:

(1) If Reagan or Anderson wins the election, then if it's not Reagan who wins it will be Anderson.
(2) Reagan or Anderson will win the election.
(3) If it's not Reagan who wins, it will be Anderson.

This new argument is really weird. The first premise in fact adds nothing at all to the argument, for it is symbolized as

(1) $(R \vee A) \supset (\sim R \supset A)$

Like each of the supposedly missing steps the tortoise foists onto Achilles, this premise does no work, for it simply states a logical truth. (To see this, note that '$\sim R \supset A$' is truth-functionally equivalent to '$R \vee A$', hence the premise says no more than '$(R \vee A) \supset (R \vee A)$'.) Removing the first premise, the argument reduces to

$R \vee A \vdash \sim R \supset A$

which is certainly valid, for the premise and the conclusion are equivalent to each other. But common sense rebels. If Reagan had not won, it would have been Carter, not Anderson, who won. How can logic legitimize a plainly wrong conclusion?

The trouble is that what made it true to say that Reagan or Anderson would win is that Reagan was way ahead in the polls and was, in fact, going to win the election. Indeed, whenever 'A' is true, it will be true that 'A v B', simply given the truth-table for 'v'. So 'A v B' will be a logical consequence of 'A'. In parallel to this fact about consequence is a rule found in all systems of classical logic, one that licenses the inference from 'A' to 'A v B'. But now, as seen in the earlier example about Lance Armstrong, if 'A' is taken as a premise, and then we suppose that 'A' is false, then it will follow that B. The argument is simple:

1	(1) A	Assumption
1	(2) A v B	2, vI (the rule is often called 'v-Introduction')
3	(3) ~A	Assumption
1, 3	(4) B	2, 3 DS (the rule is called 'Disjunctive Syllogism', or sometimes by its medieval name *MPT* – '*modus ponendo tollens*')

Notice that there is no assumption which introduces the 'novel' element, 'B', into the above argument. The only assumptions made in the argument are that 'A' and '~A' are both true. It is from this contradiction that it apparently follows that 'B' is true, no matter what formula or sentence 'B' stands for. So now we can see how logic ensured that Anderson got into the conclusion of McGee's argument when he never got into office.

How does this surprising result square with the notion that a valid inference is truth-preserving – that the truth of the premise or premises guarantees the truth of the conclusion? We seem to have here a very special case – where the guaranteed falsity of the premises (they contradict each other) guarantees the truth of the conclusion. This result has worried logicians for centuries, and we look at it in more detail in Chapter 6. Among contemporary theorists, some logicians – the *intuitionists* – reject the classical rule of 'or'-introduction, while others – the advocates of *relevant logic* – prohibit sentences or formulas occurring in the conclusion of arguments unless they already occur in one or more of the assumptions (in other words, the conclusion has to follow in a relevant way from the premises). For classical logic, however, since ϕ is a logical consequence of A_1, A_2, A_3, . . . provided there is no case in which A_1, A_2, A_3, . . . are all true while ϕ is false, we can always ensure that we have a valid argument by making its premise or premises contradictory. For then there is no chance of the premise(s) being true, hence no possibility for the premise(s) to be true when the conclusion is false.

Given the way the hook connective is defined, it is always the case that when the argument

$A \vdash B$

is valid, then the conditional

$A \supset B$

expresses a logical truth (and vice versa). Corresponding to the bizarre inference from 'A' and '~A' to 'B', is the weird logical truth '(A & ~A) ⊃ B'.

A satisfactory definition of logical truth – as we saw earlier – can be given in terms of the relation of logical consequence: those formulas and sentences which are logical consequences of no assumptions at all are the logical truths. The obvious notation for showing this is to write –

$\vdash A \supset B$

to show that 'A ⊃ B' is a logical truth. However, the ways of notating logical truth are not nearly as fascinating as are the puzzles about what to count as logical truths, and whether these are to be regarded as sentences or formulas that are true in virtue of the meanings of the logical constants. We will come back to this topic at the end of the chapter, but first we will quickly sketch out some more details of what a system of first-order logic looks like.

2.5 NAMES, QUANTIFIERS AND VARIABLES

By digging deeper into the structure of sentences, the power of logic to reveal valid inferences and true propositions is increased immensely. Bert is single and no single man has a wife. Hence Bert lacks a wife. Simple though this argument is, its structure and validity cannot be revealed by the notation developed so far. We need to uncover more structural features of language. In particular, we need the ability to represent particular things and their properties by means of our logical notations. We can refer to Bert by using a name for him – one that functions just like the name 'Bert' in English. So we can start to symbolize the argument just given by writing

b is single
No single man has a wife
So *b* does not have a wife

Here we are using the symbol, '*b*', to perform just the same role as the name 'Bert' – that is, to refer to exactly one person, namely Bert. If we had a way of representing the properties of being single, and of having a wife – say, by using the capital letters 'F' and 'G' to represent the property of being single and the property of having a wife, respectively – we still could not quite get the whole argument formalized, for we would have

Fb
No person who is F also is G
So ~G*b*

Notice that we have reversed the normal word order of English in the first premise. 'Bert is single' has become, in its logical version, 'Is single Bert'. Most notations for classical logic carry out this reversal, and we simply follow suit here: but nothing special depends on the order of the symbols.

To understand how the second premise is normally symbolized, two new ideas are helpful: the notion of an *open sentence*, and a notation of *quantifiers and variables*. The first is a really simple idea. Think of a sentence, containing a proper name, and which is true or false: 'Laurence wrote part of this book'. Now take out the proper name, 'Laurence', and replace it with a letter that marks the gap where the name was: 'x wrote part of this book'. Whereas the sentence about Laurence is true, the open sentence 'x wrote part of this book' is true of some people and false of others. It's true of Max that he wrote part of this book, and it's also true of Joe that he wrote part of it. So if we replace the letter 'x' by the name 'Max', or the name 'Joe', we get a closed true sentence, while if we replace the letter 'x' by the name 'Chad', we get a closed false sentence. An open sentence may be true or false of something, or even true of nothing at all (like the sentence 'x is completely round and square at the same time').

Closing an open sentence by replacing the variable 'x' with a name is only one possibility. Consider the true closed sentence: 'Something wrote part of this book.' Using a special symbol to represent a *quantifier*, with the meaning 'there is at least one thing, x, such that . . .' (written for short as '∃x') we can put

(∃x)(x wrote part of this book)

We read this as 'there is at least one thing x such that x wrote part of this book', or – more briefly – 'for some x, x wrote part of this book'. Provided the open sentence 'x wrote part of this book' is true of at least one thing in the universe, then the closed sentence '(∃x)(x wrote part of this book' is true).

Max, Joe and Laurence are not just things – they're also people. If we take the conjunction of two open sentences

x is a person & x wrote part of this book

then we can close this in the same way

(∃x)(x is a person & x wrote part of this book).

Provided the conjunctive open sentence is true of at least one thing, then the last sentence is true. Brackets have been used to indicate that the very same variable, 'x', is picked up by the quantifier '∃' at all the places where it occurs in the sentence. The sentence just symbolized reads 'for some x, x is a person and x (the very same thing) wrote part of this book'. By contrast

(∃x)(x is a person) & x wrote part of this book

is an open sentence and hence not true or false. This latter sentence reads in English

There is at least one person, and x wrote part of this book

or, more literally

(For at least one thing, x, x is a person) and x wrote part of this book

where the brackets show that the 'at least one' quantifier does not pick up the final occurrence of the variable 'x'. There's a neat way of talking about this. Call the shortest sentence following a quantifier + variable expression the *scope* of that expression. The variable that is attached to the quantifier, only picks up – or *binds* – the instances of that variable which occur in the scope of the original quantifier + variable expression.

Our '∃' quantifier is very expressive when combined with negation. Take 'F' and 'G' to represent the properties of being a frog, and being green, respectively. To represent 'some frogs are green', or 'at least one frog is green', we simply put

(∃x)(Fx & Gx)

Now, can you see what

(∃x)(Fx & ~Gx)

would mean? It states that there is at least one thing which is a frog and is not green, in other words that some frogs are not green. And if we want to express the claim that no frogs are green, we can simply put the negation where it has a wider scope, namely

~(∃x)(Fx & Gx)

This claims that it is false that there is at least one green frog: in other words, it expresses the thought that no frogs are green.

That done, we're in a position to symbolize the argument about Bert as follows, remembering this time to read 'F' as 'is single' and 'G' as 'has a wife':

Fb
~(∃x)(Fx & Gx)
~Gb

The formulation of the second premise says that no thing is single and has a wife. To capture the claim that no man is single and has a wife, we'd need to flesh it out a bit by writing

~(∃x)(Mx & Fx & Gx)

with 'Mx' read as 'x is a man'.

For convenience, logic texts usually introduce a further quantifier, '∀. . .', to represent 'everything . . . is such that . . .', 'each . . . is such that . . .' or just 'for all. . .'. Materialism is the philosophy that claims that everything is material. With 'Mx' for 'x is material', we can symbolize the materialists' core claim as '(∀x)(Mx)'. While the particular quantifier '∃' is normally used in front of complex sentences which contain '&' as their main connective, the universal quantifier '∀' has an affinity for '⊃'. That all frogs are green would be symbolized as

(∀x)(Fx ⊃ Gx)

and not as '(∀x)(Fx & Gx)'. Why not use the latter? '(∀x)(Fx & Gx)' would be true provided the open sentence 'Fx & Gx' were true of everything in the universe. But it is plainly false that everything in the universe is both a frog and green! By contrast, think of the open sentence 'if x is a frog, then x is green'. This is satisfied by something provided that thing is green if it's a frog. The universal closure of this sentence reads: 'For anything at all, x, if x is a frog, then x is green.' It's not a perfect translation but a lot more plausible than the conjunctive reading. Now suppose the universe sadly contained no frogs. In such a universe, provided there are things at all, it will be true of each and every one of them that if it is a frog, then it is green (remember that the truth-table for 'A ⊃ B' gives the conditional the value true whenever the antecedent is false). In the frogless universe our universal claim that all frogs are green turns out to be true (and it's also true in that universe that all frogs are grey, they're all brown and that all of them are underground trains as well). This oddity is best discussed along with other problems about the meaning of '⊃' (see Chapter 6).

In the universe we inhabit there are frogs. So the universal conditional form seems to give quite a good account of what we mean when claiming that all frogs are green: to refute the claim, we need simply find just one thing which is a frog and not green. Indeed, the claim formalized as '(∃x)(Fx & ~Gx)' explicitly contradicts the claim '(∀x)(Fx ⊃ Gx)'. So writing '~(∃x)(Fx & ~Gx)' is just another way of saying the same thing as '(∀x)(Fx ⊃ Gx)', while writing '~(∀x)(Fx ⊃ Gx)' is just another way of expressing the same as '(∃x)(Fx & ~Gx)'. You will see now why having both the particular and the universal quantifiers is a bit of a luxury: in theory, provided we have negation and the other truth-functional connectives to hand, we can express all the universal and particular truths we want by simply using one of the quantifiers. By the way, it's a bit of a luxury to have so many truth-functional connectives, for we really don't need so many either. For example, we could do without '⊃', if we wanted, because '~A v B' has exactly the same truth conditions as 'A ⊃ B'.

2.6 IDENTITY

A complete system of elementary logic usually has one other ingredient in addition to the notational devices introduced so far. In order to formalize numerical claims, and to express some other everyday pieces of valid reasoning, it is useful to have a symbol for identity. Suppose that Max is more handsome than any other man. We can express this by saying that Max is more handsome than any man who is not identical with Max. Identity in this sense is more than similarity. In everyday speech we talk about 'identical twins', meaning twins that are genetically the same, but are different – though extremely similar – people. For such twins, what is *identical* in the logical sense is the structure of their DNA, not their bodies, their faces, or their location. In the strict sense of identity, the expression '4 + 5' names the very same number as the expression '12 – 3', namely the number 9. Likewise, once it was discovered that the 'star' seen in the west at evening is the same planet (namely Venus) as can often been seen in the eastern sky at dawn, it became clear that the evening star is identical with the morning star. With 'e' as a name for the evening star and 'm' as a name for the morning star, the identity can be symbolized as 'e = m'.

It's very easy to add the rules for identity to a system of formal logic, for there are only two principles to consider. One is that each thing is identical with itself (in symbols, ∀x(x = x)). The other says that if 'a = b' then any predicate true of a is also true of b. Suppose 'Max' and 'Dr Deutsch' are names for one and the same person. Then, since it is true that 'Max = Dr Deutsch' and also true that Max wrote Chapter 4 of this book, it follows that Dr Deutsch wrote Chapter 4 of this book. As that chapter shows, identity is linked with a series of puzzles about names, and – as the chapter following that shows – these puzzles are also linked with a set of problems about modality, that is, the notions of necessity and possibility. The last two or three decades of work on identity, names, necessity and truth has revolutionized many aspects of philosophy well beyond the field of formal logic. The ideas of possible worlds and necessity introduced in the following two chapters even have implications – as we will see – for what contemporary thinkers believe about the nature of philosophy itself and the status of philosophical claims.

2.7 INFERENCE AND MEANING

Throughout this chapter we have focused on two ways of thinking about consequence: one in terms of truth, the other in terms of proof. We first introduced logical consequence in terms of the preservation of truth from premise or premises to conclusion. Sometimes, this is referred to as a semantic notion of consequence. Proof or deduction, conceived as manipulation of symbols according to rules, provided a second account of consequence: if ϕ can be derived by deduction rules from A_1, A_2, A_3, . . . and so on, then ϕ is a consquence of A_1, A_2, A_3, . . ., etc. This is sometimes called the syntactic notion of consequence.[10] The consistency and completeness of first-order logic guarantees that both forms of consequence coincide.

The tight connection between semantic and syntactic consequence means that problems and puzzles often appear twice over – as semantic ones, expressed in terms of truth, and again as syntactic ones, in terms of proof. But there may be benefits too. It might be thought that since logicians have stipulated both the semantic way of defining the connectives (by truth tables) and the rules of proof for them, there should not be much to choose between different ways of specifying what the logical constants themselves mean. Just as many of the puzzles we've looked at so far have two aspects, the semantic and the syntactic, maybe the meanings of logical constants also have the same two aspects. Logical truths (and valid deductions) are true (and valid) in virtue of the meanings of the logical constants. So perhaps we can specify the meaning of logical constants either by reference to their semantic or their syntactic roles. Since both of these roles are to some extent stipulated by people who have thought long and seriously about logic, it would not seem too difficult to carry out the required specification of meaning.

Any bright hopes of this sort are over-optimistic. An easy, but imprecise, way to say what logical constants are consists in listing them together with a brief account, either in semantic or syntactic terms, of the role they play. This is what has been done in this chapter so far. Beyond that we are liable to get mired in quicksands. The history of logic in the twentieth century was one of repeated bafflement about how to deal with the definition of the constants. Rudolf Carnap rather boldy ventured the following thoughts:

> Up to now, in constructing a language, the procedure has usually been, first to assign a meaning to the fundamental mathematico-logical symbols, and then to consider what sentences and inferences are seen to be correct in accordance with this meaning. . . . The connection will only become clear when approached from the opposite direction: let any postulates and any rules of inference be chosen arbitrarily, then this choice, whatever it may be, will determine what meaning is to be assigned to the fundamental logical symbols.[11]

What Carnap means by the 'fundamental mathematico-logical symbols' are just the logical constants. Think of rules like MP as themselves part of the definition of proof: for a line, or a sequence of lines, to be a proof, the formula at that line has to follow – by one of the rules of proof – from the formulas listed as assumptions at that line. In some standard deduction systems, there are just two rules for each logical connective – one that introduces it and one that eliminates it. To introduce the conjunction operator '&' for example, there is the rule that from 'A' on its own, and from 'B' on its own, it follows logically that 'A & B'. The and-elimination rule states that from the conjunction 'A & B', it follows logically that 'A' and it also follows logically that 'B'. From the point of view of a system of proof, these two rules tell us everything the system requires from '&'. (Some people, Gerhard Gentzen for one, have argued that the introduction rules alone define the meaning of the the operator '&'.) For Carnap, such rules – even if chosen arbitrarily – would specify the meaning of conjunction within a particular deductive system.

A very simple argument apparently shows that Carnap was wrong about this. There are dozens (actually, infinitely many) ways of formulating sentences that are equivalent to conjunctions, conditionals and disjunctions. For starters 'A ⊃ B' is equivalent to '~(A & ~B)' and to '~A v B', while 'A & B' is equivalent to '~(~A v ~B)' and to '~(A ⊃ ~B)'. Suppose that we define the connective 'et' so that 'A et B' is equivalent to '~(A & ~B) & ~(~A & B) & ~(~A & ~B)'. Now 'et' so defined will – strangely enough – have just the same introduction and elimination rules as '&'. But since to understand 'et' we need to understand not only 'and' but also 'not', it would be wrong to claim that 'et' and '&' mean the same thing.[12] Carnap is mistaken, then, when he claims that the inferential role of '&' (or of any other symbol) can completely determine its meaning.

This looks like a knockdown argument against the views of

writers like Carnap and Hilbert. Yet there are considerations that point the other way. Consider this imaginary case. Ted and Mary live in different places and don't even speak a common language yet engage in pretty competent reasoning. In fact each of them is disposed to accept the validity of very similar sets of inferences, so similar, in fact, that if we formalized their reasoning, we would find that Ted accepts the truth of '(A & B) **o** C' whenever Mary accepts '(A & B) ⊗ C' and vice versa. Likewise, for a whole range of further inferences, the logic of Ted's connective '**o**' completely matches the logic of Mary's '⊗'. Should we not say in this case that Ted and Mary mean the same thing by their two different connectives?

Before agreeing that Ted and Mary mean the same thing by their two connectives, think again about the argument about '&' and 'et'. The fact that these two connectives have the same introduction and elimination rules show that they do equivalent work, but not that they mean the same. Likewise, although it seems that '**o**' and '⊗' do equivalent work, it need not follow that there is no more to the meaning of these signs than is given through their role in inferences. After all, '**o**' may be Ted's symbol for '⊃' while '⊗' is Mary's term for '~ . . . v . . .'. In this case, we can say that Ted and Mary agree in an important respect: their terms play exactly similar roles in inference. But we cannot safely deduce that therefore their terms have exactly the same meaning.

The question of what logical words mean is certainly not a straightforward one. Heroic efforts can be made to try to give precise definitions of the logical constants, ones which attempt to capture the intuition that logical truth and logical validity are due to the meaning of these constants.[13] It certainly seems clear that connectives, quantifiers and other logical constants have definable roles in inferences – specified quite clearly in the rules for their introduction and elimination. Yet it also seems clear that we grasp these rules and learn to work with them because we already have an antecedent grasp of conjunction, disjunction, existential quantification, and so on. Formal logic may help us assess arguments, it can help express ideas and relations more precisely, but it cannot from its own resources provide an account of meaning that itself fully explains the notion of logical consequence. As we saw through analysis of what the tortoise said to Achilles, the logical competence of reasoners is already assumed as given by anyone who starts to investigate logical argument. As Wittgenstein emphasized, justifications have to come to an end somewhere, and grasping a rule is exhibited in obeying, or breaking, it in actual circumstances.[14] Unless we come to logic with some existing grasp of rules – a certain level of logical know-how – the definitions, explanations and conventions of the formal system will be lost on us.

SUGGESTIONS FOR FURTHER READING

Most introductory textbooks on formal logic have useful material on truth-tables, proof, and some have neat discussions of the theorems proving completeness and consistency; see in particular Smith (2003) and Sainsbury (2001). Graham Priest's *Very Short Introduction* gives a good overview of some of the problems discussed in the present chapter (Priest 2000), and for a bit more technical detail, see Chapter 3 of Read (1995). Timothy Smiley gives a helpful account of the notion of consequence in his encyclopedia entry (Smiley 1998). The approach to logical consequence taken in this chapter is profoundly influenced by Etchemendy (1990) – but this is definitely not a book for the beginner.

CHAPTER 3

TRUTH

3.1 RESPECT FOR TRUTH

Dick does not really see the point of telling the truth, and tends to lie whenever it suits him. Grace thinks that this is one of Dick's more irritating characteristics, and thought that she might try using some behavioural psychology to cure him. Grace asked Bert to be her witness, and announced to Dick: 'Every time you say something untrue, Dick, I'm going to punch you on the nose, but every time you tell the truth, I'm going to give you a dollar.' 'That's very generous of you' said Dick, and generous Grace immediately gave him a dollar. '$2+2=4$', said Dick, and Grace handed over another dollar. Dick was really excited about making money so easily, and said 'Now you're going to give me another dollar'. But Grace punched him on the nose. Ouch! Dick was confused. He had assumed that Grace would give him another dollar, so the last thing he said would have been true, and he would have been entitled to that dollar. But equally, Grace, by not giving him a dollar, made the last thing Dick said untrue, so she was entitled to punch him on the nose. For a while, Dick ruefully rubbed his sore nose, perplexed and upset, and was afraid to say anything. Finally he said to Grace 'Now you are going to punch me on the nose'.[1]

Grace is nonplussed. How should she respond to that last statement of Dick's? If she were to punch him on the nose, then what he said would have been true, and she had undertaken to pay him for a truth with a dollar, not with a punch on the nose. On the other hand, if she does not punch him on the nose but gives him a dollar, then what he said was untrue so, according to her promise, she should not give him a dollar, but punch him on the nose. Bert is no help at all. He just shakes his head and murmurs 'It's amazing, Grace'.

What we have here is a paradox, and it belongs in the same family as does the Liar Paradox mentioned in Chapter 1. What relates them is that they both revolve around the concepts of *truth* and *falsity*. Is Dick's last statement (that Grace will punch him on the nose) true or false? If it is true, then Grace will punch him on the nose. But she has undertaken to punch him on the nose only for untruths, therefore what he said must be untrue. However, if what he said really is untrue, then he will get a punch on the nose from Grace (that's the deal) so, since what he said was that he would get that punch on the nose, what he said is true! In summary: if Dick's last statement is true, then it is untrue; if it is untrue, then it is true!

One's first reaction to a paradox like this is to think that it is too silly to be worth bothering about. One's second reaction is to think that since the reasoning relied only on a few basic principles, and involved only intuitively acceptable assumptions, the fact that we arrive at an absurd conclusion must indicate either that there is something deeply and fundamentally wrong with how we reason or that one or more of our basic intuitions must be mistaken. Whatever the problem is, it becomes an urgent matter to locate it and to find a solution. This is why paradoxes, far from being regarded as mere recreations, have been treated with the utmost seriousness by philosophers through the ages.

Just what assumptions did we make in our discussion of Grace's attempt to cure Dick's habitual prevarication? Well, we assumed that Dick's last statement was either true or false and this led to the crazy conclusion that, if true, it's false; if false, then true. But perhaps that assumption is unreasonable. Could it be that Dick's last statement was neither true nor false? That does not really seem plausible. After all, if Dick says 'Now you are going to punch me on the nose' and Grace, forgetting her promise and forgoing any complicated reasoning, punches him on the nose just because she feels like doing so, then what Dick said was plainly true. If she does not punch him on the nose, then what he said was plainly false. So Dick's statement was true or false; not neither. But what about Grace's utterance when she was trying to lay out for Dick the details of her behavioural therapy programme? The first bit of her utterance was: 'Every time you say something untrue, Dick, I'm going to punch you on the nose.' One way of putting this into logic-speak is:

(G) For each sentence that Dick utters, 'Grace will punch Dick on the nose' is true if and only if what Dick says is not true.

Suppose that, on some occasion, Dick utters the sentence 'Pigs can fly'. Then, by substituting that sentence for the phrase 'what Dick says' in (G), we get the following instantiation:

'Grace will punch Dick on the nose' is true if and only if 'Pigs can fly' is not true.

BOX 1 : Universal Instantiation

A very obvious logical principle is at work here. It is the principle of Universal Instantiation: $(x)Fx \vdash Fa$. It means that, from the premise that every (or each) x has the property F, we can infer that any particular thing has the property F. Small letters from the beginning of the alphabet, 'a', 'b', 'c' . . . are conventionally used as abbreviations for names of particulars. The case under discussion is a little complicated. Here, the variable 'x' ranges over sentences uttered by Dick, 'a' is an abbreviation for the name of one of Dick's sentences, and 'F' is the predicate 'Grace will punch Dick on the nose' is true if and only if . . . is not true'. 'F' is called a one-place predicate, because by filling in the one blank with a noun (here the name of a sentence) we obtain a complete sentence. A much more straightforward example of a one-place predicate is '. . . is clumsy'. Note that we have been using 'sentence uttered by Dick' and 'what Dick says' interchangeably. But, as we shall soon see, that may not be a wise thing to do.

So it doesn't take any great genius to work out that, when Dick says 'Pigs can fly', he'll get a punch on the nose from Grace. The weird case arises when the occasion in question is the one when Dick says 'Grace will punch Dick on the nose'. Here we get the following instantiation of (G):

'Grace will punch Dick on the nose' is true if and only if 'Grace will punch Dick on the nose' is not true.

To say the least, that sentence is very odd. What can we infer from it? That Dick will get a punch in the nose from Grace? That he won't? The sentence seems to tell us nothing true and nothing false; it seems to be utterly vacuous. If I say to you 'Bert is in the garden if and only if Bert is not in the garden', then I have told you nothing about Bert's whereabouts; in fact, I have told you nothing about anything. You might be inclined to judge that I have uttered a perfectly grammatical English sentence, but that the sentence is empty, has no content, expresses no proposition, fails to yield a statement. If this is the line you are inclined to take, then you might want to say the same about the words that Grace originally said to Dick. Because part of her sentence was, in paraphrase, (G), and part of (G) – an instantiation of it, more accurately – is some bizarre and empty sentence.

We have been examining, even challenging, the assumption that Grace's original utterance was a *bona fide* statement. It was a perfectly grammatical sentence and it had a meaning – we understood it – and on the evidence of the first few interactions between Grace and Bert, we took it to be true. Had Dick said 'Lions are animals' and received a punch on the nose from Grace, then we should have immediately acknowledged that her original utterance was false. But then we saw that one response of Dick's froze Grace into inaction. Dick's utterance seemed to be false if true, true if false, so if it is either true or false, then it is *both* true and false. This worried us.

But here we come to another assumption that was made in our discussion. Why should we have been worried? Isn't it just an assumption that a statement cannot be *both* true and false?[2] A natural response to make at this point is that, while a movie can be both long and interesting, and a person can be both kind and intelligent, a statement *cannot* be both true and false just because of what 'true' and 'false' mean. But what do 'true' and 'false' mean? Even if we discover that we cannot give definitions of 'true' or 'false' (simple words like 'blue', 'one' and 'true' may not be amenable to any revealing definition) they still mean something, otherwise we could not understand sentences containing them. What does 'true' mean, or, to counter the impression that we are going to spend time quibbling over the meanings of words, let us put the question this way: What is truth? What is it that all truths share, but all non-truths lack? This is the central concern of the present chapter. We shall not be concerned with whether Grace eventually succeeded in instilling in Dick a respect for the truth, nor with the moral question of what exactly is valuable about being truthful. Other books have been written about the latter.[3]

3.2 THE BEARERS OF TRUTH

We can say that a particular bicycle wheel is true, and this means that the rim lies in a plane. When we say that Grace's love for Dick is true, we mean that she is not faking it. To say that Bert's aim is true means that it is on target. So there are some noun-phrases to which we can meaningfully attach the predicate 'is true' and, as we have seen, the predicate means something different in each of the three cases mentioned. But such cases are rarities and, anyway, involve senses of 'true' and 'false' with which we are not here concerned. It does not make sense to say that my coat is true, nor that my socks, the president of the United Nations, Sunday, the number 16, the storage capacity of a refrigerator are true. These things are not the bearers of truth or falsity. Try substituting any word – an adjective, adverb, interjection or what have you – for 'X' in 'X is true' and the result will almost invariably be nonsense. What, then, can we sensibly say is true or is false; what are the real bearers of truth and falsity (for short: the truth-bearers)?

One way to approach this question is *via* a consideration of the expression 'is true of'. All of the following are perfectly meaningful:

> The phrase 'is stupid' truly applies to Dick. OR 'Is stupid' is true of Dick. *OR* That he is stupid is true of Dick.
> The phrase 'is prime' truly applies to 16. OR 'Is prime' is true of 16. *OR* That it is prime is true of 16.
> The phrase 'follows Saturday' truly applies to Sunday. OR 'Follows Saturday' is true of Sunday. *OR* That it follows Saturday is true of Sunday.

The word 'satisfies' has a technical sense, meaning the converse of 'is true of' ('X is true of Y' = 'Y satisfies X') so we can rephrase the first of these examples as:

> Dick satisfies 'is stupid'.

But it is clear that we can avoid all these technical terms and circumlocutions by a suitable rephrasing, viz.:

'Dick is stupid' is true. *OR* It is true that Dick is stupid.

and similarly for the other examples.

It now looks as if we are close to answering our question about truth-bearers. Quotation marks are usefully regarded as pointing devices – they point at what lies between them. In

'Dick is stupid' is true

what lies between the quotation marks is not a single word, but is a complete sentence. Likewise, in

It is true that Dick is stupid

what follows 'It is true that' is a complete sentence. So isn't the answer this: the bearers of truth and falsity are sentences? Unfortunately, life is not so simple.

Nobody would claim that a word-salad, such as 'Next three number the lives Saturday to door' conveys anything that can be assessed for truth or falsity, but even with a grammatically impeccable sentence like 'Saturday lives next door to the number three', we might not be happy about ascribing either truth or falsity to it. If 'Saturday' is here intended to name a day of the week, then to say that Saturday lives next door to something (especially to the kind of entity that could itself not live in a house) is, not to mince words, nonsense. It is a sortal error, Saturday and the number three not being the sorts of thing that could walk through your door. Someone who utters that sentence produces a grammatically correct string of words but the person says nothing, fails to produce anything that can be assessed for truth or falsity.

You might, however, wish to disagree with that verdict. You might want to say that, since the sentence is definitely not true, it must be false. Perhaps you have further reasons for your view that the sentence is not nonsensical but plain false. So the matter is controversial. But, it is important to see that, even if we confine our attention to sentences that are grammatically and sortally impeccable, there are acute problems with the claim that sentences are the bearers of truth and falsity. Consider the sentence: 'After he had said this, he left her as he did the day before.'[4] Were I to ask you whether this sentence is true or false, you would be stumped. You would, quite rightly ask 'After who said what?', 'Who is the 'her' being referred to?', 'Is the person who spoke or wrote that sentence talking about the repetition of the man's action or about the manner of his leaving, or about the condition of the woman who was left?' In the previous section we said something about the distinction between sentence and statement. The point is that thousands of people might write or utter this sentence but be making different statements. In one situation, writer A(usten) might be saying truly of Darcy that he left Elizabeth in the same condition of revulsion as he left her in on the previous day; in another situation, speaker B(arney) might be saying falsely of Fred that he went off to work on consecutive days without giving Wilma a kiss. And so on. If the same sentence, uttered by one speaker is true and by another is false, then it can hardly be right to say that the sentence *itself* is true. Or that it is false.

This brings us to an important distinction. Writer A issued her sentence in a particular context, at a certain time and place. Speaker B made his utterance at an entirely different time and place. Both A and B used different instances or exemplars of the same sentence. Using terminology introduced by Charles Sanders Peirce, we can say that A and B used different *tokens* of the same *type* sentence. This distinction is not a difficult one to grasp. When I write 'I'm a penguin', 'I'm a penguin', 'I'm a penguin', 'I'm a penguin', 'I'm a penguin' I have written five distinct tokens of the same type sentence.

What we showed above is that it is implausible to maintain that type sentences are truth-bearers, because some instances (tokens) of a given type sentence can yield truths, while others yield falsehoods, so it would not be reasonable to say that the type sentence itself was true or false. But what about token sentences? Could they be the bearers of truth or falsity? We have already said that, when we take into account the particular context in which a given token sentence is used, we are usually in a position to figure out whether what the speaker is saying is true or false. And token sentences are reassuringly concrete – ink marks on paper, vibrations in the air around a speaker's mouth, etc., so they induce no ontological anxieties. Unfortunately, however, we still need to tread carefully. Consider a really concrete token – a tombstone in a cemetery which contains the carved inscription 'Here lies Alfred Lord Tennyson', marking Lord Tennyson's grave. If I creep into the cemetery, pick up that tombstone and place it above Mary Pickles' nearby grave, then someone subsequently reading the tombstone would receive *false* information. So it is not the concrete token that is properly called 'true'.[5]

What this example suggests is that the truth-bearer is not a concrete token, but is the *use of a particular token on a certain occasion.* This suggestion, though a bit vague (the use of a token to do *what*?) is certainly a step in the right direction. But we should not forget that people can have true thoughts and beliefs which, though they might be expressed (out loud or in writing) as sentences, may themselves not involve sentence-tokens. Consider a person looking at the newly situated tombstone and, reasonably, having the thought 'This is where Alfred Lord Tennyson lies' while another person, passing by, says to his friend 'That is the resting place of Lord Tennyson'. In quite a clear sense, what the first person thinks is the same as what the tombstone discloses and what the passer-by says. The thought, the disclosure and the words of the passer-by have the same content, and in, this case, that content is false. Philosophers use the word 'proposition' in a bewildering variety of ways, but often it is used synonymously with 'content', and therefore, cleaving to this sense of the word, we can now answer the question with which we started. It is propositions that are the primary bearers of truth and falsity. When we say that a certain statement is true, or a certain belief false, we are talking about the *content* of the statement or belief.

Notice that the words on the tombstone are not the same as the words we used to express the thought of the person who read those words, nor are they the same as the words of the passer-by. Yet they all express the same proposition. Notice too that, in the case of the tombstone, the vehicle for the proposition is a lump of granite; in the case of the person whose thought is provoked by reading the tombstone the vehicle is, er . . ., we don't really know, but it's certainly not a hunk of granite; and, in the case of the speaker, the vehicle is the vibrating air. So it would obviously be a mistake to identify a proposition with any concrete vehicle by means of which the proposition is expressed. Does this mean that propositions are mysterious, unscientific abstract entities? Not at all – any more than is the height of my table, even though I cannot physically prise its height off the table.

In a typical speech situation, a speaker utters some sentences in the presence of a hearer. The speaker may use a certain language, speak loudly or softly, elegantly or coarsely, may have a variety of intentions (including, of course, the intention to be understood), may be pointing at various objects in the vicinity, may know a great deal about the beliefs of the hearer (including the hearer's beliefs about the speaker's beliefs) and may trade on this knowledge when choosing his words. The speaker produces what J. L. Austin called 'the total speech act in the total speech situation'. For certain purposes, practical or theoretical, we focus on some features of this performance and ignore others. Thus, a sound engineer wanting to record the speaker would ignore the beliefs of the hearer, the language used by the speaker, and so on, and would focus more or less completely on the sound of the speaker's voice. That is to say, the sound engineer would concentrate on the speaker's *phonetic act*. The phonetic act is not mysterious. It is not something produced *in addition to* the total speech act, but is produced *in the course of* producing the speech act. In a similar way, the proposition expressed by a speaker is identified by ignoring such things as the loudness of his voice and the language he employed (for he could have conveyed the same content speaking a different language).[6] So the proposition is an *abstracted* entity, where the process of abstraction is simply one of selectively ignoring various features of the situation in which a speaker speaks (or a thinker thinks), and focusing not on the medium but on the message. To say that a person's *statement* is true is not to say anything about the physical process of stating, but is to say that what is thereby stated – the message, the content, the proposition expressed – is true. Likewise, it is perfectly acceptable to ascribe truth or falsity to what a person thinks (or believes), for we are not here talking about the psychological process (or state) but about *what is thought*.

One might wish to raise doubts about whether a particular speaker's utterance can be re-expressed in our own language, especially if that speaker belongs to a remote tribe or to a remote species, and this may make us wonder about the legitimacy of the notion of a proposition, of a content that may be common to various forms of expression. One way of sidestepping this issue would be to insist on limiting attention to cases (such as our tombstone example) where, pretty clearly, a common content can be expressed in several different ways, and in several different media (American Sign Language could be added to those already mentioned). A more aggressive response is that it is just tough luck on us if our linguistic or conceptual resources do not allow us to access the contents of some of our more exotic fellow creatures' utterances. *Our* inability to do so should not count against *their* ability to express propositions.[7]

A final point to conclude this section. We said earlier that quotation marks are usefully regarded as pointing devices. But if I point in the direction of a flamingo, I may be pointing to the colour that I intend to paint my bedroom, or to a remarkable feat of balancing, or to an exotic substitute for toilet paper, etc. Ambiguity also affects the pointing done with quotation marks. If I say

'Man' is 6mm long.

then the quotation marks are pointing to the ink-mark between them. But if I say

'Man' is a noun.

then I am not saying that an ink-mark is a noun – in this context, I use the quotation marks to point to a word of the English language. And in

'Man' is a concept that children acquire quite early in their development.

the quotation marks point not to a mark or a word, but to a concept that is expressed in English by the word 'man' and in Spanish by the word 'hombre'. We argued earlier that the bearers of truth and falsity are propositions. So, in saying

'Grace is generous' is true

the quotation marks point to a proposition, and which particular Grace is being referred to is typically determined by the circumstance in which that proposition was expressed. It would be an aid to perspicuity if we had different kinds of quotation marks for the different kinds of pointing, and in fact various kinds have sometimes been proposed. In the present text, however, we are sticking to the standard quotation marks, but, in cases of the predication of truth or falsity, shall take it for granted that those quotation marks are pointing to propositions. Alternatively, we could use an operator locution. For example, in

It is true that Grace is generous

'It is true' is an operator – it operates on the proposition that Grace is generous.

3.3 TRUTH AS CORRESPONDENCE

At a famous symposium that took place in 1950, J. L. Austin advocated a theory of truth that makes essential use of the sentence/statement distinction. Some words have a natural connection with what they are about. It is a fact of nature that flying bees make the sound /bzzzzzzz/, so there is a naturalistic connection between the verb 'buzz' and what that verb signifies. But there is no such connection between the word 'dog' and the animal it describes; it is a matter of convention – a 'descriptive convention' as Austin calls it – that English uses the word 'dog' for that animal (whereas French uses 'chien', German 'Hund', etc.). Just as the word 'dog' is linked, in this conventional way, to many animals of a certain sort, so, Austin contended, a whole sentence is linked, in a similar way, to many situations of a certain type. Consider the sentence 'The dog is in Stanley's garage'. There are, of course, plenty of dogs in the world and numerous individuals called 'Stanley', and our sentence fits a type of situation in which some dog is in the garage of some Stanley.

Now consider an actual historical occasion in which a certain speaker says to her best friend 'The dog is in Stanley's garage'. They will be talking of an individual known to both of them as 'Stanley' and, as a matter of common sense and common conversational practice, even if they know more than one Stanley, the one to whom they will be referring will be the one about whom they have been conferring, or who, for whatever reason, has acquired a prominence in their recent dealings. That is a matter of conversational convention. Equally obviously, they will be referring to a particular dog which is in the close vicinity geographically or conversationally. In virtue of these sorts of conversational conventions, the speaker's statement, in this particular context, picks out, refers to, or 'demonstrates', a particular state of affairs – that state of affairs in which the particular dog that is the subject of the conversation is in the garage of someone by the name of Stanley, an acquaintance of the speaker and hearer.[8] (Austin sometimes used 'fact' instead of 'state of affairs', though he recognized that the term was philosophically problematic, and he wrote a paper called 'Unfair to Facts' (Austin 1961) to try to iron out some of the problems.)

With this preamble in place, Austin's statement of his version of the correspondence theory of truth (Austin 1950, pp.152–3) should make sense:

> A statement is said to be true when the historic state of affairs to which it is correlated by the demonstrative conventions (the one to which it 'refers') is of a type with which the sentence used in making it is correlated by the descriptive conventions.

A diagram may help to make the theory even clearer:

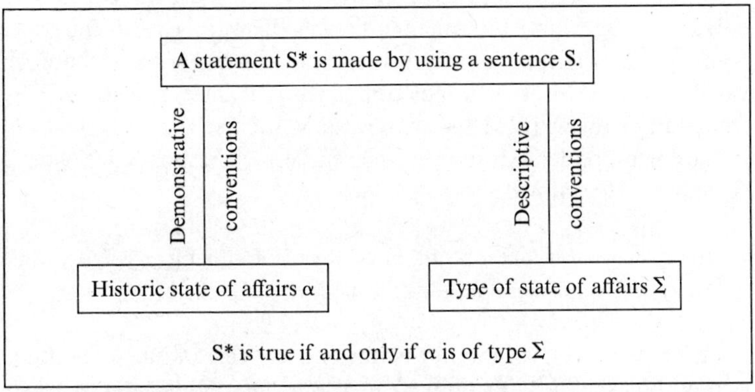

Although expressed in rather technical language, there is something very appealing and commonsensical about Austin's theory of truth. It is a correspondence theory in spades: the idea is that, when a speaker uses a sentence to make a statement, there is a *particular* state of affairs in the world to which a speaker's statement corresponds, and a *type* of state of affairs to which that speaker's sentence corresponds; the statement is true just if that state of affairs is of that type. Look at the sentence 'The street leads from the square to the main government building'. You understand the sentence and so know the type of situation to which it refers. If you hear a woman uttering a token of that sentence in London while she is showing a tourist how to get from Trafalgar Square to the Houses of Parliament, then it is clear that what is being pointed out really is an instance of that type. On the other hand, if she were pointing out Charing Cross Road, then what she would be saying is false, because Centrepoint, the office block at the end of Charing Cross Road, is not a government building. So the state of affairs indicated in the latter case is not of the street-leading-from-square-to-main-government-building type.

Before criticizing Austin's particular version of the Correspondence Theory, let us say a few words about what makes Correspondence theories of truth in general appealing. A statement, unless it is self-referring, is about things outside itself and we tend to think that if the things outside are the way that the statement states them to be, then the statement is true. On this conception, it is in virtue of things in the outside world corresponding to how they are stated to be in the statement, that the statement is true; if the way things are outside fails to correspond with how the statement states them to be, then the statement is false. Truth, then, is a matter of correspondence between words and the world; a proposition is true (or false) *because of* how things are in the world. This seems intuitively correct, so we could call it 'the correspondence intuition'. The earliest 'correspondence' view is Aristotle's. He claimed:

> To say of what is that it is not, or of what is not that it is, is false, while to say of what is that it is, and of what is not that it is not, is true.[9]

Even in the Greek original, it is not entirely clear what Aristotle is saying, but scholarly examination of various of his texts suggests that the best way of interpreting him is to read his 'To say of what is' as 'To say of what is thus and so'. So, to take a particular instance, Aristotle would be claiming that to say of what is yellow (e.g. a certain banana) that it is not yellow is false, whereas to say of what is yellow that it is yellow is true. It is hard to dispute this. The theory does not say much, but what it does say seems to be correct.[10] Mediaeval authors, taking their lead from Aristotle, devised more pert formulations of the view. A common formulation was '*Veritas est adaequatio rei et intellectus*'. This says that truth (*veritas*) is the agreement or correspondence (*adaequatio*) between things (*rei*) and the intellect or mind, a correspondence between how things are in the world and how they are said to be in a (mental) sentence. Unlike Aristotle's definition, this formulation makes explicit mention of correspondence.

Notice an important difference between Aristotle's version of the Correspondence Theory and Austin's. Aristotle speaks of things being thus and so, and the things he is talking about are the objects we refer to when we use *names*, such as 'Socrates' and *nouns*, such as 'banana', and the properties we ascribe to them, such as being homosexual and being yellow (respectively).[11] But Austin's theory invokes states of affairs or facts, and these are supposed to be what *statements* refer to. They are on the 'world' side of the correspondence relation. In our discussion of Austin, we deliberately chose an example that looked unproblematic: the state of affairs corresponding to the particular utterance of 'The dog is in Stanley's garage' that we considered seems to be a neat, clearly bounded chunk of the world and the type of state affairs corresponding to the sentence seemed likewise clearly delineated. But what about the statement 'The dog is outside Stanley's garage'? If, as Austin's theory requires, there is a state of affairs corresponding to that statement, where is it located? How far beyond Stanley's garage does it extend? Worse, what about the statement 'The dog is not outside Stanley's garage'? What state of affairs could correspond to a negative statement? Even worse, what about a conditional statement such as when you say to a child 'If you eat that filth, you'll get a stomach ache'? It is hard to think of what state of affairs could correspond to that statement, yet the statement may well be true.[12]

Austin's theory posits a relation of correspondence between a statement and a state of affairs. We have just seen that to invoke states of affairs is to invite problems. States of affairs seem to have unclear boundaries, and we find it hard to grasp what a negative state of affairs, or a conditional one, could be. But what about the relation of correspondence itself? There are problems with that too. The trouble is that we can think of many kinds of *correspondence with* and *correspondence to*, yet none of them seems to be anything like the relation of statements to the world. A key corresponds to a particular lock; the reflection of a face in a mirror corresponds to that face, the way that Myrtle was murdered corresponds, in every detail, with the way that Mona was murdered. None of these correspondences seems to provide a good model of the sort of correspondence between words and the world that is required by a correspondence theory of truth. The early Wittgenstein held that the correspondence between a statement and a (possible) state of affairs is one of *picturing*, but he later came to see that this idea would not fly. We could contrive a written sign language in which sentences present some sort of picture of what they are about, but the sentences of ordinary language do not picture in any ordinary sense.[13]

Another radical idea is that the correspondence in question is one of *identity*. This theory has an immediate attraction. When we make a true statement or have a true thought, what we say or think is what is the case – is just the way things are – is identical to the way things are – coincides with the facts. However, one trouble with this theory is that if facts really are just identical with true statements, then the correspondence in question is between a true statement and that true statement, in other words, between something and itself. Thus the theory does not capture the 'correspondence intuition' that there is a relation between, on the one hand, statements and, on the other, the world.[14]

Another theory which many people, including its author, classify as a version of the Correspondence view is Alfred Tarski's *Semantic Theory of Truth*. Tarski's theory is much closer to Aristotle's than to Austin's. For a start, Tarski does not include states of affairs or facts as part of his theoretical apparatus (though he does use these expressions when chit-chatting informally about the theory). At the core of his theory is the notion of *satisfaction*. The predicate 'is white' is satisfied by many things, including snow. Thus satisfaction is the converse of the relation *being true of* that we encountered in Section 3.1: Snow satisfies the predicate 'is white'; the predicate 'is white' is true of snow. And snow satisfies the predicate 'is white' if and only if snow is white.

Semantics is the study of meaning, of the relation between discourse and what we discourse about. Clearly the word 'satisfaction' (in the technical sense in which we are using it here) is a term belonging to semantics since, in a properly informative statement such as 'Snow satisfies the predicate "is white"', we are told that a bit of language, the predicate 'is white', stands in a particular relation (the relation of being true of) to some worldly stuff, snow. But notice that in the equivalence we just mentioned, viz

> Snow satisfies the predicate 'is white' if and only if snow is white.

the semantical term 'satisfies' occurs on the left hand side of the 'if and only if', but the right hand side is entirely free of any semantical terms. Now, imagine that, for any occurrence of a sentence containing the technical semantical term 'satisfies', we can find an equivalent sentence that contains no semantical terms whatsoever. We would then have defined 'satisfies' in wholly non-semantical terms, in the sense that, whenever we encountered a sentence containing the word 'satisfies', we would be able to supply an equivalent sentence that does not contain that word or any other semantical term.

Of course, attempting to perform this task by looking individually at all the infinite sentences that contain 'satisfies' is a non-starter, and the bulk of Tarski's seminal paper (Tarski 1933) is taken up with showing how the task can be undertaken elegantly (and in a finite amount of time). (The actual details of the definition are complex and quite formidable; we shall not consider them here.[15]) Once a definition of 'satisfies' is in place, it is a trivial matter to define 'true of' because the two are closely related, as we pointed out a couple of minutes ago, and once we have a definition of 'satisfies' or of 'true of' it is but a small step to defining a truth predicate.

By what criterion would we determine whether our proposed definition is correct? Well, suppose that we have arrived at a definition of some predicate that we shall write as 'is Tr'. The condition that Tarski laid down for this predicate to be a *truth* predicate is that the definition entail all instances of (what has come to be called) the T-schema:

S is Tr if and only if p

where what can be substituted for 'p' is any sentence of the language, and for 'S' any name or description of that sentence. *Prima facie*, this looks to be an eminently reasonable criterion. If you have defined a predicate 'is G' that you take to be a truth predicate, and then someone points out that your definition does not imply

'Snow is white' is G if and only if snow is white[16]

then you had better abandon your definition fast and get back to the drawing board.

There is an important difference between Tarski's theory and all the others we are considering in this chapter. Very near the start of his monumental paper (1933) Tarski presents a version of the Liar Paradox, and quickly arrives at the conclusion that this paradox gets off the ground because the language in which it is couched has the resources for unrestrictedly talking about itself – in English we can say things like '"is a horse" is a predicate' and 'This very statement is false'. Consider a sentence of ordinary language (we'll call this sentence Saul) that says of itself that it is not true – in other words, the sentence 'Saul is not true' has the name Saul. If we plug this sentence and its name into the above T-schema (reading 'Tr' as 'true') we get

> Saul is true if and only if Saul is not true

Hence, assuming that Saul is either true or false, we get the contradiction that Saul is true and that it is not true. Tarski concluded that any language with these resources for talking about itself is prone to paradox. But all natural languages are like that. So Tarski gave up on ordinary languages and produced his definition of truth for an artificial language, where all the talking about that language is done in a meta-language (and all talk about the meta-language is done in a meta-meta-language, etc.). So Tarski is investigating a hierachy of languages, where each language in the hierarchy has its own unique truth predicate.

Since Tarski's day, various solutions to the Liar have been put forward that do not require a Tarskian hierarchy, so the project of providing a rigorous definition of our ordinary predicate 'true' may not be as hopeless as Tarski thought, especially if, as Stephen Read has argued (Read, forthcoming), the T-schema is not truistic but *defective*. Another criticism of Tarski is that, in the formal language with which he deals, the denotation of each word is fixed. His formal language does not contain indexical or demonstrative expressions (words like 'I', 'here', 'now', 'next', 'that', the denotation of which varies with their context of utterance) and this, in turn enables Tarski to treat sentences (linguistic expressions, not concrete marks[17]) as truth-bearers and thus to ignore the important role of context in the determination of truth. This role was described in our exposition of Austin's theory.

3.4 ALTERNATIVES TO THE CORRESPONDENCE THEORY

3.4.1 Coherence Theories

Some people do not believe in the existence of a world that is independent of the workings of the mind. Philosophers who defend this (dis-)belief are called Idealists. In the previous section, we saw just how difficult it is to make precise what conception of correspondence could satisfy the requirements of a correspondence theory. But, if you are an Idealist, you avoid this problem entirely – you do not have to work out the nature of the relation between the mind's contents and the world's contents because you think the distinction can't be drawn! Propositions may stand in relations to other propositions (for example two propositions together might entail a third) but not to a non-propositional reality, according to this brand of Idealism.[18]

What theory of truth would appeal to an Idealist? When Idealism flourished, in the late nineteenth century, the theory of truth to which its main practitioners were attracted was the *Coherence Theory*, which states that a proposition is true if and only if it forms a coherent whole with the other propositions we embrace. They stressed that propositions are interconnected – for example, the proposition that the sun rises in the east in the northern hemisphere connects with propositions saying how the sun is constituted, with theories (bundles of propositions) about the rotation of the earth, etc. and itself supports other propositions such as that shadows start being cast across the streets of Accra at 4.30 in the morning at the beginning of May. Our proposition about the sun rising in the east is true if and only if it sits comfortably with all those other propositions.

One of Bertrand Russell's (1906–7) objections to the Coherence Theory was that a manifest falsehood, such as that Bishop Stubbs was hanged for murder, would be deemed true by that theory since one could find a bundle of propositions with which that scurrilous one about the bishop is consistent. It should be clear, however, even from our brief sketch of the Coherence Theory, that Russell's objection misses its target. Coherence, as the Coherence Theorists understood it, is not just a matter of consistency with an arbitrary bundle of propositions. Writers such as F. H. Bradley, Harold Joachim and Brand Blanshard conceived of human investigation as a quest for the Big Truth, a complete system of beliefs answering to its own standards of justification and explanation, which standards themselves evolved, becoming more refined and stringent as investigation proceeded. Grasping the Big Truth is, for the Idealists, comprehending the whole of Reality because, remember, for them Reality is not something external of which our judgements are merely a copy but is identical to our judgements.[19] In holding that our true judgements are *identical* to parts of Reality, the Coherence Theory thus subsumes an *Identity Theory* which, as we saw in 3.2, can be regarded as a limiting case of the Correspondence Theory of Truth. The matter is further complicated by the fact that, insofar as any particular proposition or judgement is not the Big Truth, it is only part of the truth. The nineteenth-century Idealists, however, subscribed to the quite different view that any proposition is only partially true, that it has only a certain *degree of truth*. (Whether they were confused about the distinction between these two views, it is hard to say. It would certainly be a confusion to infer from the fact that a witness did not tell the whole truth that the witness's statements were partially true. What the witness did was to refrain from disclosing some pertinent truths, or to insert into his testimony some deliberate falsehoods. But these truths and falsehoods are truths and falsehoods *simpliciter*, not propositions that are true to various degrees.)

Few people would dispute that, in many circumstances, we *test* whether a proposition is likely to be true by checking whether it is consistent with other propositions that we have good reason to believe are true.[20] So coherence (in the limited sense of *consistency*) can well be regarded as a *test* of truth, and was so regarded by philosophers such as Otto Neurath (1931) and Carl Hempel (1935) – logical positivists diametrically opposed to Idealism.[21] However, this is not the same as regarding consistency as giving us the definition of truth or an account of the nature of truth. For one thing, such a definition is circular – two propositions being consistent means that they can be *true* together, so defining truth in terms of consistency boils down to defining truth in terms of . . . truth! To accept the nineteenth-century Coherence Theory as an account of the *nature* of truth, 'that systematic coherence which is truth', as Joachim (1906, p.76) puts it, means buying into a metaphysics that most philosophers nowadays (if they understand it) reject. However, the strand of the theory that makes it an *Identity* view, has enjoyed a recent revival, and the doctrine of degrees of truth has been seized upon and modified by philosophers who advocate a particular type of solution to the Sorites paradox (described on p.17 of Chap.1).

3.4.2 The Pragmatist Theory

Pragmatism is the philosophical view that emerged at the hands of some extremely interesting American writers of the late nineteenth and early twentieth centuries. These included Charles Sanders Peirce, William James and John Dewey. Their views on truth differed from each other, but were united in their emphasis on practical consequence as against abstract theorizing.[22] Peirce recommended that 'instead of saying that you want to know the "Truth" you were to say that you want to attain a state of belief unassailable by doubt' (Peirce 1905, p. 279 of Hartshorne and Weiss). The paradigm method of doubt-elimination is scrupulous scientific inquiry and, indeed, in an early work, Peirce had envisaged such inquiry converging on both the truth and a clear conception of reality: 'The opinion which is fated to be ultimately agreed by all who investigate is what we mean by the truth, and the object represented in this opinion is the real' (Peirce 1878, p.55 of Schmitt).[23] James, too, stressed doubt-elimination though verification. He is interested in truth's 'cash-value in experiential terms'. 'True ideas', he says 'are those that we can assimilate, validate, corroborate and verify. False ideas are those that we cannot.' Whereas previous theorists who had thought of truth as a property believed it to be a property possessed by a truth-bearer, James wants to regard truth as a process. 'The truth of an idea is not a stagnant property inherent in it. Truth *happens* to an idea. It *becomes* true, is *made* true by events. Its verity *is* in fact an event, a process: the process namely of its verifying itself, its veri-*fication*. Its validity is the process of its valid-*ation*' (James 1907, p.60).

The pragmatic attitude is 'cut the bull, get down to brass tacks and focus on what practically matters' (Lynch 2004, p.61); it's a kind of philosophy for engineers. It may be difficult to see how this attitude can be brought to bear on the problem of truth, but Michael Lynch offers a very helpful analogy with moral philosophy (Lynch 2004, p.66). For utilitarians, when you have a choice of what to do, the morally right action to take is the one that leads to the greatest happiness. So 'right' is *defined* in terms of 'happiness', the maximization of happiness is *constitutive* of rightness. Likewise, for a pragmatist, when you have a choice of what to believe, the true belief is the one that delivers the most practical benefit, the one that is most useful – and usefulness comes in a variety of forms. So 'true' is *defined* in terms of usefulness – it is its usefulness that makes a belief true. (Note that, in the muscular spirit of pragmatism, we have dropped talk of propositions – too airy-fairy – and are speaking instead of beliefs.) (But this is just window-dressing because, even if beliefs are physical states of the brain, it is the content of a belief-state, i.e. a proposition, that is true or false.)

Interestingly, by pursuing Lynch's analogy we can discover one of the things that is *wrong* with the pragmatic theory. If you perform some action – perhaps you murder your grandmother – then if someone asks you whether that was the right thing to do, if you are a hard-headed utilitarian, you might reply 'Well, it might not seem right to you right now, but you should not be too hasty in your judgement – wait until you are in a position to evaluate all the consequences of my killing her and you may discover that, in the long run, it produces a geat deal of joy'. So the utilitarian would say that an action may be morally right, even though we may have to wait a long time before knowing that it is morally right. But *contrast* that with the question of whether a certain belief is true. Here's a belief: I believe that I am writing a chapter on Truth for a book on the Philosophy of Logic. That belief is true *quite irrespective* of any discoveries in the future about whether having that belief is of practical benefit to me or to anyone else. If having that belief turns out to have no practical benefit at all, or to have severe practical disadvantage, that could not possibly render my belief false. It would be crazy (wouldn't it?) to declare retrospectively that Hitler did not murder six million Jews on the grounds that maintaining that he did has turned out to be of net practical disadvantage.

Another problem about equating truth with practical benefit or usefulness emerges when you think of yourself walking in the countryside, and asking a farmhand for directions to the nearest pub. Your practical need of quenching your thirst will not be met if your rustic informant gives you the wrong directions. *His answer will be useful to you only if it is true*. Now see what happens if you make the pragmatist substitution of 'useful' for 'true' in that italicized sentence. You get 'His answer will be useful to you only if it is useful'. And that's no use at all.

No doubt, William James would reject such criticism as 'impudent slander'. He says 'The unwillingness of some of our critics to read any but the silliest of possible meanings into our statements is as discreditable to their imaginations as anything I know in recent philosophic history' (James 1907, p.72). But his complaint seems to be that critics have interpreted the pragmatists' conception of usefulness as mere pleasantness. If you think of (for example) truth in science, says James, you will see that the practical benefits at issue include elegance, economy – in general, good scientific taste – and, above all 'consistency both with previous truth and with novel fact'

(James 1907, p.66). However, inspection of the arguments against the pragmatic theory given above shows that they assume no such thin conception of usefulness or practical benefit, so, although one might share the pragmatists' general outlook, their views on truth remain problematic.

3.4.3 Deflationism

So far, we have been looking at what might be called 'substantive' or 'robust' theories of truth. All these views share the assumption that truth is something (perhaps a property, a relation, a process) and that it is the theoretician's task to say what truth consists in – to disclose the nature of truth (or to declare its nature a mystery, if you are a primitivist). But, if we adopt a hard-nosed, pragmatic attitude, another possibility comes into view. People talk about striving for the truth, or aiming at the truth. But perhaps that is just a load of pretentious claptrap. What we really want are beliefs that are useful to us, and which we can justify if challenged. To assess whether a proposition is true is only to assess whether it has a solid justification. If this is right, we will concern ourselves with the quality of the evidence that people provide in support of the propositions they assert, and will try to find ways of distinguishing good justification from bad, but we will cease caring about truth. Truth is a nothing and so, in particular, we would be wasting our time if we went searching for a theory of truth. This is the position associated with Richard Rorty (1991, 1998, 2000, 2002).

There is another very simple consideration that also makes such a position attractive. Take the statement 'It is true that Berlin is the capital of Germany'. That statement seems to have no more or less content than the statement 'Berlin is the capital of Germany'. We might just as well delete 'It is true that' for its presence adds nothing to what is said by the words following it. Of course, simple deletion will not work in all cases. For example, in 'The truth is out there' and 'Although what Dick just said is true, he usually lies', the simple deletion of 'truth' or 'true' results in nonsense. But suppose that, even in all cases like this, it were possible to so paraphrase any sentence containing 'true' or its cognates that the 'true'-words vanished, yet the meaning was preserved in the paraphrase. That would show that 'true' is redundant, in that it possesses no content. It would be a bogus predicate.[24] Hence, although this view (which is usually attributed to Frank Ramsey, though both Frege (1918) and Wittgenstein

(1979, p.9, entry for 6.10.14) got there first) is termed the *Redundancy Theory*, it is really an anti-theory theory, for it says that there is no problem of truth, because the predicate 'true' does not stand for anything.[25] In Ramsey's words: 'There is no separate problem of truth but merely a linguistic muddle' (Ramsey 1927, p.142).

Unfortunately, it is by no means clear that paraphrases of the sort required by Ramsey are generally available. Even a very simple claim such as 'What the bishop said is true' resists paraphrasing. One might try 'There is some proposition, and the bishop expressed it, and it', but that doesn't make sense. It would if we added the words 'is true', but that would defeat our object of paraphrasing 'true' away.

A perhaps more fundamental problem with the Redundancy Theory is that it asks us to read the biconditional

> It is true that Berlin is the capital of Germany if and only if Berlin is the capital of Germany

as showing that the predicate 'is true' is redundant. But isn't it equally, or even more plausible to read the biconditional as showing that the proposition to the left of the 'if and only if' requires a truth-maker (e.g. Berlin, Berlin's being large, the fact that Berlin is large, the state of affairs in which Berlin is large) which is indicated by the proposition to the right? And that is just what the *Correspondence Theory* says (Vision 2003)!

The Redundancy Theory is obviously deflationary, because it deflates our ambition to find a substantive account of truth. There are various other deflationary views that acknowledge that the word 'true' has *some* useful function, but not the function of ascribing a property to a truth-bearer. For example, Peter Strawson, in an early paper (1949), held that a speaker typically uses the word 'true' for performing the act of endorsing, or signalling agreement with, what another speaker has said – the theory is thus called the *Performative Theory*. There is an obvious difficulty with this theory. When I say 'If Creationism is true then dinosaurs roamed the Earth less than 15,000 years ago', there is no endorsing of the antecedent. Another problem: I normally endorse some claim because I believe it to be true. That perfectly reasonable explanation would translate, on the Performative Theory, into the non-explanation 'I normally endorse some claim because I . . . endorse it', which would leave my hearer completely in the dark.

That phrase 'in the dark' provides us with a convenient entry point into another deflationary view, the *Prosentential Theory*, first so-called in Grover, Camp and Belnap (1975) but anticipated, to a large extent, by other writers, including, notably, Arthur Prior (1971). The word 'the' in a sentence is usually followed by a noun, but it would be a mistake to think that, in the phrase 'in the dark', the word 'dark' is a noun that names some thing. After all, we could usually, without any loss of sense, replace that phrase with 'unenlightened' or 'mystified'. The Prosententialist claims that, in any sentence containing the predicate 'true', that predicate can be displaced by the phrase 'it is true' or 'that is true'. Those phrases are not predicates. So just as, by replacing 'in the dark' by either 'unenlightened' or 'mystified', we can forestall dumb questions like 'In which dark were you left?' or 'For what object does the word "dark" stand in that phrase?', so too we can, by rephrasing sentences containing the predicate 'true' with sentences containing 'it is true' or 'that is true', forestall dumb questions like 'For what property does the word "true" stand?', because those two phrases are clearly not adjectival or predicative. In good deflationary spirit, the Prosententialist can say: 'The predicate "is true" is entirely dispensable in favour of those other two phrases; it does not stand for any property, so we do not need any theory about the nature of the property for which it stands.'

'It' is a pro*noun*. Let us embellish the vocabulary of English by adding the word 'itt', which is a pro*sentence*. Here's how it works. Instead of the laborious

1. 'Bert believes that the chemical composition of salt is one part sodium to one part chlorine, and (indeed) the chemical composition of salt is one part sodium to one part chlorine'

we could write

2. 'Bert believes that the chemical composition of salt is one part sodium to one part chlorine and it is true'

or, using our embellished English,

3. 'Bert believes that the chemical composition of salt is one part sodium to one part chlorine and itt'

Comparing 1 and 3, we note that the 'itt' replaces the whole sentence 'The chemical composition of salt is one part sodium to one part chlorine'. Reverting now to the example 'What the bishop said is true' that we used against the naïve Redundancy Theory, this translates, according to the Prosentential view, as 'The bishop said something and itt'. Now that is a perfectly grammatical sentence, for it is just short for 'The bishop said something and it is true'. Further, it does not contain the word 'true' functioning as an adjective but merely as a non-explicit part of a prosentence. The speaker is using 'itt' here to (blindly) assert whatever it was that the bishop said. So the Prosentential Theory seems to offer a clever way of vindicating the deflationary view.

But does it really? There are serious doubts about whether all sentences containing 'true' apparently predicated of a truth-bearer can be paraphrased in the Prosententialist style. Or, if there is only a very messy paraphrase, one begins to suspect that it is the original expression that is an accurate expression of (and perhaps a precondition of) the associated thought, the paraphrase just being a sort of tedious exercise in expressing the thought differently – it shows nothing other than that such exercises can be performed. How would a Prosentential paraphrase of 'Goldbach's Conjecture is true' go?[26] (One thinks of the baroque translation of simple arithmetic statements like '1 + 1 = 2' into the language of formal logic and set theory.)

Another problem arises when you stop to think how, if you spoke embellished English, you would read aloud sentence 3 above. My guess is that you would put heavy stress on the 'itt'. It is a fact, seldom remarked, that when one wants to say that something is true without using the word 'true', one uses stress, or adds words like 'indeed' (as we did in sentence 1 above) or 'really'. If the predicative function of 'true' can always be taken over by such devices, that does not show that 'true' has no predicative function, except in a trivial sense. What seems likely is that such devices exist because we need to signal when we are committing ourselves to the truth of a proposition as opposed to merely mouthing or entertaining it. We pointed out that when a speaker claims 'The bishop said something and itt', that speaker uses 'itt' to *assert* whatever it was that the bishop said. But to assert is just to acknowledge a proposition *as true*. So, unless the Prosententalist can show otherwise, we have to conclude that the Prosentential Theory makes essential use of a concept defined in terms of the predicate 'true'.

This last objection can also be lodged against the now very popular *Minimal Theory*, which has received its most extended defence at the hands of Paul Horwich (1998). Unlike Grover, Horwich does not deny that 'true' stands for a property (although he denies that the property it does stand for is an ordinary ingredient of reality (1998, p.2)) nor does he take the 'primitivist' line of Frege, Davidson and others of holding that the meaning of 'true' is unique and indefinable.[27] Horwich's view is that the only purpose of the truth predicate is to allow us to express attitudes towards a proposition when, as Horwich puts it, 'we are thwarted by ignorance of what exactly the proposition is' (Horwich 1998, p.2). We have already encountered such cases. I trust the bishop, so, although I might not have properly heard his last remark, I say 'What the bishop said is true' or 'I am sure that what the bishop said is true' and perhaps add, more lavishly 'I believe that everything the bishop says is true'.

Suppose that the bishop's last remark was about God, though I did not realize this. Then, when I say 'What the bishop said is true', my claim is about the bishop's proposition (and is indirectly about God). If *my claim* about what the bishop said is true, then what he said is true, and vice versa. Likewise, and equally obviously, the proposition that snow is white is true if and only if snow is white. Here we have a biconditional, an equivalence. There is thus an equivalence template or *schema*

(E) The proposition that p is true if and only if p

or, in Horwich's notation (1998, p.8)

<p> is true iff p

and that, according to Horwich, tells us the complete story about truth. (E) is just a schema, because it contains the schematic letter 'p'. But substitute for both occurrences of 'p' any sentence you like, and you get an equivalence, e.g.

The proposition that ants shout is true if and only if ants shout

It is the totality of such equivalences that implicitly define truth. Horwich says 'The entire conceptual and theoretical role of truth may be explained on this basis'; 'truth is metaphysically trivial' (Horwich 1998, pp.5, 146).

Notice the similarity between (E) and Tarski's Convention (T) that we discussed in Section 3.2 above. But there are two big differences. First, in any instance of (E) we get truth predicated of a *proposition*, whereas in Tarski's theory it is *sentences* that are the truth-bearers. Second, for Tarski, it is a criterion of the adequacy of a theory of truth that all instances of Convention (T) be derivable within that theory. For Horwich, all the (infinite) instances of (E) are the *axioms* of his Minimal Theory.

Horwich's short book (1998) is an excellent read. After explaining the Minimal Theory in a very few pages, Horwich considers thirty-nine objections to it and he attempts to rebut them all, mostly successfully and succinctly. For example, to the objection that the Minimal Theory does not square with the 'correspondence intuition', Horwich points out that it is undeniable that, for example, the proposition that snow is white is true *because* something in the world (snow) is a certain way (white). We appeal to science to explain why snow is white, and only then, invoking the relevant equivalence (between 'Snow is white' and 'The proposition that snow is white is true'), do we deduce, and thereby explain, why the proposition that snow is white is true (Horwich 1998, pp.104–5).

In Section 3.1, we discussed Dick's lack of respect for truth, and we (I hope) agreed with Grace that respect for truth is important. But if, as the Minimal Theory claims, truth is not a substantial property, then it is not clear that it could be the object of respect. This looks to be a serious defect of the theory.[28] In that section, we also discussed semantical paradox and, although he wants to set aside the difficulties raised by these paradoxes, it must be said that Horwich is particularly vulnerable to them. The derivation of the Liar contradiction depends, as Horwich himself shows, on the use of a Horwich-equivalence (see also our derivation of the 'Saul' contradiction in 3.2), and he is led to concede that 'only certain instances of the equivalence schema are correct' (Horwich 1998, p.42), Horwich wants to stay calm about this, but others argue that it is a fatal defect of his position (Simmons 1999).

3.5 RELATIVISM

In this chapter, we have been discussing the concept of truth as it occurs in statements of the form 'The proposition that p is true'. But there are some philosophers who deny that, in many cases, it is correct to say that a proposition is simply true or simply false: what we should say is that the proposition is *true for X* (e.g. one proposition may be true for you, false for me). This view is known as *Relativism*.[29] Many people who use the 'true for X' locution are simply confused. A certain proposition may be *believed to be true* by you and *believed to be false* by me. Typically, in such a case, the proposition is (simply) true or (simply) false and at least one of us has an incorrect belief. Thus a postmodern relativist, following Michel Foucault, might claim that truth is what passes for truth and what passes for truth depends on who holds power at the time (particularly when that power is strong enough to shape the very meanings of our words). But from this relativistic perspective – here I quote Lynch (2004, p.39) – '[i]t follows that in the American South of the 1960s and 70s, African Americans really were morally and intellectually inferior to whites because that was the view of the white political power structure at the time'. And, as Lynch rightly says, '. . . this is unintuitive: surely such racist views were false then *and* now'.

A smart-ass rebuttal of Relativism is 'Yeah, it's an interesting theory, but it's just not true for me'. Needless to say, such a rebuttal does not do justice to serious versions of Relativism. Propositions such as 'Licorice is tasty', 'Popocatépetl will probably erupt within ten years' and 'Cheating on one's spouse is bad' are not obviously about objective matters (Kölbel 2002, p.19) and the 'widespread prejudice against relativism' (Kölbel 2002, p.128) needs to be replaced by a more considered response (Lynch 2004, pp.31–44).

SUGGESTIONS FOR FURTHER READING

Künne (2004) is a labour of love that is bound to inspire you, as will the collections of classic papers on truth (Blackburn and Simmons 1999) and Horwich, Paul (ed.) (1994) *Theories of Truth*. Aldershot: Dartmouth.

CHAPTER 4

THE LOGIC OF PARTS OF SPEECH

4.1 INTRODUCTION: THE MEANING AND REFERENCE QUESTIONS

This chapter concerns some of the philosophical puzzles and problems generated by *proper names*. Proper names are names of individual persons, places, and things. Examples include 'Max Deutsch', 'France', and 'Arnold Schwarzenegger'. One interesting feature of proper names is that they are designed for the purpose of making reference to *particulars*. In this, they differ from general terms like 'author' and 'country', which are designed to apply to more than one thing. To mark this contrast, philosophers and logicians describe the class of terms to which proper names belong as *singular* terms. As we shall see, it is precisely this singularity of proper names, and especially the way in which it is achieved, that is the source of their philosophical perplexity.

There are two basic questions to be asked about proper names (henceforth, simply *names*), questions that we will call the *meaning question* and the *reference question*. Let's start with the meaning question, since properly formulating it involves resolving a complication that does not arise in relation to the reference question.

4.1.1 The meaning question

Asked of a name, say 'France', the meaning question, in its simplest form, is this: what does 'France' *mean*? But here is where the complication appears, for there are many meanings of 'means' and its cognates (like 'meaning'). To avoid ambiguity, we must select one of these. For example, according to one common conception of meaning, the meaning of a name like 'France' is potentially different for every speaker of the language, something akin to the set of subjective associations each speaker makes with the name. This is not the sense of 'meaning' that will concern us here. What is the relevant sense and why?

Language is primarily a means of communication, and philosophers, logicians, and linguists are mainly interested in this communicative function of language. Hence, the relevant sense of 'meaning' is (very roughly) that which identifies the meaning of an expression with *what that expression communicates*. It should be clear that this communication sense of 'meaning' is some distance away from the subjective associations sense described above. Perhaps you think of baguettes and imagine the Eiffel Tower when saying or hearing the name 'France'. Nevertheless, it is implausible to suppose that you manage to communicate these associations simply by uttering a sentence with 'France' in it. Communicating those associations would take special effort on your part.

But, while the communication sense of meaning is different from the subjective associations sense and more closely related to the aims of theorists of language, it is too roughly characterized to be of much use in clarifying the meaning question asked of names. This is because, strictly speaking, names don't communicate anything at all. What gets communicated is that various things are or are not the case – that France is far away, that I'm not happy with my haircut, that two scoops of ice cream are better than one, etc. Names don't, on their own, say whether anything is the case. It is *sentences* that do that. Sentences are the basic units of communication. Sentences are the basic units of communication because it is sentences that *carry complete pieces of information*, or, to use some terminology familiar to you from earlier chapters, *express propositions*. Given this, the communication sense of 'meaning' really only correctly applies to sentences: the meaning *of a sentence* can be identified with *what gets communicated by it* and this, in turn, can be identified with *the proposition the sentence expresses*.[1]

However, most sentences are complexes; they have parts. It is therefore natural to suppose that sentences have the meanings they do in virtue of the way in which their smaller, 'subsentential' parts combine or compose. This supposition is reinforced by noticing the ways in which the meanings of certain groups of sentences appear to overlap. The meaning of 'France is far away' overlaps with that of 'Timbuktu is far way' and also with that of 'France is a democracy' but at a different point. This compositionality and overlap in meaning can be explained, it would seem, by the fact that the subsentential parts of a sentence make separable meaningful *contributions* to the proposition expressed by the sentence as a whole. Accepting this explanation allows us to characterize a notion of meaning for subsentential expressions that derives from the notion of sentence meaning described above. We can identify the meaning of such an expression with *what that expression contributes to propositions expressed by sentences containing it*.

We now have a univocal way of interpreting simple versions of the meaning question asked of names. We can take the question of what 'France' means to be equivalent to asking what *propositional contribution* 'France' makes to propositions expressed by sentences containing it. But what, exactly, is it to ask after the propositional contribution of a given expression? It is difficult to give a simple answer to this question, applying as it does to all of the various kinds of (subsentential) expressions in a language. Fortunately, our scope in this chapter is limited to names, and names are singular terms; they refer to particulars. So, for them, we can put the meaning question like this: does a name like 'France' contribute just its *referent*, i.e. the particular to which it refers, to propositions expressed by sentences containing it? Or does the meaning of a singular term somehow 'go beyond' what it refers to? In later sections, we will examine opposing answers to these questions, and we will try to get clearer about what it might be for the meaning of name to go beyond its referent.

4.1.2 The reference question

Let's turn now to the less complicated reference question. The reference question is not a question about *which* thing a particular name refers to since, in most cases, the answer to that question is obvious. 'Arnold Schwarzenegger' refers to Arnold Schwarzenegger. One doesn't need philosophy or logic to confirm this fact. Instead, the reference question is a question about the *mechanism of reference* for names. How does a name *come to have* the referent it has? How does a name *achieve the feat* of referring to some particular? Later in the chapter we will look at some specific proposals and assess their merits.

4.2 NAMES: A SMATTERING OF DISPUTES

The meaning and reference questions have received various and incompatible answers. The purpose of this chapter is to expose you to some of the most interesting and important of these. But before getting to the gritty details of these answers, it will be good to give you just a taste of some of them. The following subsections provide sketches of some of the major disputes over the answers to the meaning and reference questions. These sketches will be developed into longer versions later in the chapter.

4.2.1 The meaning question and Frege's Puzzle

For a long while, Gottlob Frege (Frege 1892) had most philosophers and logicians convinced that the meaning of a name must somehow go beyond its referent. After all, Frege would have argued, (1) is potentially *informative* whereas (2) is not.

(1) Bob Dylan is Robert Zimmerman.
(2) Bob Dylan is Bob Dylan.

That is, one might *learn something* upon hearing (1).[2] We can imagine Robert Zimmerman's high school teacher being very surprised indeed to learn that (1) is true. (2), on the other hand, can't teach anybody anything. You, for example, knew it before you read it here (even though you may never have considered the matter) and the same could be said for any random reader of (2). If, however, names contribute just their referents to propositions expressed by sentences containing them, then, since 'Bob Dylan' and 'Robert Zimmerman' refer to the same person, (1) and (2) must express the same proposition. But if (1) and (2) express the same proposition, then it seems that they must be either *both* informative or else *both* not. But (1) and (2) differ in their informativeness. (1) is informative but (2) isn't. Hence, concluded Frege, there must be more to the meaning of a name than its referent.

Times change. What was once a consensus view is now, we suspect, a minority position. Nowadays, a theory of names known in some circles as the *theory of direct reference* (and in others as *Millianism* or *Russellianism*) holds sway and it rejects the Fregean argument described above. This relatively new theory rejects not just the argument but its conclusion as well. According to the theory of direct reference, a name contributes just its referent to propositions expressed by sentences containing it, nothing more and nothing less. We will later look in more detail at this dispute between the old, Fregean view and the newer direct reference theory, focusing in particular on the shift from the former to the latter and the arguments that brought this shift about.

4.2.2 The reference question and the causal theory

The preceding subsection describes what is clearly a dispute over the correct answer to the meaning question for names. But the reference question for names has also been hotly debated. In answering the reference question for names, a traditional view, again associated with Frege, makes an interesting semantic link between names and another class of singular terms known as *definite descriptions*. Definite descriptions are complex noun phrases which, in English, typically begin with the word 'the'. Examples include 'the star of the *Terminator* movies' and 'the famous folk-rock singer with the gravelly voice'. According to the traditional view, a name refers to the particular it does because that particular is (also) the referent of some appropriate definite description, a definite description that serves to 'fix the reference' of the name. So, according to the traditional view, 'Arnold Schwarzenegger', for example, refers to Arnold Schwarzenegger because Schwarzenegger is the referent of some such definite description, 'the star of the *Terminator* movies' perhaps.

This too has been recently challenged. A new theory, due to Saul Kripke (Kripke 1972/1980) and known as the *causal theory of names*, rejects the idea that definite descriptions play an essential role in explaining how a name comes to have its referent. According to the causal theory, a name is given to its bearer at an initial 'dubbing' or 'baptism' and those present at this primordial event then pass the name along to others in their community who then pass it along to the world at large. When I use the name 'Arnold Schwarzenegger', it refers to Schwarzenegger, according to this theory, because it is Schwarzenegger who was initially dubbed with the name, and my use of it is causally connected to this initial dubbing through a 'chain' of other users. There is no particular description that can be said to be the 'reference fixer' on this theory.

4.3 DESCRIPTIVISM AND THE THEORY OF DIRECT REFERENCE

Recall the Fregean argument that since (1) and (2) can differ in informativeness, the answer to the meaning question for names cannot be that names contribute solely their referents to the propositions expressed by sentences containing them.

(1) Bob Dylan is Robert Zimmerman.
(2) Bob Dylan is Bob Dylan.

Assuming for the time being that the argument really does show that names can't simply mean what they refer to, what is needed now is a positive theory: if a name's meaning is *not* its referent, what *is* it? To put it somewhat differently, given that the difference in informativeness *cannot* be explained if the names involved contribute just their referents, how *can* that difference be explained?

Frege grappled with this question at several points in his career. His early (Frege 1879) attempt to explain how sentences like (1) and (2) can differ in informativeness was to claim that 'identity sentences' – sentences that say that one thing is identical to another – do not concern the things referred to by the names appearing in them, but instead concern the names themselves. Applied to (1) and (2), the idea would be that (1) and (2) do not, in fact, concern the man, Robert Zimmerman (a.k.a. Bob Dylan), but instead concern the names 'Robert Zimmerman' and 'Bob Dylan'. What (1) expresses, the early Frege would have held, is the proposition *that 'Bob Dylan' refers to the same thing as 'Robert Zimmerman'*. Frege would have taken (2), on the other hand, to express the proposition *that 'Bob Dylan' refers to the same person as 'Bob Dylan'*. The latter proposition is seemingly trivial while the former is clearly potentially informative. Thus, the difference between (1) and (2) would be explained. Later, Frege came to reject this possible explanation, saying, in effect, that sentences like (1) and (2) are clearly about *objects* and not merely the *names* for objects.

Whether this is clear or not, Frege was certainly right to reject his early proposal. The early proposal is simply not general enough. Frege conceived of the informativeness puzzle as a puzzle about *identity*, and his early solution applies only to identity sentences. The trouble with this is that there are sentences that are not identity sentences but which nonetheless pose precisely the same informativeness puzzle as (1) and (2). Consider (3) and (4):

(3) Bob Dylan weighs no more than Robert Zimmerman.
(4) Bob Dylan weighs no more than Bob Dylan.

(3) is potentially informative while (4) is not. It should be obvious, however, that making a fuss over the functioning of 'is' goes nowhere

towards solving this version of the puzzle. Something more general is needed.[3]

4.3.1 Descriptivism

In a famous paper called 'On Sense and Reference', Frege proposed that every name has, in addition to its referent, a *sense*, and that it is this sense that serves as the name's propositional contribution. Frege described the sense of a name as a *mode of presentation* of its referent. Expositors of Frege have further explained a name's sense as *a way of thinking about*, or *conceiving of* the referent of that name. Although there is some debate on this point, many commentators have suggested that Frege held that the sense of a name can be 'given by' a definite description. (In English, definite descriptions are noun phrases beginning with 'the'.) Some of Frege's own examples support this interpretation and it is, in any case, a natural way of cashing out the conception of sense as *a way of thinking about* an object. 'The best country for buying baguettes', for example, does seem to indicate a way of thinking about, or conceiving of, France.[4]

On this later Fregean theory, the explanation for the difference in informativeness between (1) and (2) is that while 'Bob Dylan' and 'Robert Zimmerman' share a referent, they differ in sense. The two names express different conceptions of their shared referent and it is these differing conceptions that the names contribute to the expressed propositions, not simply their (shared) referent. Perhaps the sense of 'Bob Dylan' is given by 'the famous folk-rock singer with a gravelly voice' while the sense of 'Robert Zimmerman' is given by 'the only person from Duluth, Minnesota to make it big'. If so, then we could say that (1) is equivalent to (1*) and (2) to (2*):

(1*) The famous folk-rock singer with a gravelly voice is the only person from Duluth, Minnesota to make it big.

(2*) The famous folk-rock singer with a gravelly voice is the only famous folk-rock singer with a gravelley voice.

And if this is right, then it is at least *clearer* how and why (1) is informative while (2) is not.[5]

No less a philosopher and logician than Bertrand Russell also held that definite descriptions were crucially semantically related to names, though for reasons quite different from Frege's.[6] In fact, according to Russell, names are *disguised definite descriptions*. 'Bob

Dylan', Russell would have said, is simply *short for* some definite description or other, perhaps 'the famous folk-rock singer with a gravelly voice'. Thus, Russell's explanation of the difference in informativeness between (1) and (2) is virtually identical to Frege's.

BOX 1: Russell's Theory of Definite Descriptions

Both Frege and Russell held that if we view names as equivalent to definite descriptions various puzzles about names, like the informativeness puzzle, are solvable. But how, exactly, does the meaning of a definite description manage to go beyond what it refers to? One of Russell's most famous and important contributions to the philosophy of language and logic is a theory of descriptions, which, among other things, answers this question.

Russell proposed treating sentences containing definite descriptions not as ordinary subject-predicate constructions (as they appear to be) but instead as constructions that are *quantificational* in nature. A quantificational sentence says, more or less precisely, *how many* things possess a given feature or property. 'Someone is a former bodybuilder', 'At least ten people are former bodybuilders', and 'Everyone is a former bodybuilder' are all examples of quantificational sentences. As Russell (and before him, Frege) realized, it would be a mistake to take the grammatical subjects of these sentences – 'someone', 'at least ten people', and 'everyone' – as singular terms that make reference to particulars. 'Someone is a bodybuilder', for example, does not say of some individual person – Ralph, say – that *he* is a former bodybuilder. Rather, what it says is made true by anyone at all being a former bodybuilder, Ralph, Suzette, Marcus, whoever. Russell held that descriptions, while singular terms, achieve their singularity in a striking manner: sentences that contain descriptions are equivalent to a conjunction of quantificational sentences, none of which, individually, makes reference to any particular.

Consider sentence (S):

(S) The star of the *Terminator* movies is a former bodybuilder.

According to Russell's theory, (S) is equivalent to the conjunction of (S1), (S2) and (S3):

(S1) Someone is a star of the *Terminator* movies.

(S2) At most one person is a star of the *Terminator* movies.
(S3) Everyone who is a star of the *Terminator* movies is a former bodybuilder.

As it happens, Arnold Schwarzenegger is the star of the *Terminator* movies. But none of (S1), (S2), or (S3), on its own, makes reference to Schwarzenegger. Instead, the conjunction of the three produces a kind of 'zeroing-in' effect, and the person zeroed in on happens to be Schwarzenegger, the referent of 'the star of the *Terminator* movies'. More generally, Russell's theory claims that any sentence of the form 'The *F* is *G*' is equivalent to one of the form 'Something is *F*, and at most one thing is *F*, and anything that is *F* is *G*'. See *Suggestions for Further Reading* for more on Russell's Theory.

This convergence of opinion between two of the founders of modern philosophy of language and logic deserves a label. Most commentators call the point of convergence *descriptivism*. Descriptivism, just to be clear, is a thesis about the meaning of a proper name. The thesis is simple: *a proper name is equivalent in meaning to a definite description*. Descriptivism, as we have seen, has the resources to solve Frege's informativeness puzzle. We are going to look, in the next section, at Saul Kripke's attack on descriptivist theories of names, but before we do, we ought to catalogue some of the other virtues of descriptivism so that we know just what we lose if descriptivism turns out to be unable to sustain that attack.

Descriptivism appears able to solve another puzzle about names, one related to the informativeness puzzle, namely the *puzzle of substitutivity*. This puzzle has to do with the behaviour of names in *attitude contexts*, that is, in sentences that ascribe mental states like belief (the philosopher's favourite) to agents. As before, the puzzle arises by assuming a direct reference theory for names. If the names 'Superman' and 'Clark Kent' contribute just their shared referent to the propositions expressed by (5) and (6), then (7) and (8) ought to express the same proposition and, hence, ought to share a truth-value.[7]

(5) Lois Lane believes that Superman can fly.
(6) Lois Lane believes that Clark Kent can fly.

But (5) is true, while (6) is false (or so it seems). If, however, descriptivism is true, and the names in (5) and (6) are equivalent in meaning to descriptions (which are not equivalent to each other), the puzzle diminishes. Perhaps 'Superman' means what 'the caped hero of Metropolis' does while 'Clark Kent' means what 'the mild-mannered reporter for the *Daily Planet*' does. If so, then (5) and (6) are equivalent in meaning to (5*) and (6*) respectively:

(5*) Lois believes that the caped hero of Metropolis can fly.

(6*) Lois believes that the mild-mannered reporter for the *Daily Planet* can fly.

And, if those equivalences hold, it is at least clearer how and why (5) might differ from (6) in truth-value.

It seems plain that, if descriptivism were true, a variety of semantic puzzles would be solvable. But besides its puzzle-solving capacity, there is this bit of more straightforward-seeming evidence for descriptivism: the production of a definite description is the most natural reply to a question of the form 'What does 'N' mean?', where 'N' is a proper name. If one were asked to say what the name 'Bob Dylan' means, for example, a natural reaction would be to come out with a definite description: 'It means the famous folk-rock singer with a gravelly voice.' Why, the descriptivist might ask, should we not take this sort of reply literally?

4.3.2 Kripke's attack

With all that going for it, what possible reason could there be for not accepting descriptivism? In 1972, Saul Kripke published a now famous series of lectures in a book called *Naming and Necessity*. The book changed the course of analytic philosophy in almost all of its various branches, but some of its central theses concern the philosophy of language and logic and, in particular, the meaning question for names. Most of what Kripke says about names is negative; he doesn't provide a positive answer to the meaning question. Instead he argues that descriptivism is the *wrong* answer. In fact, *Naming and Necessity* contains *three* distinct anti-descriptivist arguments. It is to these arguments that we now turn.

4.3.2.1 The modal argument

Bob Dylan might not have been famous. He is talented, it's true. But talent will only get you so far. It also seems true that Bob Dylan might have forgone a career in singing and songwriting entirely, living out his days in obscurity as a truck driver or a logger (or something). These simple facts about what might have been pose an interesting difficulty for descriptivism. Let's suppose that the definite description that the descriptivist takes to give the meaning of 'Bob Dylan' is 'the famous folk-rock singer with a gravelly voice'. If the supposition were true, we ought to be able to replace any occurrence of 'Bob Dylan' in any given sentence with 'the famous folk-rock singer with a gravelly voice' without altering the sentence's meaning or truth-value. After all, the descriptivist takes the description to be a *synonym* for the name. But as we have, in effect, already noted, there are sentences describing *possibilities* – 'modal sentences' as the philosophers say – for which this is not true. Consider (7):

> (7) It is possibly not the case that Bob Dylan is famous.

(7) is true. But now look what happens when we replace the 'Bob Dylan' in (7) with its alleged descriptive synonym to get (7*):

> (7*) It is possibly not the case that the famous folk-rock singer with a gravelly voice is famous.

(7*) is false. In fact, it seems *contradictory*. Surely anyone who counts as the famous folk-rock singer with a gravelly voice also counts as famous. You can't be a famous folk-rock singer without being famous.[8] But if (7) differs from (7*) in truth-value, then the two sentences do not mean the same thing; they express different propositions. But if that is right, then, contrary to our descriptivist supposition, 'Bob Dylan' must differ in meaning from 'the famous folk-rock singer with a gravelly voice', since it is only in the exchange of the description for the name that (7) and (7*) are differently put together.

Thus runs one version of Kripke's modal argument against descriptivism. The version just presented can be summarized by saying that what it shows is that descriptivism mistakenly implies that certain possibilities – like the possibility that Bob Dylan is not famous – are *im*possibilities. Another version of the modal argument shows that descriptivism mistakenly implies that certain contingencies are non-contingencies. A *contingent truth* is one that is true in fact but possibly false. A *non-contingent*, or *necessary*, truth is one that is true in fact and impossibly false. Now consider (8):

(8) It is necessary that Bob Dylan is famous.

(8) is false. That Bob Dylan is famous is only contingently true. But, if we make the same descriptivist supposition as before, taking 'Bob Dylan' to mean what 'the famous folk-rock singer with a gravelly voice' does, then (8) ought to be identical in meaning and truth-value to (8*):

(8*) It is necessary that the famous folk-rock singer with a gravelly voice is famous.

Unlike (8), (8*) is true.[9] Hence the two sentences differ in meaning and it looks as though we can reason to the same anti-descriptivist conclusion as before: 'the famous folk-rock singer with a gravelly voice' is not a synonym for 'Bob Dylan'.

4.3.2.2 The epistemological argument

Where the modal argument involved the notions of possibility and necessity, the epistemological argument involves the notion of *knowledge*. In particular, it involves a traditional philosophical distinction between two *kinds* of knowledge – *a priori* versus *a posteriori* knowledge. Philosophers call the sort of knowledge that one gains via the senses '*a posteriori*'. Anything learnt by sight, touch, smell, and so on is considered *a posteriori*. Characterizing *a priori* knowledge is somewhat controversial, but perhaps the most neutral way to do it is negatively, by reference to *a posteriori* knowledge: *a priori* knowledge is simply knowledge that is *not a posteriori*. Traditional examples of *a priori* knowledge include knowledge of mathematical and logical truths, one's knowledge of one's own mental states, and knowledge of 'conceptual truths' like the truth that all doctors are physicians. While such knowledge might depend on experiences of various sorts, they do not depend on *sense* experience. Knowing that all doctors are physicians, for example, seems to depend only on reflection on the concepts that constitute that proposition.

How is this distinction relevant to descriptivism? Kripke's epistemological argument is that if descriptivism is true, then some sentences that *ought* to be *a posteriori* will turn out to be *a priori* and vice versa.[10] Let's let Bob Dylan be and turn to a different example. Suppose that the descriptivist proposes that 'Aristotle' is equivalent in meaning to 'the last great philosopher of antiquity'. This proposal conflicts with the fact that it is *a posteriori* that Aristotle was a philosopher. How so? Well, on that proposal, the *a posteriori* sentence (9) is equivalent in meaning to (9*):

(9) Aristotle was a philosopher.
(9*) The last great philosopher of antiquity was a philosopher.

But the trouble, of course, is that (9*) is not *a posteriori*, it's *a priori*.[11] One need not 'look out into the world', i.e. use one's senses, to ascertain the truth of (9*). It would seem to follow, then, that (9) and (9*) differ in meaning. How could they both express the same proposition if only (9) is *a posteriori*? But if they do so differ, then, once again, it looks as though we must conclude, contrary to our descriptivist proposal, that 'the last great philosopher of antiquity' is not synonymous with 'Aristotle'.

4.3.2.3 The error argument

Thales was a pre-Socratic philosopher who seems to have believed that everything is made of water. Virtually nothing else is known by historians about Thales. So if anything counts as the descriptive synonym for the name 'Thales', it is pretty likely 'the pre-Socratic philosopher who believed that everything is made of water'. Now consider some claim about Thales, like that made by (10):

(10) Thales was fat.

If descriptivism is true, then (10) means just what (10*) does:

(10*) The pre-Socratic philosopher who believed that everything is made of water was fat.

But now suppose that what historians 'know' about Thales is a mistake and that, in fact, no philosopher ever believed that everything is made of water. On this supposition, (10*) is false, or, at the very least, not true.[12] The supposition implies that there is no referent for the description 'the pre-Socratic philosopher who believed that everything is made of water' and that, it seems, suffices to make (10*) false (or at least not true). The problem for descriptivism is that the supposition does not appear to have a similar effect on (10).

Thales might have been fat, and hence (10) might be true, regardless of whether any philosopher ever believed that everything is made of water. Notice also that on the supposition that there was no philosopher who believed that everything is made of water, the descriptivist apparently must endorse the truth of (11):

(11) Thales never existed.

But the non-existence of a philosopher who believed that everything is made of water is hardly sufficient for the truth of (11). It seems far more natural to say that *if* Thales existed, then, given our supposition about what the historians (fail to) know, a mistake has been made about him. He has been wrongly taken to have a very strange view about the nature of the world. But if that is right, then the question of the existence of Thales is *independent* of the question of the existence of a philosopher who believed that everything is made of water. The trouble with descriptivism is that it denies this independence.

Matters get even worse for the descriptivist if we suppose that the historians are wrong not about the *existence* of a philosopher who believed that everything is made of water, but about *who* that philosopher was. It seems perfectly coherent to suppose that someone other than Thales was the pre-Socratic philosopher who believed that everything was made of water. Let's suppose that this other pre-Socratic philosopher was named 'Zorba'. Again, descriptivism delivers the wrong results. For example, it predicts that (10) is true just in case *Zorba* was fat (because we are imagining that it is Zorba who was the pre-Socratic philosopher who believed that everything is made of water). But that is crazy. (10)'s truth depends on Thales's fatness, not Zorba's.

The examples involving Thales are some of the ways of making the *error argument* against descriptivism, perhaps the most compelling and straightforward of Kripke's three anti-descriptivist arguments. The basic thought behind the error argument is that the meaning of a name can't be given by those descriptions that we associate with the name, since *we might be mistaken* about which properties the referent of the name possesses. And in those cases in which we are mistaken, like in the Thales cases imagined above, descriptivism predicts the wrong truth-values for sentences involving the name.

4.3.3 Cluster-theory descriptivism

It might be thought that the modal, epistemological, and error arguments are effective only against a rather naïve form of descriptivism and that a more sophisticated variant might be able to withstand them. In the presentation of each of the arguments we imagined the descriptivist selecting a single, relatively simple description as synonymous with a given name. Perhaps it is not so surprising that this simple version of descriptivism can be shown to be false. How, then, might descriptivism be appropriately complicated? A suggestion that can be extracted from the work of the philosopher John Searle (Searle 1958) is that descriptivism should be conceived as the thesis that a name is synonymous not with a single description but instead with a 'cluster' of them.[13] The referent of the name is whatever object counts as the referent of 'sufficient number' of the descriptions in the cluster. Importantly, the members of the cluster can change from occasion to occasion, but are, generally, whatever descriptions are 'commonly associated' with the name. So, in the case of 'Aristotle', the cluster would probably include 'the last great philosopher of antiquity', 'the most famous student of Plato', and 'the author of *De Anima*', as well an indefinite number of others.

There are many questions that would have to be answered to make this 'cluster-theory descriptivism' precise,[14] but the brief sketch it has been given here is probably already enough to see how this new-and-improved descriptivism might reply to at least some of the Kripkean arguments we have recently examined. To the modal and epistemological arguments, the cluster-theory descriptivist would most likely say that, in general, any particular, individual description may be left out of the meaning-determining cluster. Consider sentence (8) again. (8) is clearly false, and since it is, we clearly cannot take 'the famous folk-rock singer with a gravelly voice' to give the meaning of 'Bob Dylan'. But there are other descriptions commonly associated with the name 'Bob Dylan', and for the purposes of evaluating (8) we can take 'Bob Dylan' to be equivalent in meaning to these others, or so the cluster-theory descriptivist might say. Just so long as these other descriptions do not express the property of *being famous*, there will be no problem with the contingency of (8). Or consider sentence (9) once more. The problem with (9), remember, is that it is *a posteriori* not *a priori*, as the simple descriptivism we were supposing earlier implied it to be. The more complicated cluster-theory will say that (9) is indeed *a posteriori* and, since it is, no serious user of (9) could take the 'Aristotle' in it to be synonymous with 'the last great philosopher of antiquity'. But it could be taken as synonymous with some cluster of descriptions commonly associated with the name that does not include 'the last great philosopher of antiquity'. Just so long as those descriptions don't express the property of *being a philosopher*, there will be no problem with the *a posteriority* of (9).

Unfortunately, these replies to Kripke's arguments are not very good, as Kripke himself has shown. Here is why: consider a sentence that has 'Bob Dylan' in its subject position and has, in its predicate position, a long disjunctive listing of *all* of those descriptions that are commonly associated with 'Bob Dylan'. Schematically, the imagined sentence looks like (12):

(12) Bob Dylan is the *F*, or the *G*, or the *H* . . .

Whatever cluster of descriptions the descriptivist takes to be synonymous with 'Bob Dylan', (12) will turn out (a) not possibly false, and (b) *a priori*. But, intuitively, (12) is neither. In other words, versions of the modal and epistemological arguments apply with as much force to cluster-theory descriptivism as they do to the simple descriptivism with which we started.

What's worse, cluster-theory descriptivism simply lacks the resources to deal with the error argument. It's clearly possible that we might be wrong about *all* of the properties had by a particular object or person, but such a thing is ruled out by both simple and cluster-theory descriptivism. In fact, the Thales examples are equally effective against both, since we were imagining that 'the pre-Socratic philosopher who believed that everything is made of water' is the *only* description associated with 'Thales', and thus the only member of the single-membered 'cluster' of descriptions associated with 'Thales'.

In the main, contemporary philosophers and logicians agree with this assessment of the dispute between Kripke and the descriptivists. Kripke won; that is the almost universal consensus. But remember that Kripke's conclusion is purely negative; it tells us only that names are not 'descriptional', as it is sometimes put. What can be positively said about the propositional contribution of a name? If it is not a descriptive conception of the name's referent, what is it? These days, many philosophers endorse a direct reference theory for names, the theory – just to remind you – that a name's sole contribution is its referent. But what, then, of the Fregean considerations that drove us away from the direct reference theory in the first place? How the direct reference theorist might contend with those considerations is the topic of the next section.

There is one final issue to settle before moving on, however. Remember the straightforward-seeming piece of evidence for descriptivism having to do with the fact that descriptions are produced when the meaning of a name is asked for? What can the anti-descriptivist say to that? Once again, Kripke's *Naming and Necessity* contains the answer. One of the many important distinctions in Kripke's book is a distinction between 'giving a synonym' and 'fixing the reference' of a name. Suppose that one were to introduce a certain name 'Penny' *via* a definite description like so: 'Let "Penny" name the pen sitting on Max Deutsch's desk.' Kripke argues that even for names like 'Penny', i.e. those introduced *via* description, descriptivism is incorrect. It certainly seems true that a version of the modal argument applies to descriptivism about such names. For example, it is surely not a *necessary* truth that Penny is sitting on Max Deutsch's desk. It could have been a different pen sitting on that desk, or no pen at all. So it seems that we had better not take 'the pen sitting on Max Deutsch's desk' to be synonymous with 'Penny' (since, if we did, we would have to count 'Penny is the pen sitting on Max Deutsch's desk' as necessary). Nevertheless, the description is clearly playing some sort of meaning-relevant role *vis-à-vis* 'Penny', a role aptly described by Kripke as *fixing the reference* of the name 'Penny'.

Reference-fixing that is not synonym-giving is close to what is going on when someone produces a description in response to a query about the meaning of a name. In fact the phenomenon is even simpler than reference-fixing since the latter involves *determining* or *giving* a name its referent but the former does not. In a case in which one replies 'the famous folk-rock singer with a gravelly voice' in answering a question about what 'Bob Dylan' means, one is simply *telling the questioner what 'Bob Dylan' refers to*. There is no need to see one's reply to the question as the production of what is literally a synonym for the name and, thus, the apparent evidence for descriptivism is neatly explained away.

4.3.4 The theory of direct reference

The theory of direct reference for names claims that the propositional contribution of a name like 'Aristotle' or 'Bob Dylan' is its referent. 'Aristotle' means Aristotle and 'Bob Dylan' means Bob Dylan. That's it. The theory is popular, mostly due to the influence of Kripke's anti-descriptivist arguments. But despite this there are surprisingly few positive arguments in favour of it. Among its supporters, the majority of effort and ink has been spent defending the theory from certain powerful-seeming objections. There is an interesting question about how to regard the theory if it turns out that these objections can be met in a plausible, convincing way. Ingenious defences of false theories have been given before, after all. At some point, it seems, someone will have to argue not just that various reasons for thinking the theory of direct reference to be false are bad, but that the theory is *true*.

That being said, we will focus here on how, and how well, the theory has been defended from one of the above-mentioned objections. The objection we will examine is the objection encapsulated by what we were earlier (in section 4.2) calling the puzzle of substitutivity, the puzzle having to with the behaviour of names in attitude contexts. This puzzle, along with the objection to the direct reference theory that can be derived from it, is perhaps the single most often discussed issue in the contemporary philosophy of language.

4.3.5 The substitutivity puzzle

Let's return to the version of the puzzle we were discussing earlier. If the names 'Clark Kent' and 'Superman' contribute just their referent to the propositions expressed by sentences involving them – as the theory of direct reference insists – then (5) and (6) should have the same truth-value:

(5) Lois Lane believes that Superman can fly.
(6) Lois Lane believes that Clark Kent can fly.

The trouble is that it seems that (5) is true while (6) is false. The descriptivist, remember, was able to solve the puzzle by saying that things are as they seem: (5) *is* true and (6) *is* false. The direct reference theorist is prevented from saying this. He or she must say that the appearance of a difference in truth-value is *merely* an appearance, for on the theory of direct reference, (5) and (6) *cannot* differ in truth-value.

An interesting and not often noted initial difficulty for the direct reference theorist is that he or she must decide, in cases of 'puzzling pairs' of sentences like (5) and (6), *which* truth-value it is that they share. In the case of (5) and (6), which is a favourite example in the literature on the theory, every direct reference theorist says that both are *true*. Our inclination to say that (6) is false is based, they say, on a mistake. We will come shortly to just what sort of mistake this is supposed to be, but first we should ask whether the direct reference theorist has some principled reason to declare (5) and (6) true as opposed to false. One thing that could be said here is that there is good evidence for the truth of (5): if one were to *ask* Lois whether she believes that Superman can fly, she would say 'yes'. But the problem is that there appears to be equally good evidence for the falsity of (6): if one were to ask Lois whether she believes that Clark Kent can fly, she would say 'no'. So no simple appeal to Lois's behaviour will give the direct reference theorist the principled reason he or she needs. In fact, that simple appeal to Lois's behaviour reveals something that perhaps counts as a further difficulty for direct reference theorists who hold that (5) and (6) are both true. He or she must deny that Lois's reaction to 'Clark Kent can fly' is good evidence for the falsity of (6), and that is a tough spot in which to be. Typically, we take someone's firm denial of a given sentence to be close to a guarantee that he or she fails to believe the proposition expressed by that sentence. But let's leave this problem unsolved and turn now to the matter of how the direct reference theorists can explain our inclination to say (mistakenly, by their lights) that (6) is false.

To explain this, direct reference theorists appeal to a distinction between the proposition(s) *semantically expressed* by a given sentence and the proposition(s) it *pragmatically conveys*. Very roughly, the distinction corresponds to a distinction between what the uttered sentence means and what the utterer of the sentence means in uttering it. Frequently, of course, the two coincide, and what one means in uttering a certain sentence is just what the sentence itself means. When they do, one is 'speaking literally'. But often, perhaps even typically, the two kinds of meaning come apart. Consider, for example, someone who sarcastically utters (13), below:

(13) George W. Bush is an incredibly polished public speaker.

In the case of a sarcastic utterance of (13), the speaker does not mean what (13) means. In fact, the speaker probably means close to its opposite – that GWB is *not* an incredibly polished public speaker. Now whether (13) is true or false depends on whether the proposition *it* expresses is true or false. Since it expresses the proposition that GWB is an incredibly polished public speaker, it is false. (There can be no arguments on *that* score.) But this does not prevent a speaker from *using* (13) to convey something true. In fact, the sarcastic utterer of (13) is just such a speaker, for, in uttering (13), she conveys the true proposition that GWB is *not* an incredibly polished public speaker.

Direct reference theorists argue that a similar sort of thing – a difference between what the sentence itself means and what gets conveyed by it – is going on in the case of (6). As far as what it itself means (what it semantically expresses), that is just the true proposition expressed by (5). But (6) pragmatically conveys a different, false proposition. When we judge that (6) is false, we are mistakenly taking this pragmatically conveyed proposition as relevant to the truth-value of (6). But the only proposition that is relevant to the truth-value of (6) is the one that constitutes *its* meaning, and that proposition, once again, is simply the true proposition expressed by (5).

But *which* merely pragmatically conveyed proposition do we wrongly take to be relevant to the truth-value of (6)? With respect to this question, there is a range of proposals made by different direct-reference theorists. We will here consider the simplest and clearest of these, a proposal that is suggested by the direct reference theorist Nathan Salmon in his book *Frege's Puzzle*.

In that book, Salmon suggests that sentences like (6), which report a person's beliefs, typically convey that the subject of the report would assent to the 'content clause' of the report. A content clause of a belief report is simply the embedded sentence that characterizes the belief being reported; 'Clark Kent can fly' is (6)'s content clause. The suggestion, then, is that because we recognize that Lois would *not* assent to 'Clark Kent can fly' we take (6) itself to be false. But this, says the direct-reference theorist, is to confuse pragmatics with semantics. It is not part of the very meaning of (6) that Lois would assent to a certain sentence of the English language. (6) could be true even if Lois were a monolingual speaker of Italian. So, at best, a sincere utterance of (6) manages to pragmatically convey the proposition that Lois would assent to 'Clark Kent can fly'. And, if such an utterance does pragmatically convey that proposition, then no wonder many of us find (6) itself to be false.

There are various difficulties both with this particular proposal and for the idea that our judgements about the truth-values of belief reports are clouded by a conflation of the merely pragmatic with the genuinely semantic. Considerations of space prevent us from examining them, but there is a last, more general issue concerning the theory of direct reference for names that deserves mention here. Many people find the theory of direct reference highly counterintuitive. Indeed, the reaction that they have is quite a bit stronger than the label 'counterintuitive' suggests. Many would say (5) and (6) simply do not share a truth-value and that this should be taken as a datum for any theory of names to accommodate. On the other hand, as we have seen, Kripke's anti-descriptivist arguments are extremely compelling. In their light, it looks to be a rather serious mistake to think of the meaning of a name as a descriptive conception of its referent. But if *both* of these attitudes are correct, then we are faced with a puzzle. On the one hand, the meaning of a name can't simply be identified with its referent. On the other, it can't be a descriptive conception of that referent either. But now how *else*, besides being a descriptive conception of a referent, could the meaning of a name go beyond what it refers to? This puzzle has plagued philosophers of language since the publication of Kripke's book and it is, as yet, unsolved.

4.4 THEORIES OF REFERENCE

Despite its misleading name, the theory of direct reference is not a theory of reference. It is a theory of meaning for names, or, more precisely, a theory about what propositional contribution a name makes to propositions expressed by sentences containing it. Neither it nor its competitor, i.e. descriptivism, answers the reference question for names; both theories are silent about how a name comes to have the referent it does. In section 4.2, we briefly introduced two opposing answers to the reference question. The first, which was described there as the traditional Fregean view, takes definite descriptions to play a crucial role in bestowing reference on a name. This traditional view was contrasted with the Kripkean 'causal theory of reference' which claims that descriptions are not crucial at all, and that the correct answer to the reference question mentions 'initial dubbings' and 'causal chains' of usage. It would be natural to assume that the descriptivist about the meaning of a name must also hold a descriptivist theory of reference, and that the direct reference theorist must accept something like the causal theory. But this is not true. It is perfectly consistent to hold that names get their references *via* description, while nevertheless holding to a direct reference theory concerning a name's propositional contribution. Likewise, it is consistent to be a descriptivist about the meanings of names while maintaining that their references are acquired as the causal theory says they are. What this demonstrates is the relative independence of the meaning and reference questions. No decision about how to answer the former necessitates a particular answer to the latter. For the same reason, no objection to, say, the theory of direct reference is automatically an objection to the causal theory of reference. The answers to the reference question we will examine here must be assessed on their own terms.

4.4.1 The traditional view

Definite descriptions play a central role both in a traditional theory of meaning for names (the 'descriptivism' already discussed in section 4.3.1) and in a traditional theory of reference for names. In order to distinguish the latter from the former, let's call the latter view 'reference descriptivism'. The basic claim of reference descriptivism is that the referent of a name is determined *via* description: some description, or collection of them, is identified as the reference-determiner for a given name, and whatever satisfies that description, or descriptions, counts as the referent of the name.

Presumably, a reference descriptivism modelled on what we were calling 'cluster-theory descriptivism' in Section 4.3.3 is the most plausible version of the theory. It is not being the referent of some *single* description that makes it the case that 'N' names N. Rather, it is being the referent of some significant cluster of descriptions that does the reference determining job.

There is an initial question about how the cluster itself comes to have the reference determining descriptions in it.[15] The easiest reply is to say that the cluster is constituted by those descriptions that are associated with the name by the various speakers who use the name. There is a difficulty with this proposal since it is possible that the cluster of descriptions that *I* associate with 'N' refer to something different from what is referred to by the descriptions that *you* associate with 'N'. What, then, would count as *the* referent of 'N'? To reply by claiming that 'N' simply refers to something different for you than it does for me deepens the problem. For one thing, it is possible that the descriptions that a *single* speaker associates with a given name pick out more than one individual. For another, it is counterintuitive to suppose that you and I speak about different things when using 'N' simply because we differ in our beliefs about N's attributes, as reflected in the differing descriptions that we associate with 'N'. Indeed, the proposal appears, implausibly, to rule out the possibility of disagreement about the attributes possessed by the referent of a name. Such 'disagreement' would amount, on the proposal, to cases of talking past one another.

A potential solution to these problems is to insist that the reference-fixing descriptions are the ones that are typically – that is, by a *majority* of speakers – associated with the name. There are related problems with this proposal, but they are, perhaps, less severe. In any case, we will, in what follows, take reference descriptivism to be the thesis that the referent of a name is determined by that cluster of descriptions that are typically associated with it.

Although reference descriptivism and meaning descriptivism are distinct theories with different explanatory aims, it turns out that one of the objections to meaning descriptivism also qualifies as a powerful objection to reference descriptivism. What we earlier called the 'error-objection' to meaning descriptivism applies to reference descriptivism as well. If you will recall, the examples we discussed in connection with the error objection featured a certain ancient philosopher, Thales, and his name, 'Thales'. In one version of the objection, we supposed that although 'the ancient Greek philosopher who believed that everything is made of water' is the only description typically associated with 'Thales', there is, in fact, no one who ever held such a strange view. The trouble with this supposition for meaning descriptivism is that some sentences involving 'Thales' would turn out false when they ought to turn out true, while others would turn out true when they ought to turn out false. The suppposition poses analogous difficulties for reference descriptivism. If the referent of a name is determined by those descriptions typically associated with it, then, since the only description typically associated with 'Thales' lacks a referent, 'Thales' itself must lack a referent. But, intuitively, our supposition should not have this result.

Even given the supposition, it could be true that there was an ancient Greek philosopher named 'Thales' (i.e. that 'Thales' has a referent) about whom a pervasive mistake has been made. More generally, the descriptions typically associated with a name might fail to determine the referent of that name because of the possibility of error. Clearly, if speakers typically associate the description 'the F' with 'N', but N is not the F, then 'the F' doesn't count as a reference-determiner for 'N'.

4.4.2 The causal theory

In *Naming and Necessity*, Kripke combines his arguments against meaning descriptivism with some of the above complaints against reference descriptivism. But, where Kripke is silent about what might replace descriptivism as a theory of meaning, he offers something close to a new theory of reference. Kripke's proposal, briefly introduced in section 4.2.2, has come to be called the 'causal theory of reference'. According to the theory, a name first acquires its referent at an initial 'dubbing' or 'baptism'. Some speaker simply stipulates that some object shall have a certain name. The speaker *might* identify the object-to-be-named *via* description – 'Let *the F* be named "N"' – or she might not. In what sort of case might a speaker not identify the object-to-be named *via* description? In a case in which the speaker is in perceptual contact with it – she can see it, or otherwise perceive it. In such a case, the speaker may simply demonstrate the object, by pointing, say. She *need not* identify it descriptively. It is perhaps this aspect of Kripke's theory that has led to it being called the 'causal theory', since being in perceptual contact with an object is one way of being in causal contact with that object. But, if so, the label is somewhat misleading, since Kripke allows for the obvious possibility of naming *via* description. When it comes to explaining how an object acquires its name, Kripke's theory allows that descriptions may play a role; it is just that they need not. Names can acquire their referents non-descriptionally as well.

The causal part of the causal theory really only emerges at the next stage, in the way in which the theory explains how some non-original use of a name has the referent it does. Why does my use, say, of 'Arnold Schwarzenegger' refer to the famous movie actor and not some other person? Reference descriptivism says that the explanation involves the descriptions typically associated with the name. The causal theory denies that those descriptions play this reference-determining role. It says instead that I 'borrow' the referent of 'Arnold Schwarzenegger' from other users of the name in my linguistic community. All such users are connected *via* a communicative (and, hence, causal) chain that traces back to the initial dubbing of Arnold with his name. Perhaps I picked up the name from Bob, who in turn picked it up from Sally, who in turn picked it up from Ron, and so on, back to the original users of 'Arnold Schwarzenegger' responsible for giving the man his name (Arnie's parents, most likely). The causal theory is causal because of the emphasis it places on such communicative links in which a name is passed from speaker to speaker.

However, so far, the theory does not suffice to answer the question of why my use of 'Arnold Schwarzenegger' refers to Arnold Schwarzenegger and not some other thing. I may have picked up the name from somebody who uses it to refer to Arnold Schwarzenegger, but that, clearly, does not guarantee that *my* use of it will refer to the same thing. I might choose to use it to refer to something else, my dog, or a rock, for example. For this reason, Kripke says that, ordinarily, a speaker uses a name with a certain implicit intention, namely the intention to use the name to refer to what others in that speaker's linguistic community use it to refer to.

An obvious virtue of the causal theory is that it easily avoids the version of the error objection that plagues reference descriptivism. The descriptions typically associated with the name 'Arnold Schwarzenegger' may fail to refer to Arnold Schwarzenegger. On the causal theory, I can nevertheless talk about Arnold Schwarzenegger using 'Arnold Schwarzenegger' because to whom I refer with such uses is independent of the descriptions associated with the name. The other difficulties with traditional reference descriptivism also fail to apply to the causal theory. There is clearly no problem, for example, selecting which descriptions make it in to the cluster of reference determining ones, since descriptions do not determine a name's referent on the causal theory.

A now common complaint against the causal theory turns on the fact, mentioned a paragraph back, that it requires the presence of an intention to refer, with a given name, to what other users use it to refer to. For what is 'the thing referred to by other users of the name "Arnold Schwarzenegger"'? but a description that I associate with 'Arnold Schwarzenegger'? It looks as though reference descriptivism is being allowed in through the back door. So, is the causal theory a genuine alternative to reference descriptivism, or is it simply a kind of reference descriptivism in disguise? These are questions that any causal theorist must answer.

Another often cited difficulty with the causal theory is that it is ill-equipped to deal with the phenomenon of *reference-change*. A name can clearly change its reference, referring at one time to *x*, and at some other time to *y*. But the causal theory appears unable to accommodate this fact. The philosopher Gareth Evans (Evans 1973) first raised the problem of reference-change for the causal theory, introducing the problem with the example of 'Madagascar'. Today 'Madagascar' names an island off the east coast of Africa. But it didn't always. It used to name a portion of mainland Africa. Legend has it that Marco Polo was the first to use the name to refer to the island but that he did so while labouring under the false impression that his use was correct – that other users of 'Madagascar' also used the name to speak of the island. Now, eventually, Marco Polo's use became entrenched. 'Madagascar' now names the island, not the mainland. The trouble for the causal theory is explaining how this came to be. After all, Marco Polo presumably intended to use the name as other users then did; he did not intend to be introducing a new use for 'Madagascar'. But these other users meant 'Madagascar' to apply to the mainland. So, given that Marco Polo intended to use the name as others then did, and given that these others then used the name to refer to the mainland, the causal theory predicts that Marco Polo's use refers to the mainland. Furthermore, since we present-day users of 'Madagascar' ultimately acquired the name from Marco Polo, the causal theory entails that *our* uses of the name refer to the mainland as well. But this conflicts with the plain facts: our uses of the name refer to the island.

Is there a compromise position, a view that combines the virtues of the causal theory and reference descriptivism while dropping their vices? Some say that there is, but debate on the matter continues. No theory has yet been recognized as the clearly correct account of the reference of a proper name.

4.4 SUMMARY

The meaning question and the reference question are very much live issues in the study of proper names. Progress has been made on them – the theory of direct reference and the causal theory are examples of this progress, at least insofar as these newer theories serve to pinpoint some of the difficulties faced by their predecessors. But along with that progress has come new problems. The nearly universal rejection of Frege's meaning-descriptivism has turned the substitutivity puzzle back into a real threat. The inability of the causal theory to cope with the phenomenon of reference-change seems as severe a problem as reference-descriptivism's inability to handle the problem of error.

Is this reason to despair? Are the problems surrounding names and naming bound to go forever unsolved? Perhaps the problems can be solved, but only by adopting some more radical approach to them than those that have been examined here. Wittgenstein (1953) held that the Fregean/Russellian approach to the problems of language was entirely wrong-headed, one of its main defects being the tendency to 'reify meaning', to conceive of meaning and meanings as kinds of *things*. In contrast, Wittgenstein claimed that there is no more to the meaning of an expression than the way in which it is *used*, and he urged theorists of language to abandon the idea that the main semantic notion is that of *standing for* or *referring to* some object or other. The approaches to the meaning and reference questions that we have looked at in this chapter are, in essence, variations on the Fregean/Russellian approach. Of course, the claims made by one or another of the theories we have examined differ from those made by Frege and Russell; the theory of direct reference, for example, denies that the meaning of a name is descriptive. But this disagreement is not a disagreement about the *nature* of meaning. Frege and Russell disagree with the direct reference theorist over *which* kind of thing counts as the meaning of a name, but, at a perhaps more fundamental level, they agree that it is appropriate to conceive of the meaning of a name *as a kind of thing*.

Perhaps it is time to consider the possibility that Wittgenstein was right and that the Fregean/Russellian approach to the problems of names and naming is what is preventing a satisfactory solution to those problems. Genuinely new approaches to the problems are only just beginning to emerge, however. A handful of papers that we think take a new approach to the meaning and reference questions are indicated in *Suggestions for Further Reading*.

4.5 A BRIEF DISCUSSION ON VAGUENESS

In traditional grammar, a simple sentence is said to consist of a subject and a predicate. In the preceding sections, we have been considering two kinds of subject term – names and definite descriptions – but we have said little about predicates. Perhaps surprisingly, predicates do not seem to raise many awkward questions in the philosophy of logic. There are *metaphysical* questions, such as 'Do all predicates stand for properties?' (In the previous chapter, we spent a little time debating whether 'is true' is a genuine property. Does 'exist' stand for a property? What about 'is red if examined before 8 January 2007'?) And a metaphysical question that has plagued metaphysics for centuries is whether properties exist independently of individual things, inhere in them or do not exist at all. But, for the philosopher of logic, predicates have not generally caused a big headache, the major exception to this generalization being *vague* predicates. This is a major exception because, when you come to think about it, *most* of the predicates we use in everyday discourse are vague and, as we indicated in Chapter 1, vague predicates are a breeding ground for paradox. Let's work with the predicate 'tall' and start by considering these two statements:

(14) A person who has a height of 200cm is tall.
(15) For any (natural number) $x>0$, if a person with a height of $x+1$ cm is tall, then a person with a height of x cm is also tall.

Now let P_x be the sentence 'A person with a height of x cm is tall'. So we might formalize (14) as P_{200} and (15) as $\forall x>0(P_{x+1}\rightarrow P_x)$. Both statements seem to be true, and we can infer from them P_{199}. Then, from P_{199} and using (15) again, we can infer P_{198}, and of course we can continue on and on until P_{50}, which is definitely false. In other words, from just (14) and (15), we can infer a false conclusion. So the argument cannot be sound. This means that the argument is either not valid, and/or one or more premises are false.

So is the argument invalid? It certainly does not seem to be. Consider:

(16) 200 is an even number, and
(17) For any $x>0$, if $x+2$ is an even number then x *is* an even number.

From them we can infer that 2 is an even number, and this surely is a valid argument. Isn't the argument about tallness of exactly the same form? If so, shouldn't it be valid too? Now (15) is logically equivalent to an infinite conjunction ('. . . Q and R and S . . .') where each conjunct is a conditional statement, e.g. ($P_{200} \rightarrow P_{199}$), ($P_{199} \rightarrow P_{198}$), ($P_{198} \rightarrow P_{197}$), . . . We can infer the same conclusion from these conditional statements and (14), using only *modus ponens* (P; if P then Q. Therefore Q). Aren't these all valid inferences? If so, isn't the original argument also valid?

It would appear, then, that the argument is valid but unsound. But which premise is false? Surely not (14). Someone who is 200cm high is indisputably tall. So it seems that we are forced to conclude that (15) is false. But consider (17). If (17) were false, it seems to follow that there is a number x such that $x+2$ is even but that x is not. So if we think (15) is also false, we should conclude that there is a number x such that a person with a height of $x+1$cm is tall but that a person with a height of $x$cm is not. But this conclusion is hard to swallow.

First of all, it is counterintuitive: such predicates as 'is tall' are vague, and the central idea about such vague predicates is that they have no precise boundaries of application. If a person is tall, then another one who is just a little bit higher or shorter should also be tall. But in denying (15) we are committed to a precise cut-off point for tallness. What could possibly explain why the cut-off point should be where it is? Moreover, we cannot verify where this cut-off point is: it is difficult to tell whether something is exactly 1.789653m tall, but in principle we can find out. But how do we find out where the cut-off point for 'tall' is precisely? It seems that no amount of tests or empirical information can help us. How can there be such a point if in principle we cannot verify where it is?

One popular response to this paradox is to adopt a three-valued logic. On reflection one might suggest that vague statements are neither true nor false, e.g. P_{150} is neither true nor false. This implies the rejection of *the principle of bivalence*: that every statement is either true or false. This principle entails *the principle of excluded middle*: that every statement of the form '*p* or not-*p*' is true. Classical logic assumes both principles.

However, it is not clear that the three-valued approach will solve the paradox. First, even if vague statements are not true or false (neutral), this by itself does not imply that (15) is false or that it is neither true or false. We might agree that P_{150} is not true and not false (let's say it is neutral). But still why does it follow that $\forall x{>}0(P_{x+1} \rightarrow P_x)$ is false, or neutral? It might be that 'Joe is tall' is neutral, but it seems plausible that 'if Joe is tall then he is not short' is still true. How would the three-valued approach deal with this argument: P_{150} is neutral, $\forall x{>}0(P_{x+1}$ is neutral $\rightarrow P_x$ is neutral), therefore P_{50} is neutral? We've here invoked the third value 'neutral', but arrived at a crazy conclusion. P_{50} is not neutral; it's plain false!

Second, there is still the problem of *higher-order vagueness*. The motivation for three-valued logic is that there is no precise height where a person changes from tall to not tall. But similarly there should be no precise number where P_x changes from true to neutral, or from neutral to false. One response might be to postulate further truth-values: true, borderline between true and indefinite, definitely indefinite, etc. But surely the same problem arises with any proposal that postulates a finite number of truth-values. Or one might argue that it is vague where the last true P_x is and where the first neutral P_x begins. This, though, does not seem plausible. If P_{200} is true and P_{150} is neutral then surely there must be a particular point where the change from true to neutral occurs. (A similar response would be applicable to the two-valued case.)

Fuzzy logic postulates an infinite number of truth-values, ranging from 0 (definitely false) to 1 (definitely true). This measure of truth is not to be confused with probability. Consider the series P_{200}, P_{199}, . . . P_{100}. The fuzzy logician should say that the first statement is true, the last one is false, and that each P_x is more true than the one that follows. Let [K] be the degree of truth of the statement K. One way to assign degrees of truth would be to suppose that for any real number x such that $200 \geq x \geq 100$, $[P_x] = (x/100) - 1$.

What is the value of $[P_{x+1} \rightarrow P_x]$? There is room for different answers here. But if both the antecedent and the consequent are true to degree 1 then according to classical logic the whole conditional is true. Reasoning using a conditional should not lead from truth to falsity. So presumably if the consequent has a lower degree of truth than the antecedent then the conditional should have a degree of truth less than 1, and the bigger the difference, the lower the degree should be.

But for each of the conditional, the antecedent has a degree of truth that is just a little bit higher than the consequent, so all the conditionals should have a high degree of truth. This explains why the argument seems plausible. But it also explains why the argument is not valid because each application of *modus ponens* produces a conclusion that has lesser and lesser degrees of truth. Is this the solution to the paradox? Many logicians and philosophers disagree. The problem of vagueness has in recent years produced a large volume of interesting work and a variety of fascinating theories. A route into the debate is suggested below.

SUGGESTIONS FOR FURTHER READING

Perhaps *the* text to read concerning virtually all of the topics that have been discussed here is Kripke (1972/1980). To get a sense of the pre-Kripke lie of the land, read Searle (1958) and also the classic Frege (1892). Brandom (1994) and Goldstein (2002) are examples of new Wittgenstein-inspired approaches to the problems of names and naming. The causal theory and the reference question are discussed in Evans (1973), in Devitt (1981), and of course in Kripke (1972/1980). The literature on the substitutivity puzzle and the theory of direct reference is now enormous. A good place to start is Salmon and Soames (1988), which is an edited volume of essays on these and related topics. Soames (2002) is a recent defence and elaboration of the theory of direct reference. It is difficult to find contemporary defences of meaning descriptivism but Linsky (1977) is not terribly ancient. Read Russell (1905) for the very famous elaboration of his Theory of Definite Descriptions. Neale (1990) is an excellent and clear introduction and defence of Russell's Theory. On the topic of vagueness, Williamson (1994) defends the existence of cut-off points. Sainsbury (1995, Chapter 2) introduces the major theories and many of the seminal papers are included in O'Keefe and Smith (1997) which also contains a useful introductory chapter. Some more recent papers can be found in Beall (2004).

CHAPTER 5

IS NECESSITY REALLY NECESSARY?

5.1 MUSTS AND MIGHTS

It ain't necessarily so, it ain't necessarily so.
De t'ings dat yo' li'ble to read in de Bible,
It ain't necessarily so

Gershwin, *Porgy and Bess*

If the Gershwin song is right, then some statements in the Bible, the newspaper, or a book like this one are not necessarily true; put another way, they might be false. This observation suggests an easy test for necessary truth. Think of a statement, say, 'Karl Marx is buried in the same cemetery as Herbert Spencer'. In fact, these two famous thinkers of the nineteenth century are both interred in London's Highgate Cemetery. But it *might* have been different, mightn't it? Either or both of them might not have been buried at all, or they might have been buried in different places. So the statement that Marx and Spencer are buried in the same cemetery is not a necessary truth, for it might have been false. If a statement is necessarily true then there is no 'might' about it. Still, there is a connection between *must* and *might*: if it's necessarily true that humans are not dogs, then it's not possible for someone to be both a human being and a dog. In this way the operators needed for *modal* logic (the logic of necessity and possibility) turn out to be interdefinable. Let's use a box, '□' to symbolize 'necessarily', and a diamond, '◇', to represent 'possibly'. Then we can write

$$\Box A =_{df} \sim\Diamond\sim A$$

That is, if it's necessarily the case that A, then it's not possibly the case that not-A.

Logic furnishes great examples of necessary truth: either it's raining or it's not, either Bob Dylan was originally called 'Robert Zimmerman' or he wasn't. There's no 'might' about 'p v ~p'. The truths of logic are not just true: they are true *necessarily*. So it looks as if '□(p v ~p)' is going to be a truth of modal logic. We have to be careful, however, about how we distribute boxes and diamonds through our formulas. While it seems pretty obvious that 'p v ~p' has to be true, this does not mean that '□p v □~p' is necessarily true, or even true at all. There are many propositions that are not necessarily true. Grace might never have met Bert, for example. So the proposition that Grace met Bert is not a necessary truth, nor is it necessarily true that Grace did not meet Bert. On the other hand, '◇p v ◇~p' seems like a better candidate for being obviously true. Is this just as necessarily – and obviously – true as 'p v ~p'? There certainly seems to be a case for thinking of things this way. So it may be that '□(◇p v ◇~p)' deserves to be true in modal logic. As we will see, though, what is true in modal logic is not a straightforward matter. This is because formalizing, and understanding, statements about what is necessary and what is possible is no easy matter.

In the pioneering days of modern modal logic (from around 1915 onwards), there was a lot of work focusing on what was, and was not, a necessary truth. The basic ideas were that any logical truth is a necessary truth, and that if we can show that some proposition follows logically from a necessary truth, then that proposition is itself necessarily true. The two modes of truth that the explorers of the new logic focused on were those of *must* and *might*, necessity and possibility.[1] Later on, philosophers took an interest in a whole lot of other things, like belief, knowledge, duty, treating them as modalities too. In consequence, what is now called 'modal logic' embraces not only the modes of truth and falsity (the *alethic* ones), but also the *epistemic* ones of knowledge and belief and the *deontic* ones of duty, obligation and permission. Despite some famous objections to the whole project of modal logic (notably those put forward by W. V. Quine) the analytical tools of modal logic and possible worlds became part of the standard issue of philosophy students by later in the century.[2] While Quine thought that modal vocabulary, and all talk of 'musts' and 'mights', was dispensable, this nowadays seems a particularly unpermissive kind of view. After all, it is quite natural for us to think and talk about what might have been as well as about what simply is. If Bert had not gone to study at St Andrews, he might never have met Grace. To say this seems no more peculiar than to say that Bert weighs more than Grace, or that metals expand when heated.

While our ways of thinking about the world naturally include the modes of 'must' and 'might', we also seem to require these very notions to express some of the things discussed in this book. Take, for example, the relation of premises to conclusion in a valid argument. If the premises are true, it doesn't just happen that the conclusion is true as well. One natural way to describe validity is to say that in a deductively valid argument it is not possible for the premises to be true while the conclusion is false. One recent book, for example, states that an inference is valid 'if and only if there is no possible situation in which the premises are true and the conclusion is false'.[3] Can validity amount to something less than this? Quine thought so. He argued, for example, that a valid argument was one in which – first – if the premises are true, then the conclusion is true, and – furthermore – any argument resulting from consistently replacing any of the non-logical words in the argument throughout by other words is one in which if the premises are true, then so too is the conclusion.[4] This Quinean version of validity, however, seems to get things the wrong way round. It claims the validity of

> Grace loves only generous people
> So generous people are the only ones loved by Grace

consists in two things. First, if it is true that Grace loves only generous people, then it is true that generous people are the only ones loved by Grace. Second, any consistent replacement of the non-logical words in the argument results also in an argument in which, if the premise is true, then so is the conclusion – for example

> Bert watches only sci-fi movies
> So sci-fi movies are the only ones watched by Bert

We might wonder why, if this is all that validity amounts to, validity itself is so important.[5] The Quinean account accepts that anything at all can be validly inferred from a false premise or false premises (for the 'if . . . then . . .' in the Quinean definition of validity means nothing other than '$\supset$', and any '$\supset$' statement with a false antecedent is true). What is wrong with this? The trouble is that the Quinean account gives no explanation of how the truth of the premises guarantees the truth of the conclusion, or of what is wrong with an argument like

Laurence is a dog
So prime numbers bigger than 2 are also odd numbers

Since Laurence is not a dog, then any proposition at all can be put forward as following logically from the false premise. We come back in the following chapter to the whole question of validity and related questions about conditionals.

It was not until the 1960s that thinkers had the idea of combining the formal methods of modal logic with the old intuitive idea *possible worlds* – a notion first given prominence in the seventeenth century by the German philosopher Gottfried Leibniz. Suppose we live in just one of many different possible worlds. The world we live in is the actual one. In the actual world, Grace met Bert and their friend is Dick, but it is possible that none of them ever met the others. In possible-worlds talk, what is possible in the actual world is realized in at least one other possible world. So there is a possible world in which Grace never met Bert, and Dick was not a friend of either of them. In general, if it's possibly the case that 'p' in the actual world, then there will be at least one possible world at which 'p' is true. (This possible world may – sometimes – be the actual world itself.) What about necessity? If the statement 'Grace met Bert or Grace didn't meet Bert' is necessarily true, then it is not just true at the actual world, but true at every possible world. Notice the reference here to 'at least one' and to 'every' possible world. The interdefinability of the modal operators matches the interdefinability of the quantifiers. Let's write '$\exists w$' to mean 'there is at least one world, w, such that . . .', and '$\forall w$' to mean 'Every world, w, is such that . . .', and – where 'A' is a metalogical variable standing for any formula whatever – let us write 'TA' to represent the fact that the formula has the truth value *true*. Then we get the following:

$$\Diamond A =_{df} (\exists w)(\mathrm{T}A \text{ at } w) \qquad \Box \mathrm{A} =_{df} (\forall w)(\mathrm{T}A \text{ at } w)$$

Correspondingly, '$\sim\Diamond\sim A$' says nothing more than '$\sim(\exists w)\sim(\mathrm{T}A$ at $w)$', which is to say '$(\forall w)$ $(\mathrm{T}A$ at $w)$', which is – as already noted – to say that '$\Box A$'.

Not only was logical truth an appealing case of necessary truth, but it seemed natural to regard logical consequence itself as having a kind of inevitability. This is what is captured by the claim that it's just not possible for the premise or premises of a valid argument to be true while the conclusion is false. If the premises of a valid argument are true, then the conclusion *has to be* true. Grace is a logician. If she is a logician, then she knows the definition of validity. If these statements are true, it *has to* follow that Grace knows the definition of validity. In saying this, we don't mean to say that Grace has to know the definition of validity no matter what. The necessity attaches to the inference, not to the conclusion itself. Grace, after all, might not have been a logician and certainly might not have known how to define validity. However smart she is in the actual world, there is some alternative possible world in which she is just not involved in logic at all. Our symbols make all this a bit clearer. Consider our *modus ponens* about Grace:

$$p, p \supset q \vdash q$$

By arguing that the conclusion has to be true if the premises are, we are not arguing

$$p, p \supset q \vdash \Box q$$

On the contrary, this second inference looks plain crazy. Corresponding to every valid inference is a conditional, so the necessity of the inference – rather than of Grace's knowledge of validity – can be captured by first writing the original inference in conditional form

$$(p \,\&\, (p \supset q)) \supset q$$

and then putting the necessity operator in front of the whole formula, thus:

$$\Box[(p \,\&\, (p \supset q)) \supset q]$$

This seems to catch just what might be meant by concluding that Grace *has* to know the definition of validity. Now, even though logical truths are necessary truths, and even if there is a certain necessity attaching to logical deduction, notice that the following is not valid:

$$p, \Box(p \supset q) \vdash \Box q$$

By contrast, any argument of the following form is valid:

$$(N)\ \Box A, \Box(A \supset B) \vdash \Box B$$

In C. I. Lewis's work, the necessary – or strict – implying of one formula by another was written using a special symbol (known as fishhook), so that '$\Box(A \supset B)$' was written '$A \prec B$'. The fishhook was introduced to avoid certain problems that arose in formalizing the conditional in English. As the following chapter shows, the success of this innovation was limited. None the less, principle N – that if we start from a necessary truth, and then consider what it necessarily implies (that is, what follows necessarily from it), we end up with another necessary truth – has remained a core commitment of every system of modal logic.

5.2 *DE RE* AND *DE DICTO*

Core commitments can lead to problems, and the principle just given is no exception. Suppose Dick, for a time at least, is a bachelor. It is a necessary truth that bachelors are unmarried – that, after all, is one of the defining conditions of bachelorhood. So it seems that, of necessity, Dick is unmarried. From the fact that Dick is necessarily unmarried, it should not follow that Dick necessarily exists. Yet that is what principle N seems to commit us to. Here is the reasoning. Suppose Dick is necessarily unmarried (this is a proposition of the form '$\Box A$'). In order to be unmarried (or to have any property at all) Dick has to exist. Indeed, it is a necessary truth that if Dick has the property of being unmarried, then he exists (this is of the form '$\Box(A \supset B)$'). So now it seems to be a necessary truth that Dick exists. This looks like a very silly conclusion, however. Dick might never have been born at all. So his existence is not in the least necessary.

Luckily, there is a way out of this problem. It involves recognizing that the mode of necessity can apply either to sentences, propositions, or statements, on the one hand, or to things themselves on the other. To say Dick is necessarily a bachelor is to say something *de re*, that is something about Dick himself (the Latin word '*res*' simply means 'thing'). On the other hand, to say that it is necessarily true that bachelors are unmarried is naturally understood as saying something about the proposition, 'bachelors are unmarried' – namely that it is a necessary truth. The '*dictum*' is the what-is-said. In our strange argument, a *de re* conclusion – that Dick necessarily exists – is put forward as following from a *de dicto* premise, namely the necessary truth that if Dick is a bachelor then he exists. But *de re* conclusions don't necessarily follow from *de dicto* premises. Principle N is plausible when the '□' operator is interpreted throughout as expressing *de dicto* modality but not when it ambiguously represents *de dicto* at one place and *de re* at another.

Once the ambiguity between the *de re* and the *de dicto* is recognized, all modal statements can be understood in two different ways. What is meant by saying that it is necessary that if Dick is a bachelor, then he exists? This seems naturally read as a *de dicto* assertion: the proposition that if Dick is a bachelor then he exists is a necessary truth. It is much less plausible to read this as a *de re* claim – that if Dick is a bachelor, then it is necessary that he exists. Consider, for a different example, the case of the shortest spy. Clearly the shortest spy is a spy, and this has the ring of triviality about it. So let's admit that it's a necessary truth that the shortest spy is a spy. But now beware the *de re* reading. Of the shortest spy, Veronica Little, it is not necessarily the case that she is a spy at all. She had many career choices open to her, and becoming a spy was not even her first career option. Being a spy is not a necessary property of Veronica's, even though it is a necessary truth that the shortest spy is a spy.

In his objections to modal logic, mentioned earlier, Quine distinguished a relatively harmless grade of what he called 'modal involvement' – namely one where the term 'necessarily' occurs only applied to whole sentences, and can be considered as a predicate of sentences. According to this first grade of modal involvement, to say that necessarily the shortest spy is a spy is to do no more than predicate necessity of the sentence, 'the shortest spy is a spy'. Despite his general scepticism about modality, Quine regarded this level of modal involvement as having relatively benign metaphysical implications. By contrast, an extreme, 'third grade' of modal involvement allows the necessity operator to be attached to sentences, clauses, and even to open sentences.[6] According to this grade of modal involvement,

Quine argued, claims about necessity involved attributing essential properties to things in the world.

Quine believed we could avoid confusion for the most part by steering clear of saying things about the essential properties of people and things. While predicating necessity of the sentence, 'the shortest spy is a spy', seemed to lead to few problems, attributing essential properties to Veronica Little was just asking for trouble. Consider the claim that the number nine is larger than the number seven. If truths of arithmetic are necessary truths, then it is harmless to say the following:

> 'Nine is greater than seven' is necessarily true

But now consider the claim – one with higher 'modal involvement – that nine is itself necessarily greater than seven. This attributes an essential property to the number nine. Now, if there were nine planets in the solar system, then nine would also be the number of the planets. Does this mean that the number of planets would be necessarily greater than seven? Notice that this question only arises once talk about necessity goes way beyond attributing a certain kind of truth to sentences. A sensible way out of the problem here might seem to be this. Why not say that while nine is necessarily greater than seven, the number of planets is only contingently, or accidentally, greater than seven? But before taking this way out of the problem, think again about the *de re/de dicto* distinction. If we are really talking about the number nine, and think that numbers have essential properties, then why not admit that the very number which numbers the planets is essentially greater than seven? On the other hand, if the sentence 'the number of the planets is greater than seven' is only a contingent truth, nothing follows about the status of the sentence 'nine is greater than seven'. In particular, nothing follows about whether the latter sentence is necessarily or contingently true.[7]

This all means that Quine's arguments are not an objection to the project of modal logic. While he was right to claim that treating necessity as something to be predicated of sentences does not lead into puzzles about whether the planets are essentially or accidentally greater than seven in number, this does not prohibit the use of richer notions of necessity and possibility – provided the distinction between *de re* and *de dicto* is kept firmly in mind. As a result, subsequent thinkers have been reluctant to leave all talk of necessity at Quine's first grade of involvement. Instead, they have believed that by insisting on the *de re/de dicto* distinction, it will be possible to avoid the difficulties enunciated by Quine and his supporters. Moreover, although Quine regarded the problematic modal cases as being the ones where *de re* modalities were involved, there is no general way of translating all modal claims purely into *de dicto* ones. For example, see if you can find a *de dicto* version of '$(\exists x)\Box Fx$', that is, an equivalent formula where the necessity operator attaches to a whole sentence, not just to the part 'Fx'.[8] You won't be able to do this. This does not mean, of course, that '$(\exists x)\Box Fx$' expresses a truth. It does express a well-formed claim that may be true or false. Quine's worries about the metaphysics of necessary properties are one thing; the acceptability of modal logic and its formulations are quite another.[9] If this line of thought is right, then being clear on questions of scope will help in avoiding unnecessary confusions. Scope distinctions, incidentally, can be vividly clarified by appeal to possible worlds themselves. It is true at all worlds that the shortest spy is a spy, but Veronica Little is a spy only in the actual world and – perhaps – in a few others as well. So it is not true at all possible worlds that Veronica Little is a spy.

5.3 WHAT WILL BE MUST BE, MUSTN'T IT?

While modern modal theorists usually focus on the notion of logical necessity, philosophers have traditionally worried about inevitability and fate. A short distance to the west of ancient Athens was a pleasant spot called Megara, where thinkers were apparently fascinated by paradoxes and by puzzles about inevitability. One of these Megarian logicians, Diodorus Cronus, who lived some time around the end of the fourth and the beginning of the third centuries BCE, left some intriguing fragments – the only remains of his once-famous 'Master Argument' for fatalism. He wanted to prove that whatever is true has to be true and that 'the possible is that which either is or will be'. Modern reconstructions of the Master Argument take it as going like this. First, there are two premises found in fragments attributed to Diodorus:[10]

P1 All past truths are necessary truths
P2 The impossible does not follow from the possible

Now suppose that tomorrow a meteor will land somewhere in the Gobi desert, doing little harm apart from leaving a small crater and startling a few nearby goats. Now, if that supposition is true, then it seems that it was true yesterday that the meteor was going to land on the desert. But then, this is something that is true and in the past, so by P1, this is a necessary truth. Now, if it is a necessary truth that the meteor lands in the desert tomorrow, then it is not possible that a meteor will not land in the desert tomorrow. This argument seems to show that the future is not as open as we might normally think it is. It seems possible, after all, that the meteor will not hit the desert: suppose, for example, it collides with a satellite as it nears the Earth. However unlikely, such an incident might knock the meteor off track, causing it to land somewhere else. Given P2, however, we are wasting our time even considering this kind of case. For supposing that the meteor doesn't land in the desert is just supposing that it was not true yesterday that the meteor lands in the desert tomorrow. And, according to P1, past truths are necessary. Given that the meteor does hit the desert and startle the goats tomorrow, then it is impossible for it to have been true yesterday that it would not do such a thing. And, as premise P2 makes clear, no impossibility follows from a possibility. So our speculation that the meteor might go off course, or fail to hit the desert, is not a speculation about a possibility at all!

This delightful puzzle has intrigued people ever since it was formulated. If you don't see it as having implications for free will, change the example. Instead of thinking of a meteor impacting on a bit of remote desert, suppose the supposition is that I will drink coffee some time tomorrow. But I don't drink coffee every day, and it seems possible that tomorrow I may not drink coffee at all all day. Now suppose that in fact I am going to drink coffee tomorrow. Then it was true yesterday that I would be drinking coffee tomorrow, and all past truths are necessary, and . . . and so on. If free will means anything, doesn't it mean that I can choose to drink coffee or not? Yet if past truths are fixed, then whatever was true yesterday determines whether or not I drink coffee tomorrow.

There is good news and bad news about the Master Argument. The good news is that there are many ways out of Diodorus's puzzle. The bad news is that each one seems to exact a price that we may not be very happy to pay. It is sometimes suggested that Aristotle – living not far from Megara – had a rather good solution to the puzzle, namely to give up what is sometimes called the *principle of bivalence* – the claim that every statement is determinately true or false.[11] The principle of bivalence requires it to be the case that if someone yesterday made a claim about the meteor landing in the desert – or about my drinking coffee – that claim would be either true or false. Aristotle may have thought, however, that so long as we are speaking about things that do not happen of necessity, then some of our sentences are neither true nor false. Suppose Laurence predicted, yesterday, that I would drink coffee tomorrow, while Joe insisted that I would exercise strength of will and resist all temptation to do so. Now imagine that when tomorrow comes, I give in and drink the coffee. Did either Laurence or Joe speak the truth yesterday? Denying the principle of bivalence enables us to say that neither was right and neither was wrong – for no truth or falsehood was uttered by them at the time.[12]

There are other solutions as well to the puzzle of the Master Argument, but these in general carry higher costs than abandonment of bivalence. It may be that what needs to be challenged is the premise that everything that is past and true is itself necessary. The Master Argument is one of a pair of arguments that raise doubts about the possibility of an open future. The other – known as the 'sea-battle argument' – is due to Aristotle himself.[13] (The sea-battle argument will reappear in the next chapter, in a bit of a different shape, when we consider how to sort out problems of entailment and conditionals.) In each case, the arguments rely on the idea that if some statement or proposition is true, then it must be the case that what the statement asserts to take place does indeed take place. This might at first seem no more than the fallacy of confusing '$\Box(A \supset B)$' with '$A \supset \Box B$'. It does seem right to claim that if it is true that I drink coffee on Tuesday, then I must drink coffee on Tuesday (which looks like a case of strict implication in Lewis's sense). Yet it would be crazy to say that my coffee-drinking was necessitated, and had to occur. If this is the ambiguity at the heart of these arguments, then they are not worth much study.[14]

However, there does seem to be a deeper problem signalled in the sea-battle and Master Arguments. Modern treatments of necessity and possibility are concerned with the notions of what is logically required, or permitted. So far, we have taken formulas of the form '$A \vee \sim A$' as examples of logically necessary truth. The present and the past are not necessary in anything like this sense. Likewise the proposition that I can jump from Melbourne to Perth states a logically possible state of affairs. There is no logical inconsistency in holding the proposition to be true. As Hume famously put it, even the proposition that the sun will not rise tomorrow cannot be demonstrated to be false, hence cannot be dismissed as logically impossible (Hume 1748/1999, 4, 1, ii). Logical possibility is a very generous notion, in fact too generous to cast much light on what Aristotle, Diodorus and other traditional thinkers were worried about. For them, the issue about whether the past is necessary, or whether it is possible to change the present, is about what it is in the power of human beings to do. Can anyone now change what happened yesterday? It seems not. Grace and Bert get married one day, and Dick gives a speech at the wedding. Two days later, a friend says to Dick: 'I thought you were going to make that joke about Bert being graced with Grace.' 'Gosh,' Dick thinks, 'I forgot. I wish I had told the joke.' But there is no way Dick can undo his mistake for there is no way he can reverse causation and now alter the past. There are science-fiction stories about time travel, of course, and these sometimes depict the alteration of what has happened as a possibility. But philosophers and physicists are unsure whether the alteration of the past is either a physical or a logical possibility.[15]

Now it is this understanding of inevitability or unalterability that seems to be at the centre of ancient thought on the necessity of the past. What makes the past necessary, in this sense, is that past events have happened and cannot now be undone or changed in any way. But then, if someone says something true (or fails to say something true) on some occasion, then that truth (or that failure) cannot be altered either. For Aristotle, what is in the past is necessary in this sense – fixed, unalterable and not now changeable. What about now? The present doesn't last long. As soon as I say or do something, that occurrence joins the list of things done, and is thus fixed and unalterable in just the way all of the past is. So what actually happens is just as fixed and unchangeable as what happened a hundred or a thousand years ago. The problem posed by the sea-battle argument and the Master Argument is whether there is any prospect for an open future given the unalterability of the present and the past.[16] It may be premature, then, to reject fatalism by reinterpreting the old arguments in terms of the modern notions of logical possibility. And it may be wise to treat the principle of bivalence with caution in the meantime.

The modern notion of necessity, explored by use of possible worlds examples and modal logical reasoning, is a different beast from these notions of unalterability and unchangeability that we have just been thinking about. So what is the modern notion? This question is a lot easier to put than to answer. Writers seem to face both ways at once – arguing that modal techniques are useful and valuable, while at the same time being unable to say much about what logical and metaphysical necessity are supposed to be. The sense of not knowing what is going on has become so pronounced that writers often do the literary equivalent of shrugging their shoulders and spreading their hands in incomprehension. Before confirming such a diagnosis, though, let's have a more detailed look at just what modal logic is all about, and what the modal operators mean. I will argue that there is a harmless use of the device of possible worlds to explore different kinds of possibility and necessity.

5.4 KINDS OF POSSIBILITY

'□' and '◇' are not truth-functional operators. Free from the gloom that can be induced by too much immersion in the Master Argument, we believe that when 'p' is true, '□p' may be false. Grace and Bert were unlucky when it rained on their wedding day. They were unlucky because it wasn't a necessary truth that it would rain on the day. After the wedding, Bert is a lucky man to be married to Grace. Although it is necessary that if he is married to Grace then he is married, it is contingent – just a matter of fact, not of necessity – that he was married in the first place and contingent that he was lucky enough to find Grace. Necessities are not the stuff of good and bad luck, but contingencies are.

As mentioned earlier, the meanings of the modal operators are quite flexible. Much of modal logic focuses on the alethic modalities of truth and falsehood at a world – often discussed in relation to science-fiction examples.[17] These, although fun, can also be misleading, especially if they suggest that alternative worlds to the world we live in can be accessed through time travel, holes in the fabric of space-time, or other devices. The philosophers' worlds of possibility are not generally meant to be capable of any causal connection with each other, or with the actual world in which we live, eat, sleep and dream. Instead, they provide insight into features of the actual world by depicting worlds that – like the worlds of fairy-tales – have no causal connection at all with the world in which we live. While modal essentialists, like David Lewis, argue that all possible worlds exist in just the way the actual world does (so there is a world where a wooden toy became a boy, another one where Alice visited Wonderland, one where dinosaurs and dodos failed to go extinct, and so on), other theorists think of possible worlds just as sets of propositions, fictions, pictures, or mere modes of speaking. To the extent that there is real disagreement among theorists about the status and nature of possible worlds, there is also disagreement about what claims about necessity and possibility amount to.

The actual world is not just limited to the earth or the solar system, but rather embraces everything in the universe. Things that might happen in the universe, but do not, are the things that happen in some other possible world. My father was offered a job in Kenya when I was eight years old. Had he taken it, I might have lived as a teenager in Africa, even though in fact I spent my teens (in the actual world) in Scotland. I can think about these possibilities without imagining any changes in world politics, the legal systems of Scotland and Kenya, the global economic order or any of dozens of other structures that characterize the world as we know it. However, things might be different from the actual world in much more dramatic ways. Stories which describe the transformation of wooden toys into living beings and where magic routinely happens, describe worlds in which the laws of physics and biology as we know them are violated. However, these worlds are not ones in which the same sentence is counted as true and false at the same time, so they are not logically impossible. Since they are at least logically consistent, such weird worlds belong to the set of logically possible worlds, and it is from the set of logically possible worlds that alternatives to the actual world are normally chosen.[18]

Now some of the things that we say about what is possible or impossible are concerned with physical, legal, practical or causal possibilities. Having arrived early at the bus stop, for example, Bert waits impatiently, thinking

> It's not possible that I've missed the bus.

If it is really impossible that he's missed the bus this can be explained by invoking the idea of a structure or set of worlds that cluster around the actual world. For Bert's thought to be true, then the actual world is just part of a set of worlds, W, in each of which it is true that Bert has not missed the bus. From our earlier definitions of '□' and '◇', given a set of worlds, W, and a particular world in that set, *w*,

□*A* at *w* iff for every world w^i in W, T*A* at w^i
◇ *A* at *w* iff for at least one world w^i in W, T*A* at w^i

Bert's thought is an instance of

~◇*A* is true at *w* iff for every world w^i in W, T~*A* at w^i

This set of worlds clustering around a given world is normally called the set of worlds *accessible* from the world in question. It has access to them – they are *alternatives* to it – precisely by being ones at which everything that is necessarily true at the given world is also true. And – for every sentence that is possibly true at the given world – there will be a corresponding sentence that is true at some (at least one) of the worlds in the associated set. A necessary truth at *w*, then, is true at every world to which *w* has access; a sentence is possibly true at *w*, when it is true at at least one of the worlds to which *w* has access. By cunningly restricting the range of worlds to which a given world has access, different kinds of necessity and possibility can be studied.[19] In this way, notions such as legal, political, physical, economic and other kinds of possibility can be charted. Bert is not thinking that it is logically, or even physically, impossible for him to have missed the bus. Instead, he is restricting his thoughts to the set of worlds that are transport-alternatives to the actual world – those in which timetables are the same as in the actual world, and the correlations between the timetable times and the bus-stop times are much the same as in the actual world. Relative to the worlds in this set, it is possible that the bus is very late, or even that it is not running at all, but not possible that Bert has missed it. For a different case, suppose we are interested in what is allowed or disallowed by the laws of Hong Kong at a certain time. To study this, we consider a range of worlds that differ from the actual world in terms of how people act, but in which the laws of Hong Kong are not changed at all. By thinking about which actions and behaviours are legal or illegal in this set of alternative worlds, we can start to explore what is legally possible, and legally required, by the laws of Hong Kong.

At this level of analysis, the device of possible worlds seems useful and harmless, even if the notions of metaphysical and logical necessity give rise, ultimately, to vexatious puzzles.

5.5 IDENTITY AND NECESSITY

As we saw earlier (see pages 93–5), there is a modal argument against the claim that the meaning of a name is given by some description. Philosophers who reject descriptivism usually also accept the interesting claim that identity statements, when true, are necessarily so. Recall the principles of identity introduced in the earlier chapter. Everything is self-identical ($\forall x\ (x=x)$) and if x is identical with y, then any property of x is also a property of y ('$(x=y) \supset (Fx \equiv Fy)$' holds for any property F). Now if the principle of self-identity is like other logical and mathematical principles, it will be a necessary truth, that is

$$\Box \forall x\ (x=x)$$

Now suppose one thing has two different names (as in the case of Bob Dylan and Robert Zimmerman). Since it's necessarily the case that each thing is itself, it would seem that Bob Dylan is necessarily identical with Bob Dylan. That is, the property of being necessarily identical with Bob Dylan is one that the gravelly-voiced singer indubitably has. But Robert Zimmerman will also have that property. So Robert Zimmerman has the property of being necessarily identical with Bob Dylan. In other words, if Bob Dylan and Robert Zimmerman are the same person, then Bob Dylan is necessarily identical with Robert Zimmerman.[20]

This doesn't mean that Robert Zimmerman might not have had a different performing name. He might have called himself any number of names. But given that he chose 'Bob Dylan' as his performance name, then it's necessarily the case that Robert Zimmerman is Bob Dylan. Someone who didn't know that the singer called 'Bob Dylan' was originally called 'Robert Zimmerman' would have to carry out some research to discover the fact that the two names refer to one and the same person. But the fact uncovered by the research is a necessary fact. If this strikes you as puzzling, then reflect on what to say about names of natural things, like 'salt'. The stuff called 'salt' in everyday language is sodium chloride and it's not only found in solution in sea water but also found as a mineral (rock salt). When we say 'salt is sodium chloride' – meaning that salt is identical with sodium chloride – we have also uttered a necessary truth, although it clearly took lots of detailed study to find this fact out. Moreover, it is simply a fact of linguistic history that salt is called 'salt' in English. The word 'salt' comes from the Latin word for salt (*sal*), rather than the Greek term for the same stuff (*hals*). Mineral salt, in fact, is sometimes called 'halite', a word deriving from the Greek. So sodium chloride might have been generally called 'halite'. None the less, salt, and halite, are not just the same stuff as sodium chloride: they are necessarily the same stuff as sodium chloride. For if an identity statement is true, it is necessarily so.

5.6 EPISTEMOLOGY, METAPHYSICS AND MEANING

If you are puzzled about how necessary truth can depend on historical accidents (like what name Robert Zimmerman selected as his performance handle) and can sometimes only be uncovered by doing factual and scientific research, then you are not alone. Many philosophers in the course of history have thought that what is necessarily true can be discovered simply by reasoning, does not depend on historical accident, and is not uncovered through factual and scientific studies. For them it was the hallmark of necessary truth that it was discoverable independent of sensory experience and scientific study. This kind of discoverability was labelled '*a priori*', to distinguish it from the kind of discovery that can be made only through experience – the discovery of what is knowable *empirically* or '*a posteriori*'. Notice, though, that *discoverability* or *knowability* are categories that apply to the route by which we know or discover something. They belong to the theory of knowledge, or *epistemology*. That something is necessarily the case, however, is not a fact about how that thing is to be discovered. Rather, this is a fact about the way the world is. That salt is sodium chloride, that Robert Zimmerman is Bob Dylan, is just the way things are, independent of whether we know them or not, and independent of how we can find out about them or not. Such facts about how the world is are usually called *metaphysical*. In metaphysics, those facts that are necessary are distinguished from those that are contingent. The contingent facts are ones that hold, but which might not have held. It is necessarily the case that sodium chloride is identical with salt, but it is a contingent fact that sodium chloride is called 'salt' in modern English.

In his 1951 classic essay, 'Two Dogmas of Empiricism', Quine appears to make no distinction between the *a priori* and the necessary, reflecting what was at the time a widespread and cavalier way of thinking about metaphysical and epistemological matters. In fact, in the same essay he discusses what would nowadays be regarded as a third distinction – between those sentences that are true in virtue of the meanings of the words they contain (*analytic* truths), and those whose truth does not depend on meaning in that way (synthetic truths). His example was the word 'bachelor' and the expression 'unmarried man'. As used in everyday English, these seem to mean much the same. So the sentence 'all bachelors are unmarried men' looks as if it is analytically true, that is, true just in virtue of the meanings of the words it contains. On the other hand, 'all folk singers play guitars' looks like a sentence which – if it were true at all – would certainly not be an analytic truth. If true at all, the sentence would be synthetic

All three distinctions just introduced are meant to be exhaustive and exclusive. That is, any sentence or proposition at all will be either analytic or synthetic (but not both). Any state of affairs in the world will be either necessary or contingent (but not both). And any situation that is capable of being known will be knowable *a priori* or empirically (but not in both ways). Why is it so easy, then, to get confused when talking about these very different things?[21] One problem is the relation between what is the case in the world, and the truth of sentences (or – to put it more carefully – the truth of the propositions expressed by the use of certain sentences). For example, to say that salt is necessarily identical with sodium chloride seems equivalent to saying that the proposition 'salt is identical with sodium chloride' is necessarily true. So was the statement about salt and sodium chloride expressing something about the truth of a proposition, or about the way the world is? Unclarity over this point means we slide easily from thinking about propositions to thinking about states of affairs in the world, and vice versa. A symptom of the difficulty here is the word 'fact' itself. To say that it's a fact that Robert Zimmerman and Bob Dylan were one and the same person is ambiguous. Saying this is sometimes just a way of saying that it is true that Robert Zimmerman and Bob Dylan are the same. I say 'that's a fact' when I'm agreeing with what someone has just said, as if I'm adding my endorsement to her remark. 'That's true' would serve just as well. But to say something is a fact may also be a way of saying that there is something in the world – some 'truthmaker' which makes the given sentence true. This everyday way of speaking makes it easy to confuse talking about the world on the one side and talking, on the other, about propositions, thoughts, sentences and words. The analyticity of sentences or propositions gets easily mixed up with the necessity of the states of affairs they describe. If we assume that the only route to knowing that a proposition is analytic, or a state of affairs is necessary, is through *a priori* knowledge, then it is easy to think that 'analytic', 'necessary' and '*a priori*' are almost interchangeable terms.

On closer analysis, it's hard to make sense of the idea that each proposition that is true corresponds to some fact in the world. Take as examples 'Rock salt is halite', 'Rock salt is sodium chloride' and 'Halite is sodium chloride'. If each proposition corresponds to some fact in the world making it true, then how many facts are out there? Are there really three different facts 'out there', one corresponding to each of the propositions? If we have three propositions, then conjoining any two of them forms a new proposition. But if each proposition corresponds to one fact, does the conjunction of two of them correspond to some new fact (a 'conjunctive fact')? As was shown in the chapter on truth, this puzzle provides one of several reasons for doubting that the truth of a sentence or proposition involves a relation to some corresponding fact. Whatever the perplexities in the notion of fact, it does appear to be the case that – like the notion of necessity itself – it is ambiguous between application to statements, propositions and sentences on the one hand and the way the world is on the other.[22]

SUGGESTIONS FOR FURTHER READING

Very many textbooks will give concise and clear introductions to systems of modal logic. Any of these mentioned in the text and endnotes will do a good job of introducing the main formal machineries – Melia (2003) being the easiest and least technical, Sainsbury (2001), and Girle (2003) asking for more technical dedication, and Hughes and Cresswell (1996) making even more demands. If you are already logically or mathematically trained, you may find Max Cresswell's chapter (Cresswell 2001) a good source for a fast overview and introduction to the formal treatment of modality.

Stephen Read spends some time attacking modal realism (Read 1995, Chapter 4) or modal platonism – the position that in a sense all possible worlds are equally real. How mad or dangerous this position is depends – according to Joseph Melia – on how loudly its extreme implications are proclaimed. He mounts a defence of 'quiet moderate realism' (Melia 2003, Chapter 6). The distinction between the epistemological notions of *a priori* and *a posteriori*, on the one side, and the metaphysical notions of necessary and contingent, on the other, owes much to the work of Saul Kripke (see Kripke 1972/80). Questions about scope, *de re* and *de dicto* are best approached by going back to some older collections, such as Linsky (1971).

CHAPTER 6

ENTAILMENT

6.1 ENTAILMENT, IMPLICATION AND STRANGE REASONING

Bert and Grace have been travelling together in Europe for some time. But Bert wanted to admire the Vltava from Charles Bridge in Prague, while Grace was fascinated with the exotic architecture of Budapest. So they took a few days off from each other to indulge their separate passions. Dick, unsure of the geography of eastern Europe, was trying to figure out where his friends were. 'If Bert is in Prague', he reasoned, 'then he's in the Czech Republic. But if he's in Budapest, then he's in Hungary.' He stopped a moment, wondering if he had placed the two cities in the right countries. He thought long and hard. 'What if I'm wrong?', he wondered. 'What if Bert is in Prague, but Prague is in Hungary?' Then an idea struck him. After all, he'd just been studying elementary logic to help him avoid major goofs in reasoning. So he quickly symbolized the two statements like this:

$$p \supset c$$
$$b \supset h$$

Suddenly he grinned. It didn't matter if he was wrong, for according to his recent study of logic, he could see that the following argument was valid:

$$(p \supset c), (b \supset h) \vdash (p \supset h) \vee (b \supset c)$$

'Even if I'm wrong I'm still right', he thought. 'For if it's true that if Bert is in Prague then he's in the Czech Republic, and that if he's in

Budapest then he's in Hungary, then it follows as clear as day that if he's in Prague then he's in Hungary, or if he's in Budapest then he's in the Czech Republic. Mmmhhh, I don't know why I wasted time worrying about that!'

Something has gone badly wrong here, even though Dick seems not yet to have noticed it. In terms of classical logic, the inference he wrote down is certainly valid. Yet common sense rebels at it. C. I. Lewis's version of strict implication was partly stimulated by dissatisfaction not only with inferences like Dick's but also with all the paradoxes associated with the conditional and with inferences that ran parallel to these. At the time Lewis was working on the early stages of modal logic, the '⊃' sign was often referred to as the sign for 'material implication'. Material implication gave rise to two very significant worries. First of all there was the problem of contradictions. It seems strange to claim that any statement or proposition can follow logically from a contradiction. Yet, as was seen in Chapter 2, a truth-functional conditional with a contradictory antecedent is true, and an argument with a contradictory premise is valid (see pages 45–6). Second, if the consequent of a material conditional is guaranteed to be true, then the whole conditional is itself true, and – correspondingly – any argument with a certainly true conclusion is valid.

To see how puzzling the 'paradoxes' of material implication are, just check the truth-table for '(p & ~p) ⊃ q' and observe that – just like 'p ⊃ (q v ~q)' – that formula is going to be true no matter what. A contradiction materially implies any statement (true or false), while a logical truth follows from anything you like. The trouble is that in truth-functional logic a conditional is only false when two features hold: first, the antecedent is true, and, second, the consequent is false. That's just one of the four possibilities on the truth table. Since in all other cases, the conditional is true, then a conditional whose antecedent is guaranteed to be false as a matter of logic (the first formula above), and one whose consequent is true as a matter of logic (second case) is bound to be true. To be sure, these are not genuine paradoxes – not if paradoxes are defined as pieces of apparently cogent reasoning that lead from obviously true premises to outright contradiction. But they are certainly puzzling results that cast doubt on whether truth-functional conditionals give a reasonable account of 'if . . ., then . . .' as it is normally used in everyday reasoning. Parallel to these results are the weird deductions

$p \& {\sim}p \vdash q$
$p \vdash q \vee {\sim}q$

which seem to be certainly as odd as Dick's peculiar argument.[1]

The introduction of strict implication had some limited success. The relation symbolized by Lewis's new fishhook operator was meant to capture a notion of 'following from' that was more stringent than the one captured in the standard truth-table for '⊃'. Lewis suggested that 'if p then q' should be read as saying 'it's not possibly the case that p and not q'. Put another way, strict implication was a relation of antecedent to consequent in which the truth of the antecedent *necessitated* the truth of the consequent. We can put this in terms of the possible-worlds talk introduced in the preceding chapter: the truth of 'p' necessitates the truth of 'q' when at every world where 'p' is true, 'q' is also true. Instead of using a special fishhook symbol, we can just symbolize this using the box operator of the last chapter: '□(A ⊃ B)' is read as 'A entails B', or 'it is not possible that A and not B'. Using this symbolism, and imagining that Dick was trying to reason strictly, we get this version of his argument:

$$\Box(p \supset c), \Box(b \supset h) \vdash \Box(p \supset h) \vee \Box(b \supset c)$$

But this argument is not valid. Why not? Well, the truth of the premises is compatible with the falsehood of the conclusion – that's why. The conclusion is a disjunction, and it will only be false if both of its components are false. Suppose it's necessary that if Bert is in Prague then he's in the Czech Republic. That's compatible with it being possible that it's not true that if he's in Prague then he's in Hungary. And it's also compatible with the possibility that it's false that if he's in Budapest, then he's in the Czech Republic. Likewise, the second premise is also compatible with neither part of the conclusion being necessarily the case. (If you still don't see this, check the endnote for more detailed reasoning.[2])

Helpful though this discovery will be to Dick, Lewis's work on strict implication was, unfortunately, not very useful in regard to the more serious problem posed by the 'paradoxes' of material implication. For they simply reappeared as puzzles about strict implication. A contradiction strictly implies any statement at all, and a logical truth is, regrettably, entailed by any statement. In fact, these 'paradoxes' are simply symptoms of a deeper problem altogether, namely the problem of how conditionals as used in everyday reasoning and reflection relate to the formally defined operators of logical systems. There are many disanalogies between conditionals and any kind of truth-functional operator like '⊃'. For example, conditionals in English regularly fail to be transitive,[3] while '⊃' certainly is. So, while the form '((A ⊃ B) & (B ⊃ C)) ⊃ (A ⊃ C)' always expresses a logical truth, many statements of this form seem outright false. (Think of the clumsy statement: 'If it is the case that if Bert plays football, Grace will play cricket and that if Grace plays cricket, Dick will be pleased, then – that all being so – if Bert plays football Dick will be pleased.' It is not too hard to think of a situation where the antecedent is true and the consequent false.)

Since '□' and '◇' are not truth-functional operators, and strict implication is not a truth-functionally defined kind of implication, it was hoped by the pioneers of modal logic that they might be able to capture the non-truth-functional aspects of hypothetical and conditional reasoning. They were right to notice that conditional statements have implications that go well beyond what is given by the truth-table definition of '⊃'. What foiled them, however, is a problem still not fully sorted out nowadays – the fact that the word 'if' does very different jobs in different contexts. If logicians and philosophers are to avoid the embarrassing condition of premature theorising – *speculatio praecox* – some attempt has to be made to identify and classify the ambiguities that arise in daily use of the word 'if'. Given the close relationship between conditionals, logical consequence and valid deductions, any problems about 'if' (and their solutions) will be parallel to problems and solutions about logical conseqence and valid deduction. In particular, if it is right to regard 'if' as highly ambiguous, then the notions of entailment, deduction and logical consequence will likely be ambiguous as well.

6.2 CONDITIONALS, CONDITIONAL REASONING AND COUNTERFACTUALS

Every formula in truth-functional logic is equivalent to one that can be written out using only the symbols for '&' and '~' (or for 'v' and '~'). For purely formal purposes, the conditional and biconditional operators are surplus to requirements. The 'paradoxical' logical truth 'p ⊃ (q ⊃ p)', for example, is logically equivalent to '~p v (~q v p)' which in turn is logically equivalent to 'p v ~p'. While the paradoxical formula states that if 'p' is true, then it follows from, or is implied by, 'q' (which can represent any statement you like), its simplest equivalent version simply states that either 'p' is true or '~p' is. Looking for logical equivalents can lead to the disappearance of a connective altogether. Does this mean that we can also make the paradoxes of material implication disappear by appeal to logical equivalences? The clear answer is 'No!' While 'p ⊃ (q ⊃ p)' seems puzzling, 'p v ~p' does not. This fact intensifies, rather than resolves, the puzzle. It is the system of translation from English into logical notation, and the truth-table definitions of the connectives, that provoke the paradoxes of material implication in the first place. To claim that accepting the same symbolism, and the equivalences it generates, will help the paradoxes disappear simply seems to beg the question.

The same reply would seem to rule out any simple solution to the problem of conditionals – one, for example, that insists on taking '⊃' as interdefinable with negation and disjunction (or conjunction). We cannot expect to make the vexed issue of conditionals go away simply by rewriting the puzzling formulas and statements in ways that avoid any iffyness – that is, by avoiding the use of '⊃' altogether. As in the previous case, this manoeuvre seems to beg the question – by presupposing the controversial translations of English into formal logic that are at the root of the problem.[4] The 'paradoxes' of material implication, after all, are a result of theory and symbolism, not something that was there to be resolved before logicians proposed the truth-functional definition of '⊃' as a paraphrase of the sense of the English 'if . . . then. . .'.

A better strategy might be to try for a solution to the problem before we start doing any translation into logical symbols at all. Think of it this way. Suppose puzzling conditional statements *in English* could be uncontroversially translated into non-conditional statements *in English*. We then find out if the non-conditional English equivalents give rise to puzzles like those surrounding material and strict implication, the failure of transitivity and so on. However, this approach will just not work. There is no 'natural' translation of a typical English conditional into a less problematic non-conditional form. However, there is one very common example in the discussion of conditionals that looks as if it might be resolved by application of this kind of medicine. The world was shocked when on 22 November 1963 the President of the United States, John F. Kennedy, was shot dead in Dallas, Texas. The man arrested for the killing was Lee Harvey Oswald, who was himself killed a short time later while in police custody. Now there was some scepticism at the time about whether Oswald had really killed Kennedy, or whether he was framed by some other people altogether. In a classic paper published in 1970, Ernest Adams put forward two 'conditionals', claiming that while the first was true, the second was probably false.[5] Adams's examples were

> If Oswald did not kill Kennedy, then someone else did.
> If Oswald had not killed Kennedy, then someone else would have.

These examples have been recycled ever since, even though neither of them is a typical conditional at all. Think about how to provide natural English translations in non-conditional form for each of them. Consider the first statement. This seems equivalent to the claim 'Someone killed Kennedy'. Notice that we can make this claim without any fancy translation device: we are not claiming that some logical connective captures the meaning or use of 'if'. Rather, the conditional statement seems just to be an elaborate way of stating that someone killed the president.

The second example can also be reduced to a simpler form. It just says that someone was bound to kill Kennedy. Conditionals of this form are often used to give consolation in the face of misfortune. Imagine that Bert once doubled his money by speculating on the currency market. One day he gets caught by a sudden drop in the value of the yen, having invested all his gains in a final bold – but very ill-advised – venture. 'If you hadn't lost money on the yen,' Dick tells Bert consolingly, 'you would have lost it on something else.' This is a kind of fatalist consolation: Bert is supposed to draw comfort from the thought that he was bound to lose money sooner or later. This equivalence can be put forward without making any explicit reference to features about logical translations of the English sentences. So now, without any appeal to the logical understanding of 'if', we can see that our two supposed 'conditional' sentences amount to no more than the following pair of claims:

> Someone killed Kennedy.
> Someone was bound to kill Kennedy.

Even though the first statement is true, it seems highly improbable that the second one is. The disappearance of the two conditional constructions in favour of the simpler statements does not prove that Adams's examples are 'really' not conditionals. It suggests, however, that the Adams examples may not be typical, and that it would be wise to be cautious about making premature generalizations on the basis of such cases.

Conditional sentences in which backward tense shifting occurs are often referred to as 'unreal', 'subjunctive' or 'counterfactual' conditionals'.[6] None of these terms is particularly apposite. Here is a typical example of what a 'counterfactual' conditional is supposed to be like. If Dick hadn't eaten the sauerkraut, then – Grace thinks – he wouldn't have gone down with food poisoning. In a case like this, the unreal or contrary-to-fact element in the 'if' clause is clear: Dick did eat the sauerkraut, and he did get sick. The antecedent specifies something that did not happen, inviting us to think about what would have happened had he not eaten the sauerkraut. Well, according to the truth table for '⊃', anything you like can be put in the consequent without making the resulting conditional false. Any conditional with a false antecedent is true. So from the point of view of truth-functional logic, given the fact that Dick did eat the sauerkraut, it's true that

> If Dick hadn't eaten the sauerkraut, he wouldn't have gone down with food poisoning

and also true that

> If Dick hadn't eaten the sauerkraut, he would still have gone down with food poisoning.

To common sense it seems much more likely that one of these conditionals is true, and the other is false. Faced with the clash between truth-functional logic and good sense, several logicians and philosophers turned to modal logic in the hope that it would solve the problem.[7] Maybe in these 'counterfactual' cases, the situation was something like this. Think of all the worlds in which the false antecedent actually holds – that is, all the possible worlds where Dick did not eat the sauerkraut. Now the claim that if he had not eaten the sauerkraut then he would not have become sick means this:

first, there is at least one of these possible worlds in which Dick does not become sick; second, the 'counterfactual' is true when at least one world in which the antecedent holds, and the consequent holds, is more similar to the actual world than any alternative world in which the antecedent holds.[8]

The adequacy of this account is highly contestable. While talking about similarity relations among possible worlds gives a new way of speaking about such cases, it also raises questions about whether any new insights are gained by this mode of talking. Less contested is the question of whether there is any point in calling all such conditionals 'counterfactual'. It is obvious that in many cases, back-shifting of tense is used where the speaker does not know whether or not the antecedent is true. But there is nothing in the typical uses of this construction that suggests the antecedent is false, or is taken by the speaker to be false. Bert, let us suppose, is surprised that some money has disappeared from the piggy-bank where he and Grace put their small change. He can't remember if he took it himself. 'If Grace had taken the money,' he reflects, 'she would probably have mentioned it to me.' It seems pretty clear that Bert's musings do not commit him to a firm belief that Grace did not take the money: rather, the use of the past tense reflects uncertainty. So 'counterfactual' conditionals are not always contrary-to-fact! This may seem like quite a small point. It draws attention, however, to the fact that the common term used to refer to a phenomenon can often mislead, and may encourage a biased analysis.[9]

6.3 ENTAILMENT, RELEVANCE AND REASONS

Conditional constructions are often used to state reasons. In a common case, the 'if'-clause of a conditional is put forward as stating the reasons or grounds for what is stated in the 'then'-clause. The content of the 'then' clause is explained by, or grounded in, the content of the 'if' clause.[10] This grounding need not involve reference to causes or causal systems. In fact, conditional constructions are often used where the reasoning is not straightforwardly causal – that is, in ways that are very different from the cases of the sauerkraut and piggy-bank. Suppose Bert, reading about the latest sighting of the long-dead Elvis Presley, exclaims: 'If Elvis is alive, then I'm a dormouse!' This can hardly be taken as putting forward any grounds for concluding that Bert is a dormouse. Since Bert plainly is not a dormouse, then, if we accept Bert's statement, it is equally plain (by contraposition[11]) that Elvis is not alive. The conditional construction in this case seems to be used mainly to emphasize the absurdity of thinking Elvis might still be alive. In the Oswald/Kennedy example, the conditional seems to be used as a way of emphasizing that Kennedy is really dead. Think, by comparison, of the statement

> If Grace didn't take the money, then it's still in the piggy-bank.

Here the fact that Grace didn't take the money gives a perfectly good reason for thinking that the money is still in the piggy-bank, and – moreover – gives a reason why the money is still there. In the first of the Oswald and Kennedy examples –

> If Oswald didn't kill Kennedy, then someone else did

the fact that Oswald didn't kill Kennedy would not be a reason why someone else did so. However, if it is true that Oswald didn't kill Kennedy, this would provide a reason for thinking that someone else did. By returning to one of the arguments mentioned in the previous chapter – the one about Aristotle's famous 'sea battle' – we can start to clarify just what kind of conditions are involved in conditionals. On the basis of these examples, I will make the suggestion that there are many different jobs done by conditionals. This is a controversial idea, so make sure you check on my claims by thinking up cases for yourself.

On, then, to that old sea-battle puzzle. Consider whether the following two statements are different in terms of the grounds the antecedent provides for the consequent (see Wertheimer 1968, pp.363–4):

> (a) If a sea battle occurs tomorrow then the statement 'There will be a sea battle tomorrow' is true today.
> (b) If the statement, 'There will be a sea battle tomorrow' is true today then a sea battle will occur tomorrow.

Is one of these statements more sensible than the other? Writing about a related pair of examples, David Sanford says: 'the statement about the battle, if true, is true because of the occurrence of the battle. The battle does not occur because of the truth of the statement' (Sanford 1989, pp.176–7).[12] What Sanford may mean is that the occurrence of the battle explains the truth of the statement, rather than explanation being the other way around. So (a) gets things the right way round, while (b) seems a bit strange. But we need to be careful here. I suggest that each of (a) and (b) actually gets things the right way round, provided we read them in the right way.

Let's take *S* to be the statement 'There will be a sea battle tomorrow'. Can anything be inferred from the truth of *S*? It seems so: if *S* is true today, then it is correct to infer that a sea battle will occur tomorrow. That is, even though the truth of *S* does not *explain* the occurrence of the battle, the fact that *S* is true licenses the inference to the occurrence of the event. Suppose inferences hold among statements. It would then be fine to infer from the truth of *S* today that some other statement is true tomorrow – say, 'There is a sea battle today' (when uttered tomorrow). Since 'there is a sea battle today' is true tomorrow if and only if there is a sea battle tomorrow, then we can infer from the fact that *S* is true today that a sea battle will occur tomorrow. That being so, (b) is not so strange after all. It gets things the right way round as far as inferences are concerned.

What, then, about the asymmetry between (a) and (b)? There does seem to be an explanatory difference between them. If (a) looks more sensible than (b) from an explanatory point of view, this is because the occurrence of the battle gives a reason why *S* is true. The 'if, . . . then . . .' in (a) seems to have an explanatory force that is lacking in (b). So it looks as if there are different ways in which conditionals can work: the antecedent can give grounds for making an inference, or – in case (a), but not (b) – it can actually give a reason why the consequent holds. The truth of *S* is a condition of *inferring* the occurrence of the sea battle. However, the occurrence of the sea battle is a condition of *explaining* the truth of *S*. Yet it is the very same conditional construction which is employed in both (a) and (b). The same form of words in English is thus open to very different interpretations.

If this is right, then there may be a significant ambiguity in the way conditionals are used. Further, such an ambiguity will explain why the translation of 'if' by '⊃' is so unsatisfactory. The truth-table for '⊃' gives an unambiguous specification of everything that is relevant to the connective's meaning – but only from a logical point of view. There is nothing in that point of view that makes much sense of the idea of 'following from' that seems central to the use of 'if' in English and to our use of argument in everyday life. Remember the modal definition of validity: an argument is valid when it's not possible for the premises to be true and the conclusion false. Why is it not possible for premises to be true while the conclusion is false? Put another way, *why* do premises of valid arguments necessitate their conclusions? The obvious answer is that it's not possible for the premises to be true while the conclusions are false because the conclusions *follow from* their premises, are founded on them, or explained by them. Yet the notions of *following*, *founding*, and *explanation* are alien to the logic of truth-tables.[13]

Things are also a bit tricky when it comes to the connection between conditionals and causal connections. Conditionals are often used to describe situations of cause and effect where there is bound to be a lack of symmetry between one happening and another. But there is no uniform direction of causal explanation: sometimes the 'if'-clause identifies a causal factor, but sometimes the direction of causation runs the other way (from the 'then'-clause back to the 'if' one). Bert and Grace, knowing how weak-willed they were, bought a piggy-bank with a key. As he puzzles over where the money has gone, and who has taken it, Bert examines the piggy-bank and notes that it is undamaged. He thus comes up with this conditional:

If Grace opened the piggy-bank, she used a key.

The fact that she used a key explains why Grace was able to open the piggy-bank without damage. The cause-effect connection here runs from using the key (cause) to opening the piggy-bank without damage (effect) – that is from the content of the consequent to that of the antecedent. On the other hand, that Grace opened the piggy-bank gives a ground for Dick's inference that she used a key. So there is an inferential route from opening of the bank (antecedent) to use of the key (consequent) – exactly the opposite of the cause-effect route. Here's another example, from McCawley (1993):

If John wins the race, we will celebrate.

John's winning the race gives the reason why we will be celebrating. Our celebration, however, is not likely to be the reason why he wins the race. What is the connection between the celebration and John's winning the race? Again, there is a ground for inferring: that we don't celebrate is a ground for inferring that John didn't win the race. As in the previous example, there is a gap between inferential symmetry and explanatory asymmetry. The gap is hardly suprising: inferences can run from 'if' to 'then' or vice versa, but causal explanations will mostly run in only one direction, from cause to effect.[14]

There seem to be at least three different relations we can distinguish in everyday uses of conditional statements. First is the inferential relation symbolized by the hook operator, '⊃'. To try to avoid the paradoxes of material implication some theorists have championed a stronger form of implication in which the premises have to be relevant to the conclusion.[15] But the relevant implication connective – like the one for strict implication – inherits many of the features of '⊃' that are problematic. Any operator-like hook can capture some inferential relations – ones like those we've seen in the sea battle case and the other cases just discussed. Where hook (or fishhook, or some other hook-like operator) connects two propositions, A and B, there will generally be a straightforward connection also in the opposition direction. The classic example of this is contraposition – if 'A ⊃ B' is true, then '~B ⊃ ~A' is also true.

Two further relations, however, are often captured by use of conditionals in English, but not catered for by hook and its relatives. To identify these, consider the different things that can be meant by saying

> If Grace was present, it was a good seminar.

Suppose the amazing Grace is invariably a lively contributor to any seminar she attends, always making provocative, constructive and insightful remarks. Her attendance, in other words, guarantees an interesting time for all who attend. In this case, her presence was the *reason why* the seminar was good. This looks like a kind of explanatory use of the conditional construction, where the direction of explanation runs from the content of the 'if' clause to that of the 'then' clause. This gives a second case captured by some everyday uses of the conditional.

Now think of a quite different situation. Grace is shy, according to this story, but she is someone with a talent for spotting which seminars are going to be good, even though she is always too reserved to participate in discussions. Grace's attendance at a seminar, according to this story, provides a *reason for thinking* that the seminar is going to be good. According to the earlier story, the seminar was good because Grace was at it. According to the latest one, it was the goodness of the seminar that explained Grace's presence. So it seems that 'reason for thinking' conditionals provide a third kind of use of 'if' in English. Cases of these last two kinds were first introduced in Wilson (1979). Notice that hook (as understood in classical logic) does not capture the 'reason why' relation. Nor does it capture the *reason for thinking* relation, for it permits any truth to be inferred from any other statement whatever.[16] So there seem to be at least two uses of 'if' that are not captured by the use of the hook connective, or its relatives.

The *reason why* and *reason for thinking that* conditions help to shed light on the cases discussed earlier. That Grace opened the piggy-bank without damage is a reason for thinking that she used the key, not a reason why. Our celebrating is a reason for thinking that John has won the race but not a reason why. Although there is sometimes a correlation between reasons why, on the one hand, and reasons for thinking, on the other, no generalizations about this can be safely made. If *A* is a reason why *B* occurs, then the occurrence of *B* will sometimes be a reason for thinking – but not a guarantee – that *A* has occurred. If *A* is a reason for thinking that *B* has occurred, then *B* will sometimes be a reason why – but not a guarantee that – *A* has occurred. It appears, then, that the 'if' clause of a conditional may do any of three things: (i) introduce a clause from which some consequent follows in the way modelled by an operator-like hook; (ii) state a reason why what is stated in the consequent is the case; (iii) state a reason for thinking that what is stated in the consequent is the case.

Parallel to these three ways of thinking about conditional propositions will be three ways of thinking about the relation of premises to conclusion in arguments – arguments can be thought of as (i) inferential, (ii) giving reasons why the conclusion follows and (iii) giving reasons for thinking that the conclusion follows.[17] There is no more reason, in fact, to think that arguments do just one job than there is to think that the word 'if' does just one job. Instead, questions about inference, deductions and entailment are all connected to the questions we've been asking about conditions and conditionals. So it's not surprising that thinking about any of them can benefit from taking a good look at how 'if' actually functions in everyday language.

Searching for an account of entailment that will capture our demands on the notion of logical consequence has proved to be a baffling task. Instead of finding one way in which the conclusion of an argument follows from the premises, we have found three possible ways of thinking about what follows from what. The standard, classical approach gave rise to the so-called 'paradoxes' of material implication, paradoxes that are not avoided either by systems of strict implication, or by the more recently introduced systems of relevance logic (see note 15, below). Exploring the use of conditionals has revealed three strikingly different ways in which the conditional construction in English is used. There may, of course, be more. Each of the three uses of conditionals mentioned in the present chapter corresponds to rather different ways of thinking about the relation of premises to conclusion in arguments. Logic, to the extent that it is concerned with inference only, not with reasons why or reasons for thinking, uses a notion of consequence that is purely inferential, parallel to the way that the hook operator presents a very weak sense in which a consequent 'follows' from an antecedent. This sense is so weak that the use of the word 'follows from' to describe it is not really appropriate at all. However, when we try to give an account of 'following from' that invokes reasons why, or reasons for thinking, we move the discussion out of the scope of formal logic.

So this means we face a new 'paradox' of entailment. Using truth-functional, or modal, definitions, we try to capture what it is about a valid argument that makes the premises necessitate the conclusion. Yet the logical concepts – even those involving necessity and possibility – lose the very notion of *following from* that we were trying to analyse. Suppose that where A entails B, we analyse this as meaning that it is impossible for it to be the case that A and $\sim B$. Then, according to elementary logic, if A is a contradiction, then of course it is impossible for A to hold, hence impossible for it to be the case that A and $\sim B$. By reducing entailment to some form of conditional, strict implication or relevant implication, the logical system introduces a bizarre result. Our common sense tells us that the logical reduction just does not capture the relevant connection that is supposed to hold between premises and conclusion, or the way that premises supply reasons why (or reasons for thinking that) the conclusion holds – the reasons in virtue of which the conclusion *follows from* the premises. But how can we go beyond the logical account? If we try to define validity, entailment and consequence by other means, then we are no longer doing formal logic. So the attempt to capture the notions of *entailment* and *following logically from* within logic are a failure, and the attempt to capture them outside logic would mean that we were no longer giving 'logical' definitions of these notions.

In the face of this 'paradox', what are we to say? One thought is that we should take a modest view of what logic can achieve. It can successfully formalize some inferences, lay out the structure of many arguments, and paraphrase some of the conditional propositions we put forward. But it cannot fully capture the inferential power of human minds and everyday language, let alone explain in a satisfactory manner the basic notions on which it draws and which it uses in the very first steps of building its formal systems. This is not really bad news. As we saw earlier, the study of logic will not make an illogical person into a logical one, and – as poor Achilles found from his discussion with the wily tortoise – deduction will be lost on someone who does not already accept *modus ponens.* This chapter, and the previous one, have shown how adding notions of necessity and possibility to the resources of formal logic can produce useful and interesting results and help us represent and think about many mind-boggling problems. It would be asking too much if adding these notions to logic were a way of providing definitions and explanations for the notions of logical consequence and entailment themselves. As with the cases of *modus ponens*, so with the other cases we've looked at. In order to formalize and regiment our understanding of necessity, entailment, and deduction, the understanding in question has to be there already[18]

The same point about prior undertanding also holds for a notion that we have not had time to discuss in the present book – presupposition. Logicians have long noted that presupposition is a consequence-like relation. In the nineteenth century, Gottlob Frege made the point that 'if one asserts "Kepler died in misery" there is a presupposition that the name "Kepler" designates something' (Frege 1892, p. 69). Subsequent writers have often taken this Fregean notion of presupposition to mean something like this: in order for it to be either true or false that Kepler died in misery, the proposition 'Kepler existed' has itself to be true. In general, where proposition *B* presupposes proposition *A*, then *B* is true or false *only if A* is true.

By a relatively short step, this latter formulation seems to be much the same as saying: whenever *B* presupposes *A*, then *B* entails *A* and ~*B* also entails *A*. But with presupposition understood in this way, it will clearly be no more amenable to logical definition than the other concepts just discussed.

This fact has, of course, not deterred logicians from developing calculi of entailment, presupposition, implication and so on.[19] These systems often present some insight into how the various concepts interrelate, how the extension of first-order logic by introducing modal operators leads to new ways of organizing our thought about deductive relationships, and outlines the scope and limits of systematization. At the same time, these formal treatments also throw up many paradoxes and puzzles – some of which we have just been exploring. Observe that none of these bewitching puzzles would arise if any of the formal systems gave a trouble-free, comprehensive, precise and non-paradoxical definition of the concepts we have been studying here. So formalization has provided a surprising and unexpected benefit to us – by giving rise to new problems at the same time as it tries to settle old ones. As long as logic continues to appeal to our desire for precision and system it will also stimulate us to explore the limits of such precision and to raise questions even about the role of precision as an ideal. As we have seen throughout the book, the attempts to give precise formulation to the notions of entailment, logical consequence, the role of the conditional, the nature of truth – these all run up against problems that cannot themselves be resolved by appeal to formal systems or to some new form of precise discourse. As Wittgenstein cautions, in §81 of the *Philosophical Investigations*, to think that our everyday language only approximates to some ideal language or calculus is to stand at the brink of a misunderstanding (Wittgenstein 1953). We hope the philosophy of logic as we have presented it here is a strong antidote to any such misunderstanding.

SUGGESTIONS FOR FURTHER READING

Entailment and logical consequence are extensively discussed in Read (1995), Chapters 2 and 3, from the point of view of a relevance logician. Chapters 5 and 6 of Sainsbury (2001) discuss in an interesting way many of the issues touched on in this and the previous chapter. These chapters, however, make heavy formal demands on the reader, and should only be tackled by those who have already mastered some formal logic. Conditionals are discussed by the contributors to the Jackson (1991) collection, and Vic Dudman's complaints in his chapter there to some extent complement the challenges put forward in the present chapter. Further work on conditionals is found in Woods, Wiggins and Edgington (1997). Although Bennett (2003) is comprehensive, it is aimed at an audience with considerable background in logic and philosophy. Ideally, any account of entailment and implication would discuss the related topics of conversational implicature and assertability – although limits of space have forced us to mention them only in the notes. For an introduction to this area, see Walker (1975).

CHAPTER 7

CRITIQUES OF LOGIC

7.1 INTRODUCTION

Logic is often understood as the systematic study of the principles of correct reasoning. As such, one might wonder why anyone would want to criticize logic. The theme of this chapter is indeed to argue that critiques of logic are more often than not misguided. But it is important to distinguish between different kinds of critiques, in order to see more clearly the rather different motivations that lie behind them and the diverse issues that are involved.

7.2 LOGIC AND CREATIVITY

One popular criticism of logic is that it is somehow incompatible with creativity. According to this critique, logical reasoning requires consistency and careful step-by-step reasoning. But it is doubtful whether such rigid thinking processes can enhance creativity. Logical laws certainly do not provide the recipe for generating insights. Furthermore, new ideas very often originate from vague intuitions and metaphors which might not survive rigorous critical scrutiny. Thus it might be argued that studying logic can be detrimental to one's creativity. An experiment in support of this conclusion is quoted approvingly in the *New York Times* management bestseller *In Search of Excellence* by Peters and Waterman:

> If you place in a bottle half a dozen bees and the same number of flies, and lay the bottle horizontally, with its base (the closed end) to the window, you will find that the bees will persist, till they die of exhaustion or hunger, in their endeavor to discover an opening through the glass;

> while the flies, in less than two minutes, will all have sallied forth through the neck on the opposite side. . . . It is the bees' love of flight, it is their very intelligence, that is their undoing in this experiment. They evidently imagine that the issue from every prison must be where the light shines clearest; and they act in accordance, and persist in too-logical action. To bees glass is a supernatural mystery. . . . And, the greater their intelligence, the more inadmissible, more incomprehensible, will the strange obstacle appear. Whereas the featherbrained flies, careless of logic . . . flutter wildly hither and thither, and meeting here the good fortune that often waits on the simple . . . necessarily end up by discovering the friendly opening that restores their liberty to them. (Peters and Waterman 1988, p.108).

The observation here is an interesting one, but it is doubtful that a single experiment involving bees and flies can lead to the conclusion that logical thinking is undesirable for human beings. If anything, the problem with the bees is that they do not reason enough, persisting in a strategy that does not lead to success.

In this context it might be useful to draw a rough distinction between two kinds of creativity. First, there is creativity in art, like drawing a painting, or composing a symphony. It is true that good logical reasoning is neither necessary nor sufficient for artistic talent, which depends more on aesthetic sensibilities and artistic skills. But logical reasoning is not necessarily incompatible with artistic creativity. Leonardo da Vinci was an intelligent thinker and a talented scientist and inventor, so we can safely assume that he could reason well. His creativity as an artist is certainly beyond doubt. Likewise, the famous Renaissance painter Albrecht Dürer was well known not only as a painter but also as a mathematician. These are of course exceptional cases, but there does not seem to be any evidence showing that basic reasoning skills are harmful to artistic creativity.

Outside of art, another kind of creativity that is perhaps more prevalent is 'cognitive creativity'. Cognitive creativity is creativity that is used in solving complex problems, as in the invention of scientific theories to explain new phenomena. But cognitive creativity is also required when we go about solving countless problems in our daily lives. When we have to figure out why the computer keeps on crashing, or how a relationship can be improved, we may need to make use of cognitive creativity to come up with explanations and solutions.

Contrary to what you might think, logic is crucial for cognitive creativity. In solving problems, we need not just ideas, but ideas that really work and which can solve our problems in an effective and appropriate manner. For example, one can easily propose a hundred different ways to reduce greenhouse gases in the atmosphere, e.g. shut down all factories, stop using cars every other week, etc. But these ideas are impractical and not really useful, even if nobody has thought of them before. To be truly creative in solving problems, we have to determine whether a new idea is a good one or not, and logic is indispensable for such a task. If we want to build a rocket to Mars, we had better make sure that the design principles for the rocket are consistent with the relevant laws of physics. Innovation is not just the moment of 'eureka'. The use of logic in the evaluation, testing and modification of ideas is just as integral to the complete creative process.

It is of course possible for creativity to be hindered by rigid and inflexible logical thinking. This is perhaps the moral behind the story of the bees and flies. It is not uncommon to over-analyse a problem, and not leave enough room for imagination to roam. But this is a problem with the misguided use of logic, and not with logic itself. In the first chapter of this book we drew a distinction between logic and reasoning. The principles of logic are formulated in terms of concepts such as truth, validity, consistency, and proof. As such, these principles say nothing about what we should aim to achieve in applying logic. Logic tells us that certain patterns of arguments are valid, but logic itself does not say we should never use any invalid arguments (say, for rhetorical purposes). Logic provides the tools for evaluating consistency, but logic does not say we should be consistent all the time. In fact, Cherniak (1986) has argued that the human brain is likely to consume too much computational resources if we were to check the consistency of all our beliefs exhaustively. This of course does not imply that contradictory beliefs are true. It only goes to show that we need not pursue logical reasoning at all costs in all situations, just as it is pointless to engage in logical reasoning when all we want is to sit down quietly and enjoy a good meal. If suspending logical analysis at certain points in the creative process facilitates new ideas, there is no reason not to do so. The ability to apply logical reasoning judiciously is a key element in a sharp and flexible mind.

7.3 LOGIC AND RELIGION

The distinction between logic and reasoning is of special relevance when we are dealing with critiques of logic based on religious considerations. Consider for example the following comments on logic by D. T. Suzuki, a famous writer on Zen Buddhism:

> [T]he ordinary logical process of reasoning is powerless to give final satisfaction to our deepest spiritual needs. (Suzuki 1986, p.59)

> [T]he reason why Zen is so vehement in its attack on logic . . . is that logic has so pervasively entered into life as to make most of us conclude that logic is life and without it life has no significance. (Suzuki 1986, p. 63)

It is true that courses in critical thinking and logic often emphasize the importance of logic for just about everything we do. This does not mean that logical reasoning always leads to success, since factors such as luck, knowledge, and personality are also relevant. So it is puzzling why anyone would want to say that 'logic is life and without it life has no significance'. And Suzuki has given no evidence that any philosopher or logician has ever propounded such a view. Suzuki is correct if what he means is that logical reasoning alone is not sufficient to help us discover the meaning and value of life. For that matter, logic is also not enough to guarantee fame, fortune, or fulfilling personal relationships. But this is of course not the task of logic, and it would be just as wrong to criticize chemistry or physics on the same grounds.

Suzuki sometimes speaks as if the problem with logic is that there are rules to follow, and these rules are detrimental to one's spiritual health:

> In logic there is a trace of effort and pain; logic is self-conscious. . . . Life, according to Zen, ought to be lived as a bird flies through the air or as a fish swims in the water. As soon as there are signs of elaboration, a man is doomed, he is no more a free being. . . . Not to be bound by rules, but to be creating one's own rules – this is the kind of life which Zen is trying to have us live. Hence its illogical, or rather superlogical, statements. (Suzuki 1986, p.64)

Logic is certainly not sufficient for enlightenment, but this does not mean that logic cannot help us in our quest for happiness or meaning.

Suppose someone wants to live a tranquil and self-sufficient life. But she likes to be praised and is obsessed with how other people judge her. It is important to see that her ideals are inconsistent with her actual practice, and noting the inconsistency would enable her to think more deeply about what matters most to her life. Part of what a training in logic does is to make us alert to lurking inconsistencies. Without some amount of logical thinking, a muddled person with contradictory values can end up living an unfulfilling life.

We should also recall the distinction between the principles of logic and their use in reasoning. A person who devotes his entire life to logic at the expense of everything else is unlikely to be an enlightened person. But this is a criticism of his obsession with logic and not a criticism of logic *per se*. Even if one can be a happier person by repeatedly asserting contradictory claims, this does not mean that the assertions are therefore true. In many Buddhist traditions, meditations play an important role in acquiring enlightenment. Meditation here involves entering into a special state of awareness, refraining from judgements and deliberation, yet remaining alert and focused. In such a state of consciousness, one is not supposed to carry out any logical reasoning. But this is not the same as rejecting the principles of logic as incorrect.

However, as Suzuki points out, many Buddhist texts contain frequent statements that are plainly contradictory or inconsistent. For example, in the famous Diamond Sutra (The *Vajracchedika Prajñāpāramitā* Sutra), we find many claims of the form '*x* is not *x*, therefore it is *x*', e.g.

> The world is not the world, therefore it is the world.
>
> The perfection of wisdom is not the perfection of wisdom, therefore it is the perfection of wisdom.

Similarly, we find the following splendidly inconsistent passage in Nagarjuna's *Mūlamadhyamakakārikā* (Fundamental Verses on the Middle Way),

> Everything is real and is not real,
> Both real and not real,
> Neither real nor not real.
> This is Lord Buddha's teaching.

Many people would argue that inconsistency in religion extends beyond Buddhism or Eastern philosophy. For example, many people find it difficult to accept the doctrine of the Trinity in mainstream Christianity. According to the doctrine as presented in the Athanasian Creed

> . . . there is one Person of the Father, another of the Son, and another of the Holy Spirit . . . the Father is God; the Son is God; the Holy Spirit is God. And yet there are not three Gods, but one God.

One might have thought, if the Son, the Father, and the Holy Spirit are the one true God, and there is no other God, then the Son is identical to the Father, and also identical to the Holy Spirit. Yet it was the Son who died on the cross, and not the Father or the Holy Spirit. This appears to violate a principle of logic known as indiscernibility of identicals – if x and y are one and the same thing, then whatever is true of x is also true of y. So if Aristotle is one and the same as the most famous teacher of Alexander, and Aristotle was a philosopher, then it must also be the case that the most famous teacher of Alexander was a philosopher.

There are various ways to deal with seemingly inconsistent religious claims. One might take the inconsistency as evidence for rejecting the doctrines that entail those claims. Or one might suggest that the claims in question are not to be taken literally, and reinterpret them in such a way that the apparent inconsistency disappears. Thus, in the case of Buddhism, it might be suggested that to say that an object is both real and unreal is to say that even though the object exists according to conventional understanding (so 'real' in one sense), its existence depends on contingent and fleeting conditions, and thus the object does not have a distinctive inherent essence in ultimate reality ('unreal' in a different sense). As for the problem of the Trinity, some philosophers have argued that it can be resolved using the notion of relative identity. According to this line of thought, identity is relative to a kind of entity. So, for example, one might suggest that the Eiffel Tower that existed a hundred years ago is the same tower as the Eiffel Tower today, but they are not the same physical object because many parts have since been replaced and they are physically distinct. Likewise, perhaps Jesus is the same God as the Holy Spirit, but they are different Divine Personalities. So there is no inconsistency after all, or so one might argue.[1] It is a controversial matter whether these interpretations are coherent or faithful to the original doctrines. But notice that all such attempts to restore consistency are motivated by the desire to be logical – to rescue these doctrines from their apparent incoherence.

Some authors have opted for a far more radical alternative to the reinterpretation approach by adopting some version of dialetheism, which is the view that there are true contradictions. Within classical logic, it is not possible for a statement and its negation to be true at the same time. However, dialetheists deny this, and claim that some contradictions can indeed be true. This is certainly not a popular position in philosophy and logic, but it has been suggested that dialetheism can be independently motivated, and that it provides the solution to a variety of paradoxes, such as the liar paradox (see Chapter 3). It is also suggested that dialetheism lies behind some of the most important ideas of philosophers such as Kant, Hegel, Heidegger and Marx. With respect to Nagarjuna's *Mūlamadhyamakakārikā*, Garfield and Priest (2003) have argued that the text can be understood as an expression of dialethic logic in the investigation of reality, leading to the paradoxical conclusion that the ultimate nature of all phenomena is that they have no ultimate nature.

It is beyond the scope of this book to discuss the pros and cons of dialetheism. Although it might be difficult to accept that there can be true contradictions, it is important to point out that endorsing dialetheism is not the same as rejecting logic or rational argumentation. First, dialetheists need not think that all contradictions are true, only that some are. Second, while dialetheists reject classical logic, they are still free to develop alternative systems of logic to encapsulate dialethic reasoning in a rigorous manner, and this is in fact an active research project that some logicians are pursuing. In classical logic, a contradiction entails everything.[2] A dialetheist should therefore make sure that his or her system of logic does not have such a feature, or else every statement would be true according to the system. It is hard to imagine why anyone would want to embrace such systems, for to accept every statement as true is to give up reasoning indeed, and most likely with disastrous practical consequences.

The example of dialetheism shows that one can engage in a critique of widely accepted principles in logic, without giving up on rational argumentation altogether. But it is important to provide principled justifications for one's views and to be aware of their implications. This is a lot more preferable to saying that God or ultimate reality is beyond logic, and to leave it at that. That weak and irresponsible response closes off the possibility for any constructive dialogue or serious investigation into the subject, and is unlikely to change other people's minds.

7.4 FEMINIST CRITIQUES OF LOGIC

We now turn to more recent critiques of logic from feminism. According to some feminist writers, male philosophers and logicians have long dominated the discipline of logic, propounding conceptions of logic and rationality that oppress women and the powerless. In her controversial book *Words of Power*, Andrea Nye even goes so far as to link logic with Hitler, proclaiming that 'logic in its final perfection is insane'. It is of course impossible to summarize in a chapter the diverse positions within feminism on this issue. What we shall do is focus on some of the main themes in feminist critiques of logic, bearing in mind that not all feminists are critical of logic, and that those who are might endorse only some aspects of these themes.

A significant body of feminist writings related to logic is historical in character. According to some authors, a careful reading of the history of logic and philosophy from Plato to Kant, Hegel and beyond reveals a history of misogyny and oppression. Within this tradition, men are idealized as the embodiment of reason, and women are portrayed as emotional and lacking in rationality. For example, Aristotle has been a main target of attack, despite the fact that he is a major figure in the history of logic, and his syllogistic logic is still being taught these days. Notoriously, Aristotle believed that the female is 'a mutilated male' (*Generation of Animals*, §737a 25–28), and that 'the male is by nature superior, and the female inferior; and the one rules, and the other is ruled' (*Politics*, Book I, §5.) As for Kant, women are supposed to possess a 'beautiful understanding' in contrast to men's 'deep understanding', and because of this, a woman 'will learn no geometry . . . Her philosophy is not to reason, but to sense'.[3] Feminists contend that such hierarchical conceptions of gender not only exerted a huge influence on the western philosophical tradition, they also led to detrimental practical consequences for women. If women are seen as inferior and deficient in rationality, they might be excluded from decision-making and political participation, and deprived of their own autonomy.

The association of logic and philosophy with misogyny and sexist stereotypes is indeed regrettable. But a lot of the objectionable views in question have to do with erroneous conceptions of rationality or misguided theories of gender or human nature. It is certainly legitimate to criticize them and express our indignation. But why think that logic must incorporate such objectionable assumptions? Many of the laws and principles of logic, such as *modus ponens*, are abstract in character. Some philosophers have suggested that a feature of logic is that it is topic-neutral. For example, the validity of inferring P from (P and Q) does not depend on the motive, race or gender of the person carrying out the inference. Nor does it depend on what the sentences P and Q might be about. It is difficult to see how such seemingly content-neutral principles can actually perpetuate domination.

Yet it is precisely the abstract nature of logic that many feminists have misgivings about. A recurrent theme in Nye's *Words of Power* is that logic focuses on forms rather than actual content and substance, and this pursuit of generality can only lead to the neglect of the subtleties of concrete situations. According to Nye, since generality is an essential feature of logic, logic cannot be purged of its biases and should be completely abandoned, to be replaced by the practice of reading:

> If logic teaches us to ignore the circumstances in which something is said, reading asks us to consider it carefully, if logic teaches us to forget who says something and why, this is precisely what we need to know if we are to read correctly. (Nye 1990, p.183)

Nye argues that unlike logic, reading requires careful attention to context and background, and this is essential for unmasking political rhetoric and distinguishing right from wrong. Nye is of course quite right that reading so understood is an important skill, but it would be quite wrong to think that reading can displace logic. For reading involves interpretation, and unless interpretation is arbitrary, reasons and standards would have to be invoked to determine whether an interpretation is appropriate, and in criticizing or defending particular interpretations, we would have to make use of logic.

However, the view that logic is problematic because of its formal and abstract nature is not uncommon in feminist writings. Thus, according to Cope-Kasten (1989), because logic is formal in nature, impersonality is emphasized at the expense of empathy. Aristotle's syllogism is supposed to be an example,[4] and it is argued that the fascination with formalism can sometimes 'prevent a check on aggressive impulses by isolating the agent from experiencing the victim as a real flesh-and-blood person'. Similarly, Pam Oliver complains that logic leads to over-simplification by ignoring the complexities and pragmatic considerations of human activities. Whereas 'logical deduction is orderly, tidy, clean', it results in 'simplistic decisions which can be disastrous in their consequences', such as 'the Jewish genocide . . . the Bay of Pigs invasion . . . and a now rampant technology which has long since outstripped the ability of men to use it wisely in the interests of humanity today' (Falmagne and Hass 2002, p.225–6).

To evaluate such objections properly, it is important to disentangle many different but related issues. First, there is the psychological question as to whether competence in logic is somehow incompatible with empathy and inter-personal skills. This is an empirical issue that requires carefully controlled scientific studies. But whatever the empirical facts might be about human cognitive architecture, surely the appropriate response is that a normal well-functioning individual should cultivate both kinds of skill, and strike an appropriate balance given limited time and resources.

As to the charge that logic ignores context, this seems to involve the mistaken inference that because the evaluation of the validity of an argument is *independent* of its context, arguments therefore cannot be *about* context. It is true that the validity of an argument does not depend on the motive or the identity of the person giving the argument. Indeed this point is often strongly emphasized in the teaching of logic. But this does not mean that such contextual factors are unimportant, or that logic cannot be used to analyse these factors. If someone gives an argument that has a morally objectionable conclusion, there are plenty of things we can do with logic other than to focus on the form of the argument. For example, we can give our own arguments to explain why its premises are mistaken, or we can use a different argument to criticize the motivation of the person who puts forward the objectionable argument. The principles of logic are flexible enough to be applied dynamically depending on what we want to evaluate. It would be a gross misunderstanding of logic to think that it cannot be used to analyse context or substantive issues. Of course, it is perhaps possible that a student who is learning the forms of argument might get the wrong impression that context is unimportant, but this is a matter about proper pedagogy and is not a problem of logic as such.

As to whether 'tidy' logic can apply to 'messy' real-life situations, perhaps this depends on the particular situation in question. Many complex policy or moral issues require a delicate balance of competing rights and values, and when it comes to such situations logic might not provide a method for determining the optimal solution. But there are inevitably pros and cons to any proposed solution to a complex problem, and it is not clear why logic cannot help us analyse the consistency and justification of these reasons.

To sum up, while the principles of logic are indeed general and abstract, they are quite capable of being applied to concrete situations or in the analysis of complex issues. Also, we should not forget that abstraction is a fundamental aspect of reasoning. In science and in ordinary life, we abstract away from particular experiences to form general beliefs about trends and patterns. In mathematics, we search for proofs that reveal the general properties of numbers or mathematical objects. Indeed, abstraction also has an important place within feminism, in revealing general but powerful currents of misogyny and objectionable modes of thinking which should be brought to the surface. No doubt it is possible to over-emphasize abstraction, but this is a misuse of logic, and does not indicate an inherent bias in the subject itself.

We now turn to a different set of criticisms of logic, which specifically aims to show that logic is biased in its very formal framework. According to these objections, certain notations and laws of formal logic distort reality in that they misrepresent femininity, or they incorporate problematic values that perpetuate domination and stereotyping. In this chapter, we shall focus on the critique of the law of identity and negation in classical logic.

The law of identity can be expressed by the formula $\forall x(x=x)$, which says that everything is identical to itself. Thus, Simone de Beauvoir is identical to Simone de Beauvoir, London is identical to London, etc. While one might have thought that this law of identity is trivially true, it has been suggested that the law is actually a distortion of feminine identity. According to the French writer Irigaray, woman is 'the sex which is not one', for 'she is neither open nor closed. She is indefinite . . . She is neither one nor two.' Feminine identity is supposed to be fluid, but the law of identity is determinate. Discussing Irigaray's views, Marjorie Hass writes

> . . . although sexed identity frees us from the self-substituting model of identity characterized by the logical law of identity, it is also what makes individual identity possible: 'becoming one's gender also constitutes the means for returning to the self. I am born a woman, but I still must become this woman that I am by nature.' Irigaray has identified a sense, then, in which the law of identity does not 'apply' to women.[5]

Is it really true that the law of identity does not apply to women? 'Identity' is a notoriously slippery word, and one can distinguish between at least two different readings. What Irigaray and Hass are concerned with might more appropriately be called 'gender identity', which is related to social or self-perception of gender role, such as thinking that boys should play with cars and girls with dolls. However, the law of identity is about 'numerical identity', and says nothing more controversial than that each thing is identical to itself. Numerical identity has nothing to do with gender, and if there is an object *C*, then the law tells us that *C* is identical to *C*, whether *C* is a person or not, and whatever his or her gender identity might be. Hass claims that someone born as a woman still has to 'become a woman'. This might be taken to mean that gender identity is not biologically given, a presumably reasonable claim. But obviously, the person that has yet to 'become a woman' is still identical to herself. It is therefore extremely misleading to use this as a counterexample to the law of identity.

However, Hass might not be satisfied with the answer that identity in logic is not the same as gender identity. She writes:

> Symbolic logic fails to represent the form of difference exhibited by genuine sexual difference, the form of identity proper to feminine identity, and the form of generality required to express a feminine generic. Each of these relationships remains outside logic, remains 'illogical'. (Falmagne and Hass 2002, p.84)

This passage suggests the view that if feminine identity is not explicitly represented in logic, then logic somehow denigrates such concepts. But surely this is a misunderstanding of formal logic. Just because certain concepts do not appear within the core notation of logic, it does not follow that logic lacks the resources to express these concepts, nor that these concepts have been marginalized.

A similar misunderstanding of formal logic can also be found in the critique of the language of science by Luce Irigaray. In 'Is the Subject of Science Sexed?', Irigaray claims that science must always be expressed in the language of formal logic, but formal logic is biased because it fails to include concepts close to feminist concerns, such as 'reciprocity', 'exchange', 'permeability' and 'fluidity' (Irigaray 2002, p.252).

It is true that the usual formal languages of logic do not contain symbols which express the concepts listed above. But this does not mean that formal logic is opposed to such concepts, since one can always explicitly introduce symbols that express these concepts. For example, one can stipulate that the relational expression 'R*xy*' should mean *x helps y and y reciprocates*. The reason why the standard formal languages do not mention symbols with such meanings is because these are optional concepts which might not be useful for all contexts of reasoning, and so it is better that they are introduced when they are needed.

7.5 PLUMWOOD'S CRITIQUE OF CLASSICAL LOGIC

In a series of books and articles, Val Plumwood has put forward an extended critique of classical logic, focusing in particular on the concept of negation ('not') (see for example Plumwood 1993, 2002a, 2002b). In classical logic, a statement P and its negation ~P always have opposite truth-values, and it is not possible for P and ~P to be both true. Negation is closely associated with the making of distinctions, e.g. distinguishing between things that have a certain property F, and things that do not. There is a huge literature in feminist and post-modernist thinking concerning how certain distinctions create oppression and unequal hierarchies. What is surprising and radical about Plumwood's position is her claim that such objectionable thinking is supposedly embedded in the way negation operates in classical logic. Her argument is that certain distinctions which she calls 'dualisms' possess objectionable features that are also present in classical negation.

Homogenization is one such feature, and it takes place when 'differences among the inferiorized group are disregarded' (Plumwood 1993, p.53). An example from Plumwood is how non-English foreign immigrants in postwar Australia were all branded as 'aliens' or 'wogs'. This practice involves homogenization because in branding these groups together as being outside the dominant class, their distinctive cultures, languages and social organization were completely disregarded. Plumwood believes that classical negation is also guilty of homogenization. Here is her explanation:

> It takes p as primary and treats its negation as having a secondary role, as delineating what is left over after the primary term 'p' has finished taking its slice of the universe. Classical not-p cannot be independently identified and homogenizes the Other as an oppositional remainder. (Plumwood 2002b, p.62)

To evaluate this argument, let us first note that homogenization involves two essential features: targeting a group as inferior, and ignoring diversity within the group. Are these features really present in classical negation?

Consider the first assumption that classical negation involves treating something as inferior. While it is true that ~P is 'secondary' to P in the sense that the former is defined in terms of the latter, it is not clear why not-P should therefore be 'inferior' to P. To begin with, symbols such as P, ~P by themselves do not have any meaning. Unless we know the meanings being assigned to such symbols, it does not make sense to say in the abstract that ~P is deemed to be inferior to P. For all we know, P can designate a state of affairs (e.g. everybody is suffering.) that is a lot less desirable than ~P. Furthermore, P is logically equivalent to ~~P in classical logic. If the use of negation counts as an objectionable act of homogenization, then just as ~P is homogenized by P, ~~P should likewise be homogenized by ~P. But P cannot be inferior to itself, and so homogenization cannot really be inherent in classical negation.

Plumwood acknowledges the existence of double negation in classical logic, and her response is that although 'any proposition can occupy the primary role, once this is set the behavior of its negation is completely determined'. She also criticizes classical logic for being 'centrist', where 'the center is the source of value or meaning, and all others derive their value or disvalue ultimately from their relationship or lack of relationship to the center'. The suggestion seems to be that ~P is somehow regarded as having lesser value because it is completely dependent on and controlled by P, the 'controlling-center'.

While freedom is a good thing and being 'controlled' is not, it is unhelpful to speak of classical negation in such metaphoric language.

First, what is objectionable about ~P being 'completely determined' and 'controlled' cannot be that ~P is defined in terms of P. When a definition is introduced, the defined term necessarily derives its meaning from the other terms in the definition. If this dependency of meaning is supposed to be objectionable, then one would have to reject all definitions, which obviously is untenable. So what is problematic is presumably the way in which classical negation is defined, and perhaps the objection is that the definition introduces an unjustified hierarchy in value between P and ~P. However, unless Plumwood provides a more substantive theory of value, it is hard to see how classical negation renders the (instrumental, moral or otherwise) value of ~P as being dependent on P. Suppose for example P means 'it is raining'. The symbol represents a state of affairs that perhaps has some value, such as its value in cleaning pollution from the air and nourishing plants. Now consider its negation ~P, which means 'it is not raining'. There is certainly some value in not raining, since one can go out for a picnic. But it is doubtful whether anyone would want to claim that raining 'controls' not raining, or that not raining is inferior to raining, or that the value of not raining derives solely from the value of raining. Whether rain is to be preferred presumably depends on the time and place and the consequences. Classical logic has nothing to say on this issue, and it would be absurd indeed to speak of homogenization in this context. On Plumwood's account of homogenization, homogenization requires a class of individuals or entities being treated as inferior. But this example shows that there are lots of contexts where classical negation is used but where no such judgements are involved. It would not be plausible to respond that the biases of classical logic operate only when negation is applied to a subject matter related to power. This would be an *ad hoc* response that begs the question, and unconvincing as well since the logical behaviour of classical negation does not depend on subject matter.

Perhaps the proper conclusion to draw is that homogenization is not an essential aspect of classical logic. On such a view, the use of classical negation in a discourse is not sufficient reason to conclude that homogenization is taking place. It would depend on the nature of the additional value assumptions and practice in the discourse, which may have nothing to do with formal logic. Plumwood calls this position 'externalism', which she discusses explicitly only to reject it. However, it would seem that some of Plumwood's own examples actually support externalism. Consider her example of the derogatory term 'wogs' as a label for all non-English foreign immigrants in postwar Australia. The second essential aspect of homogenization is present because the diverse cultures of the immigrants were dismissed in the use of the term. However, homogenization is not a necessary consequence of the use of the general term 'wogs'. What is objectionable (among other things) was the additional, implicit thinking that the term 'wogs' exhausts the identity of the immigrants and that further distinction is of no value. In a similar vein, one might argue that classical negation itself does not entail homogenization. The use of the term 'non-mammals' as a general category does not preclude us from recognizing the diverse types of entities that are not mammals. Although ~P is defined in terms of P, classical logic does not imply that it is not worth distinguishing between the different situations that are sufficient for ~P, even if classical logic is unable to express such distinctions. In any event, some such resources are indeed available to classical logic. So for example, situations where ~P is true can be distinguished into at least two cases: (Q and ~P), and (~Q and ~P), and one can make further distinctions as well. To sum up, we have shown that classical negation does not necessarily involve judgements of inferiority, and also it does not disregard diversity. Homogenization does not result from the use of classical negation in the marking of a distinction. Rather it comes about through the adoption of problematic moral and cultural assumptions *about* the proposed distinction. These assumptions are external to classical logic, and they grow out of the power-relations in the particular contexts in question, as when new terms are defined to reinforce class hierarchies.

Similar responses can be offered to Plumwood's other objections against classical logic. In radical exclusion, for example, 'one member of a dualistic pair, that construed as superior, defines itself against or in opposition to the other, by exclusion of the latter's inferiorized characteristics' (Plumwood 2002a, pp.25–6). An illustration provided is the definition of men as active and intellectual, and women as passive and intuitive. Such definitions make it a necessary truth that men and women have opposite psychological profiles, and so 'common or bridging characteristics are ignored, discouraged, or actually eliminated'. Again, Plumwood believes that classical negation exhibits the problem of radical exclusion in its rejection of contradiction:

> The radical exclusion aspects of classical otherness are evident in the classical treatment of contradictions as implying everything, for the effect of p&~p→q is to keep p and its other or negation at a maximum distance, so that they can never be brought together (even in thought), on pain of the maximum penalty a logical system can provide, system collapse. (Plumwood 2002a, p. 32)

It is not clear why the endorsement of progressive or feminist causes should require the embracement of contradictions, and it would be helpful if some concrete examples could be given. But whether we endorse dialetheism or not, we should be cautious in taking classical logic to be guilty of radical exclusion. Radical exclusion has to do with the use of opposing definitions that distort reality, ignoring the features shared by the defined entities and their mutual interaction. The obvious response is that classical logic does not require definitions to be formulated in such a way. For example, it is not a law of classical logic that male and female be defined in such a way that their significant features do not overlap. Of course, if 'female' is defined as 'non-male person', then necessarily males are not females, but again classical logic is silent as to the soundness of such a definition. In other words, if such definitions suffer from the problem of radical exclusion, that is only because the definitions incorporate erroneous conceptions (e.g. of gender) which are external to logic. Furthermore, classical logic contains plenty of resources for exploring commonalities. In classical logic, two inconsistent positions need not always be formulated as P and ~P. If two inconsistent positions indeed have shared assumptions, they can be identified and introduced into complex conjunctions that more accurately capture their content. Thus one view might for example be expressed as (P&Q&R), the other as (~P&Q&S), where Q would be their common ground, and the symbols R and S express the additional content distinctive to the respective positions. It is of course possible that there are subtle differences between two theories that cannot be captured in the formalism of classical logic. This only shows that classical logic is not as rich as natural language, but this is a well-known fact, and it is a far cry from the charge that classical logic is guilty of radical exclusion.

Another of Plumwood's objection to classical logic is that of 'backgrounding'. The idea is that although the dominating master is dependent on the other's services (e.g. the Athenian elites and their slaves), this dependency is hidden or denied. In the case of classical logic, backgrounding is supposed to be reflected in the way in which premises relevant for establishing the conclusion of an argument can be suppressed, and so its contribution is hidden or unacknowledged. According to Plumwood, this is 'most clearly expressed in the principle (related to Exportation), $p \& ((p\&q)\rightarrow r)\rightarrow q\rightarrow r$, which accordingly might be called Exploitation'.[6]

The technical issues involved here are interesting though complicated. For our present purpose, we shall have to limit ourselves to the following informal remarks. First, backgrounding as a moral fault is rather different from the notion of premise or assumption suppression. The former is inevitably a bad thing, but premise suppression need not be. For very often we do seem to suppress assumptions for the sake of efficiency and succinctness in expression. In certain contexts where there is a gas leak, Plumwood's principle of 'exploitation' allows us to assert 'if you smoke, there will be an explosion', rather than having to explicitly state all the supporting conditions necessary for bringing about an explosion, such as the laws of physics and chemistry and the fact that there is a gas leak.[7] In such contexts, it would seem that suppression is a virtue rather than an evil.

The suppression of premises obviously can be an evil when problematic assumptions are concealed in order to hide the weaknesses of an argument. If someone argues that clitoridectomy is permissible because this is the traditional custom of many societies,[8] this person is probably assuming implicitly that traditional customs should be respected and tolerated. If this is indeed the case, this crucial assumption should be brought to the surface. Once identified, we might object to it because traditional practices (e.g. torture, slavery, etc.) need not be morally acceptable. Classical logic helps us identify this hidden assumption because the original argument is not valid without such a premise. So when it comes to analysis that really matters, one should not underestimate the power of classical logic in revealing hidden premises.

In a monograph on relevant logic that Plumwood co-authored with the late Richard Routley and others, it is claimed that the suppression of assumption is equivalent to 'nuclear power, and other typical technological fixes in that they allow cleverness in technique to obscure the fact that very heavy costs are being incurred for an unnecessary item' (Routley, Meyer, Plumwood and Brady 1982, p.147). In that book, suppression is cited as a crucial reason why classical logic should be revised in favour of relevant logic. However, not all researchers in relevant logic agree that suppression avoidance is a necessary feature for a good logic (see for example the discussion in Urquhart (1988) and Brady (2003)). Furthermore, setting suppression aside, most systems of relevant logic[9] still include the theorem P→P. This has the effect of allowing circular arguments of the form: 'A. Therefore, A.' Should we argue that these systems are also politically incorrect because they reflect how a controlling master brushes off challenges and provides circular self-justification in order to maintain dominance? In her critique of classical logic, Plumwood claims that the popularity of classical logic reflects a 'logic of colonization'. By the same reasoning, are we to say that the majority of relevant logicians are actually not any better off?

There is actually a more plausible interpretation available, which is that different systems of formal logic have their respective strengths and weaknesses. The majority of relevant logicians most likely do not accept circular reasoning, but this does not mean that the injunction against circular reasoning should always be built into the formalism of logic. In normal circumstances, the prohibition of circular reasoning is part of the tacit principles of rational discourse and argumentation. Whether such principles should be explicitly incorporated into a system of logic depends on the use of the system, and how the cost of incorporation relates to other concerns such as simplicity and strength. Classical logic is not without its problems, and, as we have seen in Chapter 4, some philosophers and logicians argue that we should introduce more than two truth-values in light of the phenomenon of vagueness. But classical logic remains a simple and powerful system that is relatively user-friendly for many purposes, and this is probably the real reason why it is prevalent.

Plumwood believes that there is a shady political reason why classical logic is the dominant system of logic. This explanation has some plausibility if biased values are indeed inherent in the framework of classical logic. But we have seen that the arguments for this claim are not convincing, and there is a more plausible alternative explanation. The enterprise of relevant logics that Plumwood favours is certainly a fruitful and important branch of logic, and a laudable motivation for this line of research lies in the search for a formal account of proof and validity that hopefully is more faithful to our intuition of what a good inference should be. But a big question in the background is how such formal work actually relates to the advancement of feminism and other progressive causes. Plumwood admits she is not 'arguing that classical logic itself is the cause of women's oppression, and that if we just change the logical theory, all will be well' (Plumwood 2002a, p.32). But if we are correct that classical logic is not really oppressive, the remaining central issue becomes how much of the informal principles of good reasoning should be explicitly formalized, and at what cost. If we accuse those who subscribe to classical logic as misogynists, we would be misconstruing the nature of classical logic, and imposing a needlessly strict formalism by insisting that equality and rationality can only be given expression in a formal symbolic framework, a requirement that is often alien to the practical concerns of most feminists and liberal theorists.

7.6 FEMINISM, LOGIC AND RATIONALITY

This concludes our discussion of feminist critiques of formal logic. The final theme in feminist research we shall look at is not so much a critique of logic, but a project to re-conceptualize rationality and its relation to logic. The emphasis of this line of approach is not to reject any particular part of logic, but to show that rationality is not exhausted by logic. This is perhaps the most promising and fruitful part of the feminist discussion of logic. One important issue concerns the use of logic in actual reasoning and its role in rationality. Whereas many courses in critical thinking continue to stress the need to study formal logic in order to improve one's reasoning, philosophical discussion and experiments in psychology have questioned the centrality of domain-general logical principles in everyday life thinking.[10] Feminists have also participated in this debate in various ways, and the ongoing dialogue has certainly enriched our understanding of rationality.

For example, feminist theory has often emphasized the importance of context and history in practical rationality. The idea is that to make a moral judgement about people or action need not be a straightforward deduction from abstract principles. It should instead be 'informed by a detailed understanding of the whole context and history of the problem, including the histories and characters of the people involved, their cultural traditions, and so forth' (Nussbaum 1998, p.253). In other words, an adequate understanding of moral life requires an appreciation of the complexities of relevant circumstances, rather than the repudiation of logic. Feminists have also argued for the importance of community and personal relationships in cognitive development, especially in the cultivation of rationality. Finally, feminism has also contributed to a better understanding of how emotion relates to rationality. An important idea is that an emotional state is a complex mental state which usually has a judgement as its trigger or part of its cognitive component. Grief, for example, involves the belief that some desirable object or state of affairs no longer exists. Such judgements can surely be assessed in terms of truth and rationality. This observation and others help us understand the inadequacy in the simple dichotomy between emotion and reason. If we understand how justified beliefs about the world can rationally call for appropriate affective responses (which can be intense), this helps us address arguments that attempt to invoke women's emotional experiences to undermine their claims to rationality.

7.7 CONCLUSION

So, to conclude, although we have failed to find any successful feminist arguments specifically directed at the laws and principles of logic, there are lessons to be learnt about the history of philosophy and logic, the misuse of logic, and the need to rethink its connection with rationality. Feminists have made valuable contributions in emphasizing the importance of context, differentiation and relationality, but these legitimate concerns do not show that logic itself is an expression of misogyny and oppression. If anything, logic is an essential tool that helps us unmask the rhetoric and hidden practice which stand in the way of genuine equality.

SUGGESTIONS FOR FURTHER READING

Readers are encouraged to look up the books and articles mentioned in the chapter for further discussion. The feminist literature is huge, but on the topic of feminism and logic a good place to start is Falmagne and Hass (2002). Read (1988) and Mares (2004) are useful texts for relevance logic. More general discussion of feminism relating to rationality and analytic philosophy can be found in Antony and Witt (1993), Jones (2004), and the numerous articles in the online *Stanford Encyclopedia of Philosophy* at http://plato.stanford.edu/contents.html#f.

NOTES

1: REASON, UNREASON AND LOGIC

1 Please be careful of the difference between entailment (the premises of an argument may entail its conclusion) and inference. Inference is an action performed by an agent. You, or someone else, might, if you are sufficiently astute, infer that all geese are animals if you were given the premises (1) All geese are camels; (2) All camels are animals. The propositions (1) and (2) entail the proposition that all geese are animals. So entailment is a relation between propositions.

2 There is a vast literature on why, in 'concrete' situations such as this (walking down a street, pointing a house out to someone) only an idiot like Dick would make this kind of error in reasoning, whereas for arguments of the same form but more 'abstract' in content, most people make such errors. Evolutionary psychologists put this down to the fact that our reasoning abilities evolved so as better to cope with practical situations where our survival (or, worse, our prospect of mating) is under threat, especially from cheaters.

3 In a manuscript of 1848, George Boole (one of the great figures in the history of mathematical logic) wrote: 'Reasoning is for the most part carried on by the aid of signs . . . [I]t is universally agreed that the use of signs is a most important aid and that without them no extended process of reasoning could be conducted. The signs by which we conduct the processes of common reasoning are the words of our own language either spoken or thought. It has been observed that they who are debarred from the use of words are led if capable of reasoning at all to invent a substitute. Laura Bridgman, an American young lady who was born deaf and dumb but was possessed of considerable powers of intellect was accustomed to put her fingers in rapid motion when she was occupied in thought.' This manuscript, called 'The Nature of Logic', is reproduced in Grattan-Guinness and Bornet (1997); see pp. 1, 14. Boole does not say why he thinks that Laura's finger movements were an aid to thought rather than a mere by-product of her thinking. Were her powers of reasoning impaired when she was sitting on her fingers?

4 For example, considerations about practical reasoning (of the sort exemplified in our example about deciding whether to shave) might lead one to conclude that the mind must have a modular architecture, with different modules dedicated to different kinds of processing task. See Carruthers (2004).
5 For a scholarly discussion of the etymology of these terms and what they mean, see Railton (2000), esp. pp.179–88.
6 The extent of irrationality in all walks of life is quite frightening. See Sutherland (1992) and Wheen (2004). Types of irrationality include wishful thinking, acting contrary to one's own best judgement, self-deception, and believing something that one holds to be discredited by evidence. For an excellent philosophical discussion of these, one that broadly defends Freud's explanation, see the four essays by Donald Davidson (2004, pp.169–230). A big question that engages both psychologists and philosophers is whether experiments on human rationality do or do not tend to show that humans are frequently and systematically irrational. For a thorough treatment of the debate, see Stanovich (1999); also Samuels *et al.* (2004).
7 This is an adaptation of the argument in Lewis Carroll's classic miniature (Carroll 1895).
8 For a wonderfully clear and concise account of Leibniz' contribution to logic, see Kneale and Kneale (1962, pp.320–45).
9 A Bayesian calculation uses the mathematical theory of probability to calculate the degree of plausibility of a belief. See Joyce (2004). There are two chapters (11 and 12, pp.78–93) on the elements of probability theory in Priest (2000).
10 (Moore 1959, pp.219–21). For discussion, see Stroll (1994, pp.42–5). Another ambiguity, this time of the phrase 'a nature than which no greater nature can be thought', undermines St Anselm's celebrated ontological proof of the existence of God. So argues Peter Millican (2004), a difficult but rewarding article.
11 (Pirie 1985). As you'll see from this book, studying fallacies can be a lot of fun.
12 This might seem a pretty pointless activity – the conclusion of an argument contains no more than is already contained in the premises. But think of the amazing, delightful, surprising conclusions that can be deduced from Euclid's simple axioms. Deduction can be immensely fruitful.
13 Compare the rules of rationality enunciated by Robert Nozick (1993, pp.75–93), especially Rule 4 at p. 89. McGee's puzzle is a good one and you should not assume that the approach taken here is the final word on the subject. You may think that McGee really has produced an example that shows MP to be invalid (he has further examples in his article). Or you may think that MP is OK, but that some other fallacy is perpetrated in McGee's examples.
14 You might think that what is inconsistent cannot be logical, that the idea of a logic that countenances inconsistent desires is oxymoronic. But there are currently on the market *dialetheic* logics constructed on the

apparently far more outrageous supposition that some *propositions* are simultaneously true and false. See Priest (1987).

15 This conundrum is the subject of a famous short paper by Arthur Prior (1960). For a discussion, see Read (1988) but be warned that Read's discussion reaches a level of difficulty at least one higher than that of the present text.

16 You will find a short, but more thorough discussion of this example in Priest (2000, chap.2, pp. 7–16).

17 This too is why, although we can utter the words 'S is not true', we cannot use those words self-referentially to assert S. In other words, 'S' cannot be the name of the statement 'S is not true' for otherwise, in asserting S, we should, at the same time, be rejecting it (in saying that it is not true). To see this is to be well on the way towards a solution of the Liar paradox that we mentioned earlier.

18 Here we follow Michael Dummett (1981, pp.432–3); see also Hacking (1979).

2: HOW TO PROVE A POINT LOGICALLY

1 See Hilbert and Ackermann (1950).

2 See *Ten Classics* (1963), and the discussion in Karine Chemla's papers (Chemla 1997; Chemla 2000).

3 There is a discussion of the differences between these three notions in Chapter 3.

4 This is a development of a point originally made by Saul Kripke (1976), although the original insight is Wittgenstein's.

5 (Carroll 1895).

6 This is not Zeno from Citium, the Stoic, but a different Zeno – from Elea – whose brainteasers included a proof that an arrow in flight is always at rest, and that Achilles, great athlete and warrior though he was, could never beat the tortoise in a race, provided the tortoise was allowed to start moving before Achilles. Once behind the tortoise, the paradox ran, Achilles could never catch up: suppose he reached a point halfway between him and the tortoise, then before overtaking the tortoise, he has to cover half that distance again (one quarter the original gap), and before doing that he must cover half of that distance (one eighth of the gap), and so on. Since the series 1/2, 1/4, 1/8 . . . runs on infinitely, it appears Achilles can never catch up. In Carroll's logical analogue to this puzzle, it turns out that poor old Achilles cannot catch up with the conclusion of a simple argument!

7 See Thomson (1960).

8 See Smiley (1995).

9 Douglas Hofstadter has argued that the proper conclusion to draw from the tortoise's trick is that we cannot go on defending patterns of reasoning forever and that in some substrate of our hardware, perhaps even at the cellular level, there exists a formal system which limits any further regress (Hofstadter 1979, p.684–5).

10 In formal systems, there is a notation for this difference. 'A $\vdash$ B' represents syntactic consequence, while 'A $\models$ B' is used for semantic consequence. In later chapters, when talking about semantic consequence, the latter symbolism will be used.
11 (Carnap 1937).
12 This argument was given in Prior (1964), and versions of it subsequently appear in many other works, for example in Harman (1986a), and in Sainsbury (2001, Chap.6).
13 To engage in this task here would be too difficult. A helpful, but rather technical, overview of how to give precise definitions for the constants is in Chapter 6 of Sainsbury (2001).
14 See Wittgenstein (1953, §217).

3: TRUTH

1 The paradox here is a version of the Sancho Panza Paradox. See Church (1956, p.105) and Mackie (1973, p.297).
2 Graham Priest, who seems keen to emulate Socrates in corrupting the youth, summarizes the main idea of Chapter 5 of his introductory logic text (Priest 2000, p.37) as 'Sentences may be true, false, both, or neither'.
3 Notably Williams (2002) and Lynch (2004). Both these books are exceptionally well written and engage critically with the views of Nietzsche.
4 This example is taken from Wittgenstein (1953, §525).
5 For a further bizarre example, see Ellis (1990, p.172).
6 (Austin 1962, p.148). For discussion of some of the acts that are typically produced in the course of producing a total speech act, see pp.92–8. Fascinatingly, a related discussion of these matters occurs in Aristotle (Dougherty 2004).
7 Doubts about expressing the utterances of other tribes in our own vernacular ('radical translation') are expressed in Quine (1960, Chap.2). Rejection of the possibility of alternative conceptual schemes is to be found in Davidson (1974). For a rejection of Davidson on this score, see Blackburn (2004) and – on behalf of dolphins – MacIntyre (1999) and – on behalf of bonobos – Greenspan and Shanker (2004).
8 When, on a particular occasion, I utter a sentence (accompanied perhaps by some pointing) the demonstrative conventions, together with my words, serve to pick out the particular objects and the particular state of affairs to which I am referring. The identity of the statement I made is also determined by those words and objects, so there is an *internal relation* between the statement and the state of affairs. Austin appears to overlook this point. We owe this observation to Peter Cave.
9 Aristotle, *Metaphysics Γ* 7: 1011b26–7 (Kirwan 1993). As Künne points out in the course of his interesting discussion of classical correspondence (Künne 2004, pp.94–114), the first half of Aristotle's definition is lifted from Plato's *Sophist*, 240e10–241a1.
10 J. L. Mackie (1973, pp.17–63) accordingly calls his own variant of this theory, the Simple Theory. Aristotle's definition seems to apply only to

those statements in which a property is ascribed to an object and not to statements such as 'It is now raining', 'If Grace loves Dick then she doesn't love Bert'. Both Mackie and Künne (2004) seek to escape this limitation. Mackie's view is that, when a statement is true, 'things are in the world as in the statement they are stated to be' (p.50). He is not talking about a relation between things and statements, but between *how things are* and *how they are stated to be* and he says that the relation between these two is 'too close to be called correspondence' (p. 56). So his view is close to, but not identical with, the *Identity Theory* that we shall be discussing below. Künne's attempt at a symbolic formulation of the Simple (or 'Modest') view (2004, p.337) is criticized in Akiba (2004).

11 Though older readers may remember the music hall song 'I've never seen a straight banana'.

12 And we have not even considered statements of logic or mathematics, or scientific laws, where there do not seem to be any state of affairs corresponding to them. One possibility is that there are different kinds of correspondence for different areas of discourse. See Sher (2004).

13 The 'picture theory' features in Wittgenstein (1961, §2.1–3.01; §4.01–4.012), but a quite different conception of language informs the later writings. See, e.g. Wittgenstein (1953, §§7, 23).

14 Julian Dodd, who offers a subtle and spirited defence of the identity theory, is happy to abandon the 'truth-maker principle' that there is something that makes truths true (Dodd 2000, Chap.1). This is a very bold line to take. At the beginning of this chapter, we talked of Grace's action of giving Dick a dollar *making true* his statement that she would give him a dollar. This seems an entirely proper description of the situation. The statement 'The train is arriving on time' is made true by the locomotive pulling into the station at the designated time; its doing so any later would make the statement false. See also Stewart Candlish (1999) and his concise (2005).

15 The most accessible rigorous presentation, in the secondary literature, of Tarski's theory, is Soames (1999, Chaps.3 and 4), but you will probably need at least another year's study before you can treat yourself to this. Tarski presents his own informal exposition in Tarski (1969).

16 Enclosing a sentence in quotation marks is one way of forming its name, but as Tarski himself points out (Blackburn and Simmons 1999, p.119) there are others.

17 See the clarification supplied by Tarski at footnote 1, p. 156 of Tarski (1933).

18 For guidance in formulating the Idealist position, we are indebted to Stewart Candlish.

19 On first reading these nineteenth-century authors, one finds oneself on an alien planet wading through mud, enveloped in a dense swirling mist. The account given here of their positions is the crudest possible guide. Candlish and Damnjanovic (2006, §1.2) do enough scholarly exegesis to enable some rays of light to peep through. They also show that while Bradley may properly be classified as an Identity Theorist, he is not a Coherence Theorist, for, unlike Joachim and Blanshard, he does not

hold that truth *consists* in coherence, although he thinks that a proposition can be true if and only if it passes the consistency test. Ralph Walker is also good on the coherence theory. See his (1997, pp.310–19) and (2001).

20 Of course, if one insists on slavish conformity to established dogma, the result will be the inhibition of good science, as Paul Feyerabend forcefully argues (1963).

21 Ralph Walker (1989, Chap.9) shows that a coherence theory of justification does not entail a coherence theory of truth.

22 For a useful, brief exploration of pragmatist theories with an investigation of these differences, see Schmitt (2004, pp.3–11).

23 Peirce notes that he is using the word 'fated' not in any sense related to superstition but as it occurs in 'We are all fated to die'.

24 See Chap.2, 'A Bogus Predicate?' of Künne (2004) for a good discussion of different versions of this 'nihilistic' position; also the introduction to Blackburn and Simmons (1999).

25 This characterization is taken from Ayer (1936, p.119). A similar point can be made about belief. To believe that a certain proposition is true is just to believe that proposition. So, again, for Ramsey, there is no problem of truth that is separate from the problem of what it is to believe something.

26 This objection is taken from Künne (2004, p.83), who has a long chapter (pp.33–92) devoted to the question of whether 'true' is a bogus predicate.

27 See Frege (1918, p.87) and Davidson (1996). Davidson mounts an attack on Horwich's Minimal Theory, which is countered in Künne (2004, pp.327–31).

28 Horwich does address this problem at various points in his book (1998, pp.62–3, 139–41, 143–4) but does not succeed in closing off doubt, e.g. see Lynch (2004, pp.107–16).

29 Recent books defending relativism include O'Grady (2002) and Baghramian (2004) and also Kölbel (2002). Volume 12, number 3 (September 2004) of *International Journal of Philosophical Studies* is devoted to the subject.

4: THE LOGIC OF PARTS OF SPEECH

1 More precisely the meaning of a sentence *as it is used in a given context* can be identified with the proposition it expresses in that context. Some sentences mean different things in different contexts, 'I am hungry', for example.

2 As a young man, Robert Zimmerman changed his name to 'Bob Dylan'.

3 Nathan Salmon (1991) makes this point. Despite its clear truth, philosophers persist in calling Frege's puzzle 'Frege's puzzle about identity'. It is not a puzzle about identity.

4 I hope that you, dear reader, do not mistakenly think that the best country for buying baguettes is somewhere other than France.

5 Only clear*er* and not perfectly clear because we still would need to settle

on a theory of meaning for definite descriptions that would explain how *their* meanings go beyond *their* referents. This, however, seems on its face to be a far easier task. Different but coreferential definite descriptions generally seem quite obviously to differ in their semantic contribution. See the text box in section 4.3.1 for a brief introduction to Russell's Theory of Definite Descriptions.

6 Russell's reasons appear to have been more epistemological than semantic. He held that in order to genuinely name something, one had to bear a fairly intimate epistemological relation to that thing, a relation that Russell called 'acquaintance'. Things to which one is not acquainted can only be described, not named. Russell further held that the only items with which one is in the special relation of acquaintance are oneself and one's 'sense data', i.e. the mental effects of perception and sensation. Since most of the things labelled by proper names are not oneself or one's sense data, most proper names are not, according to Russell, really names. They are definite descriptions in disguise.

7 This is an instance of a more general principle connecting *meaning* to *truth*. The general principle is often put by saying that the truth-value of a sentence is a function of the meaning of the sentence and 'the way the world is'. One consequence of this principle is that sentences that differ in truth-value cannot mean the same thing. Hence, a good way of testing a semantic theory's consequences is seeing whether sentences that it claims to mean the same thing differ (or, better, *could* differ) in truth-value. This kind of test will crop up again and again in the main text.

8 There is, at least, *a* sense in which (7*) is contradictory. There are other readings of (7*) according to which it is not. For example if we interpret (7) as saying (roughly) that the famous folk-rock singer with a gravelly voice is such that, possibly, he is not famous, (7*) will strike us as non-contradictory (and true). The important point is that (7*) *can* be taken as a contradiction, can be taken to imply that there could be a non-famous but famous folk-rock singer with a gravelly voice. There seems to be *no* sense in which (7) is contradictory, however, and this suffices to show that (7) and (7*) are not equivalent.

9 More carefully, there is *a* reading of (8*) according to which it is true. As was the case with (7*), (8*) has multiple readings (see note 8, above), and according to some of these (8*) is not true. The important point is that (8*) can be taken as expressing the true proposition that it is a necessary truth that anything which counts as the famous folk-rock singer with a gravelly voice also counts as famous. On the other hand, there seems to be *no* sense in which (8) can be taken to express a truth. Hence, (8) and (8*) cannot mean the same thing.

10 Sentences are only derivatively *a posteriori* or *a priori* depending on whether the propositions they express are *a posteriori* or *a priori*.

11 In other words, 'It is *a priori* that the last great philosopher of antiquity was a philosopher' is true, but 'It is *a priori* that Aristotle was a philosopher' is false.

12 Some philosophers and logicians believe that there are sentences that are *neither* true nor false. Indeed, some philosophers believe that sentences

containing definite descriptions that lack referents – like (10*) – are paradigmatically neither true nor false.

13 This is not Searle's actual view. Searle denies that the cluster of descriptions associated with a name give its meaning. Instead, the cluster only determines the referent of the name. In other words, Searle's official view is really a view on the reference question for names, not the meaning question. Nonetheless, many have suggested that a descriptivism based on Searle's theory of reference for names can better handle Kripke's anti-descriptivist arguments.

14 Are we, for example, meant to take the meaning of a name as given by a *disjunction* of descriptions? And under what conditions, exactly, can the members of the cluster of meaning-giving descriptions change?

15 Though it was not mentioned earlier, this is a problem for the cluster-theory taken as a theory of meaning just as much as it is for the cluster-theory taken as a theory of reference. If names are equivalent in meaning to a cluster of definite descriptions, *which* descriptions count as the members of that cluster?

5: IS NECESSITY REALLY NECESSARY?

1 The outstanding pioneer of the area was the American logician Clarence Irving Lewis whose systems of modal logic were outlined in Lewis (1918), and given wide currency through the logic text of which he was co-author (Lewis and Langford 1932). For a more up-to-date introduction to modal logic see Sainsbury (2001, Chap.5), or Girle (2003). Melia (2003) gives a readable, and relatively informal, overview of the topics discussed in the present chapter. The definitive – though difficult – modern text on modal logic itself is Hughes and Cresswell (1968), updated as Hughes and Cresswell (1996). For an amusing example – only slightly technical – of the use of possible worlds as an analytical device, see Lewis (1973, Chap.1.2).

2 Quine put his sceptical views forward in some of the essays published in the collection *From a Logical Point of View*, and these are discussed in Linsky (1971). For a recent discussion of Quine's scepticism see Melia (2003, Chap.3).

3 (Smith 2003, p.44).

4 This is actually a modification of what Quine says about logical truth (see for example 'Truth By Convention' in Quine (1976)), extended so as to apply to arguments.

5 See (Melia 2003, Chap.1) for an objection along similar lines to the model-theoretic definition of validity.

6 Quine's intermediate, second grade of modal involvement takes necessity and possibility as operators on sentences and clauses, just like negation. For details see 'Three Grades of Modal Involvement', in Quine (1976) and the discussion in several papers in Linsky (1971). Melia (2003, Chap.3) is a relatively untechnical introduction to the problems raised by Quine for modal logics.

7 The reason for this is simple. Quotation blocks substitution of equivalent sentences, or co-referring terms, for each other. For example, Claudius was emperor of Rome at the time he landed in Britain in 43 CE. So, from

Claudius landed in Britain

it follows that

The emperor of Rome landed in Britain.

This is a case where one term has been substituted for another one when both terms refer to the same person. But now consider:

Grace told Bert: 'Claudius landed in Britain in 43 CE.'

It certainly does not follow from this that Grace told Bert 'The emperor of Rome landed in Britain in 43 CE'. Just as quotation prevents substitution of co-referring terms in this case, so it will also block substitution in cases like

'Nine is greater than seven' is a necessary truth.

As long as we are limited to Quine's first grade of modal involvement, it will be impossible to derive from this statement anything like

'The number of planets is greater than seven' is a necessary truth.

8 The *de re/de dicto* distinction is often defined in terms of *scope*. Recall that the scope of a negation operator is the shortest formula or sentence following the operator. Differences in scope make for significant differences in meaning, since, for example, '$\sim(p \supset q)$' has '$p \supset \sim q$' as a logical consequence, but not vice versa. Scope differences for the necessity and possibility operators are likewise significant. In the *de re* formula in the text, the scope of the '$\Box$' contains a free occurrence of the variable 'x' – one that is subsequently bound by the initial '$(\exists x)$' quantifier. Some authorities use scope to define the notion of *de re* – see Hughes and Cresswell (1968, p.184). Combining negation and modality provides fun examples. Here's one: from the truth that it's not necessarily the case that the shortest spy is a woman, it would be wrong to infer that the shortest spy is necessarily not a woman.

9 For a more detailed discussion of *de re* and *de dicto* along with reflections on Quine's scepticism, see Melia (2003, Chap.3).

10 See Kneale and Kneale (1984, p.119).

11 Hugh Rice discusses the Aristotelian and other proposed solutions to the fatalist challenge in Rice (2002). As he points out, Aristotle's rejection of the principle of bivalence is only one reading of what he argues in *Categories* and in *De Interpretatione*. (*Stanford Encyclopedia of Philosophy* article, 'Fatalism', http://plato.stanford.edu./entries/fatalism/#2)

12 Notice that this view is compatible with the idea that when tomorrow comes, it will turn out that one of them will have spoken the truth: suppose I do drink coffee, then Laurence's proposition was not true

when he uttered it (for at that time it was neither true nor false) but became true when the first sip passed my lips.

13 Suppose there will be a sea battle tomorrow. Then it is true today that there will be a sea battle tomorrow. Now suppose the present is unchangeable. What is true now is necessarily so and cannot be changed. So it is necessary that the sea battle occurs tomorrow (Aristotle, *De Interpretatione*, Chap.9).

14 See Priest (2000, Chap.6) for the suggestion that Aristotle's argument in *De Interpretatione* falls prey to this fallacy. Rice, however, gives a more subtle account of Aristotle's thought (Rice 2002). Indeed, although Aristotle may be read as rejecting the principle of bivalence, he combines that rejection with a commitment to the law of excluded middle, namely that any proposition of the form 'A v ~A' is necessarily true. Aristotle, according to Rice, holds that while it is neither true nor false yesterday that there will be a sea battle tomorrow, the claim that either there will, or will not, be a sea-battle tomorrow is not only true but necessarily so. As Aristotle concisely puts it: 'Everything necessarily is or is not, and will be or will not be; but one cannot divide and say that one or the other is necessary.'

15 For some interesting speculations see the essays in Le Poidevin and MacBeath (1993).

16 Richard Gaskin suggests that it was the medieval logician, Duns Scotus, who first tried to wriggle out of the challenge of fatalism by invoking the logical possibility that things might be other than they in fact are. Gaskin argues that this manoeuvre offers little real comfort when necessity and possibility are thought of in terms of inevitability and changeability respectively (Gaskin 1995, pp.93–4).

17 For example Rod Girle uses examples from the television series *Sliders* (Girle 2003, Introduction), Raymond Bradley and Norman Swartz begin their first chapter with the tale of Lazarus Long from Robert Heinlein's novel *Time Enough For Love* (Bradley and Swartz 1979) and Stephen Read uses Isaac Asimov's novel *The Gods Themselves* (Read 1995, Chap.4).

18 You might wonder why we can't also include impossible worlds in the range of possibilities. This is a tricky question to which there is not a short answer. In fact there are logicians who accept the *dialethic* view that some contradictions are true and who are prepared to accept that some possible worlds are impossible. Proper discussion of this question lies beyond the scope of the present book.

19 Incidentally, by playing games with different kinds of accessibility relation, we can define different systems of modal logic. Suppose that if world *w* has access to world *k* and *k* in turn has access to world *i*, then *w* has access to *i*. In this case, the accessibility relation is transitive. By making accessibility reflexive (each world has access to itself) and symmetric (if *w* has access to *i*, then *i* has access to *w*), we define the system S_5, one of the simplest, but also least plausible, of the modal logics. See Sainsbury (2001), and Girle (2003) for an introduction to a number of different systems of modal logic.

20 Jonathan Lowe objects to this argument on the grounds that the property that should be attributed to Bob Dylan is the one of being necessarily self-identical (see Lowe 2002, pp.84–9). '$\Box(\forall x)(x=x)$' states, according to him, the claim that each thing is of necessity identical to itself. Robert Zimmerman has that property too (of being necessarily identical to himself), but nothing follows from these suppositions about whether the identity of Bob Dylan with Robert Zimmerman is necessary or not. The argument in the text goes through successfully only if the property ascribed to Bob Dylan is the one of being (of necessity) identical to Bob Dylan.

21 A very helpful discussion of different senses of *a priori* is given in Kitcher (1990, pp.15–17). She shows how Immanuel Kant slides from one sense to another without apparently noticing.

22 The content and structure of this chapter owe much to suggestions from Richard Borthwick and Y. S. Lo. Y. S. Lo's suggestions also helped shape the arguments in Chapters 2 and 6.

6: ENTAILMENT

1 As anticipated earlier, the symbol '$\models$' is now being used to represent semantic consequence, rather than deducibility in terms of rules of proof.

2 The reasoning is easy so long as you recall that that 'not necessarily' is equivalent to 'possibly not'. The first premise holds at a world – presumably the world in which Dick is located. Let's pretend it's the actual world. It says that '$p \supset c$' is true at every world accessible from the actual world *w*, while the conclusion insists that either '$p \supset h$' is true at all such worlds, or '$b \supset c$' is true at them all. So let's look for a counterexample. Take the first clause of the conclusion, and think about denying it. That is, suppose that '$\sim\Box(p \supset h)$' is true at world *w*, which is to say that '$\Diamond\sim(p \supset h)$' is true at *w*. So then it will be at some world accessible from *w* that '$\sim(p \supset h)$' is true. Suppose this is world *w**. Now '$p \supset c$' is true at *w** (for it is true at all worlds accessible from *w*), and that is not incompatible with the truth of '$\sim(p \supset h)$' at *w**. After all, if it is possible at this world for it to be false that if Bert is in Prague, then he's in Hungary, then there is a world where that very falsehood is realized. So what? That can still be a world where if he is in Prague, he is in the Czech Republic. What about the second premise (that '$(b \supset h)$' is necessarily true). From it we can deduce that '$(b \supset h)$' is true at *w**. But this is not in the least inconsistent with it being true at *w** that '$\sim(p \supset h)$'. So the truth of the premises is compatible with the falsehood of the first disjunct of the conclusion.

The second disjunct of the conclusion gets the same treatment. Suppose that clause is false. In other words, suppose that it's not necessarily true that if Bert is in Budapest then he's in the Czech Republic. So it's possibly false that if he is in Budapest then he's in the Czech Republic. Let's go to that world where the possibility is realized. That won't, however, be world *w**. What is possible at a given world is realized at some alternative world. But not all possibilities need be realized in the same world. It is possible that I will see Joe on Tuesday, and also possible that I don't see him on that day. But there is no world where both of these possibilities are realized! So we can't rely on the idea that '~(b ⊃ c)' holds at world w^*. Instead, we need to consider a third world, w^{**}, where it is true that '~(b ⊃ c)'. But at w^*, it will be true both that 'p ⊃ c' and 'b ⊃ h' (for they are true at all worlds accessible from w). Their truth at w^{**} is perfectly consistent with it being true that '~(b ⊃ c)' at w^{**}. So denying the first part of the conclusion leads to no inconsistency, and denying the second part of the conclusion leads to no inconsistency either. So the whole conclusion can be denied while the premises are true. So the argument is invalid.

3 A relation is transitive if, given that it holds between one thing and a second thing, and also between the second thing and a third thing, then it holds between the first and the third. That is, *R* is transitive when: (*a* has *R* to *b* & *b* has *R* to *c*) ⊃ *a* has *R* to *c*.

4 This fact has not deterred heroic philosophers from grimly defending the standard logical translation of conditionals by '⊃' by expending enormous ingenuity in explaining away everyday uses that fail to fit the truth-functional paradigm. One way of doing this is to count certain conditional propositions – say those with obviously false antecedents – as true, but not appropriately assertible. They may not be assertible for various reasons. For example, it may be that by asserting them the speaker implies that he or she is less well-informed than he or she actually is (see Walker (1975) for an introduction to H. P. Grice's theory of conversational implicature) and see also Grice (1991). Grice's account of implicature seems to explain why some conditionals are not suitable for asserting, and it has the merit of having wide applications beyond the issue of conditionals. The extent to which it protects and preserves the standard truth-functional account of conditionals is debatable (see Read (1995, Chap.3)).

5 (Adams 1970).

6 English, unlike Latin or French, has no subjunctive construction, and a smooth account of English grammar need only postulate two tenses – present and past (Huddlestone 1984). What are often called 'subjunctive' conditionals are those where the 'modal' (in the grammarian's sense) component of the auxiliary is given past tense. For example, 'If he can open the door . . .' and 'if he could open the door . . .' differ simply in that the modal 'can' has present tense in the former case, and past tense in the latter.

7 One of the best-known treatments of these problems using ideas drawn from modal logic is Lewis (1973) where a counterfactual analysis of causal conditionals is developed.

8 This is the basic line taken in Lewis (1973). A later, and more elaborated, account of causation and conditionals is given in Lewis (2001). For an account of causal reasoning that is not sympathetic to the Lewis approach, see the appendix to Pearl (2000).

9 Jonathan Bennett, who claims that he 'holds his nose' when using the

label 'subjunctive' (see Bennett 2003, p.12), seems to agree that 'would' and 'were' conditionals are generally accepted and asserted by those who disbelieve the antecedent. He argues that 'subjunctive' conditionals are 'zero-tolerant', that is, they are perfectly well usable in contexts where speaker and audience are certain that the antecedents are false. If we overlook the fact that 'subjunctive' conditionals are often used where there is simply uncertainty about the antecedent's truth value, then there is a risk of focusing on the 'zero tolerance' aspect to the neglect of others. This partial focus may explain the one-sided account Bennett gives of whether – and in what circumstances – we can apply *modus ponens* to a 'counterfactual' conditional (see Bennett 2003, §88).

10 I owe many of my ideas about conditionals to conversations many years ago with my then Stirling colleague Ian Wilson. See Wilson (1979) for a brief introduction to his views.

11 '$\sim q \supset \sim p$' is the contrapositive of '$p \supset q$'.

12 The discussion by Sanford and Wertheimer is in terms of necessary and sufficient conditions. However, these are just variant terms in which to speak of the puzzles of conditionals, inference and entailment. There is a standard account – often found in logic texts – which runs as follows (see, for example, Blumberg 1976). When the conditional '$p \supset q$' is true the truth of the consequent, 'q', is *necessary* for the truth of the antecedent, 'p', and the truth of the antecedent is in turn *sufficient* for the truth of the consequent. The biconditional '$p \equiv q$', according to this account, states that p and q are jointly necessary and sufficient for each other.

13 It can be helpful to ditch the idea that logical methods explain or justify our grasp of consequence, entailment and validity. Instead, logic provides the tools for testing and exploring entailment and validity. Think of it like this. If (i) premises A and B entail conclusion C (i.e. C follows logically from A and B), then (ii) if A and B are both true in a situation, C is true in that situation as well. Suppose the conditional linking (i) and (ii) were itself explanatory. It would be bizarre to try to make the explanation run the other way – from (ii) to (i) – as if learning about truth tables, interpretations and possible worlds would give explanations of the notions of *entailment* and *following from*. Since explanations are usually unidirectional, then if our prior grasp of entailment explains the truth-conditional account of validity, the latter will be unlikely also to explain the former. If we drop the idea that truth tables, etc. *explain* validity and entailment, then we can see logic as a highly effective, but partial, systematization of capacities and understanding we already have, including a prior grasp of consequence and entailment. This approach to thinking about logic, influenced by Wittgenstein's later work, was advocated in some classic studies, such as Strawson (1952). This is the view which underlies my discussion of the new 'paradox' of entailment which is proposed at the end of the present chapter.

14 In feedback systems cause and effect are interlinked: the faster the engine runs, the more the governor reduces fuel flow, leading to the

engine running more slowly, leading to the governor increasing fuel flow, the engine running faster, and so on.

15 For relevant logicians, the paradoxes are puzzling because there is no element in the premise or premises that is relevant to the conclusion. A minimal condition of relevance might seem to be that the conclusion contains at least one clause that is also present in one of the argument's premises, or that there be some common content between premises and conclusion. Stephen Read points out that this condition is unlikely to work, and suggests an alternative way of ensuring relevance (1995, Chap.2). There are, unfortunately, no easy, non-technical introductions to relevant (or relevance) logics. Standard works are Anderson and Belnap (1975), and Anderson, Belnap, and Dunn (1992). Just as in the case of Lewis's work on strict implication, the relevance logicians' attempt to circumvent the paradoxes of material implication were generally unsuccessful. For example, any statement can be inferred from a contradiction in most systems of relevance logic (unless the semantics for the logic in question allow the inclusion of inconsistent worlds).

16 In moral theory, a distinction is often made between two kinds of reasons – those that explain an action, and those that justify it. Although it looks as if 'reason why' conditionals might fulfil both roles, this topic is too large to explore just now, and the present author has no idea where the exploration of it might lead.

17 More details on these ways of thinking about conditionals, and the significance of them for the understanding of necessary and sufficient conditions, can be found in Brennan (2003).

18 This result is in keeping with many things suggested by Wittgenstein and by philosophers influenced by his approach to questions of language. For instance, in his classic essay on reference, P. F. Strawson wrote that 'neither Aristotelian nor Russellian rules [he is referring to two of the giants of logical theory] give the exact logic of any expression in ordinary language, for ordinary language has no exact logic' (Strawson 1950).

19 A review of these is given in Beaver (1997), but this is only accessible to those with knowledge of formal logic.

7: CRITIQUES OF LOGIC

1 See Geach (1972, pp.238–49), Martinich (1978), and the more recent discussion in Rea (2003).

2 A (probably inaccurate) story has it that the famous philosopher and logician Bertrand Russell was once asked to prove that anything can follow from a contradiction. He was asked the question, 'You mean from the statement $2+2=5$ it follows that you are the Pope? Can you prove it?' Russell came up with this proof right on the spot:

1. Suppose $2+2=5$.
2. Subtracting 2 from both sides we get $2=3$.

3. Transposing, we have 3 = 2.
4. Subtracting 1 from both sides, we get 2 = 1.

'Now', Russell continues, 'the Pope and I are two. Since two equals one, then the Pope and I are one. Hence I am the Pope.'

3 (Kant 1764/1960, Section 3).

4 A syllogism is a certain type of argument about classes of objects. Here is an example: 'All whales are mammals. All mammals are warm-blooded. Therefore, all whales are warm-blooded.' See pages 34–5.

5 See Falmagne and Hass (2002, p.82). Similar arguments can also be found in Hass's chapter in Freeland (1998).

6 (Plumwood 2002a, p. 40, footnote 16). Presumably it should read '(p&((p&q)→r)))→(q→r)'. '→' is equivalent to hook operator '⊃' discussed in Chapter 2.

7 So 'p' abbreviates or stands for the relevant laws of physics and chemistry or other standing conditions, 'q' stands for 'you smoke' and 'r' for 'there will be an explosion'.

8 This is the practice of female genital cutting often performed without anaesthetic on young girls or female babies.

9 Such as systems R and E, and any system stronger than the very weak system B. See Mares (2004, p. 201).

10 See for example Barkow, Cosmides and Tooby (1992).

REFERENCES

Ackrill, J. L. (1963). *Aristotle's Categories and De Interpretatione*. Oxford: Clarendon Press.

Adams, Ernest (1970). 'Subjunctive and Indicative Conditionals.' *Foundations of Language*, 6, 89–94.

Akiba, Ken (2004). Review of Wolfgang Künne's *Conceptions of Truth*. *Australasian Journal of Philosophy*, 82, 525–7.

Anderson, A. R. and Belnap, N. D. Jr (1975). *Entailment: The Logic of Relevance and Necessity*. Princeton, NJ: Princeton University Press.

Anderson, A. R., Belnap, N. D. Jr and Dunn, J. M. (1992). *Entailment*, Volume II. Princeton, NJ: Princeton University Press.

Antony, Louise M. and Witt, Charlotte (eds). (1993) (2002). *A Mind of One's Own: Feminist Essays on Reason and Objectivity* (2nd ed.). Boulder, CO: Westview Press.

Aristotle (4th century BCE). *Categories*. Translated in Ackrill (1963).

Austin, J. L. (1950). 'Truth.' *Aristotelian Society* suppl. vol. 24, 111–29 (repr. in Blackburn and Simmons (1999)).

Austin, J. L. (1961). 'Unfair to Facts'. In *Philosophical Papers*, pp.102–22. Oxford: Clarendon Press (repr. in Blackburn and Simmons (1999)).

Austin, J. L. (1962). *How to Do Things with Words*. Oxford: Oxford University Press.

Ayer, Alfred Jules (1936). *Language Truth and Logic* (new ed. 1971). Harmondsworth: Penguin.

Baghramian, Maria (2004). *Relativism*. London: Routledge.

Barkow, J., Cosmides, L. and Tooby, J. (eds) (1992). *The Adapted Mind*. New York: Oxford University Press.

Beall, J. C. (ed.) (2004). *Liars and Heaps: New Essays on Paradox*. Oxford: Oxford University Press.

Beaver, D. (1997). 'Presupposition'. In van Benthem, J. and ter Meulen, A. *Handbook of Logic and Language*. Cambridge, MA: MIT Press.

Bennett, Jonathan (2003). *A Philosophical Guide to Conditionals*. Oxford: Clarendon Press.

Blackburn, Simon (2004). 'Relativism and the Abolition of the Other'. *International Journal of Philosophical Studies*, 19, 243–58.

Blackburn, Simon and Simmons, Keith (eds) (1999). *Truth*. Oxford: Oxford University Press.

Blumberg, A. E. (1976). *Logic: A First Course*. New York: Alfred E. Knopf.

Bradley, R. and Swartz, N. (1979). *Possible Worlds – An Introduction to Logic and Its Philosophy*. Oxford: Basil Blackwell.

Brady, Ross (ed.) (2003). *Relevant Logics and Their Rivals* Vol. 2. *A Continuation of the Work of Richard Sylvan, Robert Meyer, Val Plumwood and Ross Brady*. Aldershot: Ashgate.

Brandom, R. (1994). *Making It Explicit*. Cambridge, MA: Harvard University Press.

Brennan, Andrew (2003). 'Necessary and Sufficient Conditions'. In Zalta, E. (ed.). *Stanford Encyclopedia of Philosophy*. Retrieved from http://plato.stanford.edu/entries/necessary-sufficient/

Candlish, Stewart (1999). 'A Prolegomenon to an Identity Theory of Truth'. *Philosophy*, 74, 190–220.

Candlish, Stewart (2005). 'Truth – Identity Theory of'. In *Routledge Encyclopaedia of Philosophy On-line*. Retrieved from http://www.rep.routledge.com

Candlish, S. and Damnjanovic, N. (2006). 'A Brief History of Truth'. In Dale, Jacquette (ed.). *Philosophy of Logic*, vol. 11 of Dov Gabbay, Paul Thagard and John Woods (eds). *Handbook of the Philosophy of Science*. Amsterdam: North-Holland.

Carnap, Rudolph (1937). *The Logical Syntax of Language*. New York: Harcourt Brace.

Carroll, Lewis (1895). 'What the Tortoise Said to Achilles'. *Mind*, 4, 278–80. (Available online at http://www.ditext.com/carroll/tortoise.html or http://www.lewiscarroll.org/achilles.html)

Carruthers, Peter (2004). 'Practical Reasoning in a Modular Mind'. *Mind and Language*, 19, 259–78.

Casscells, W., Schoenberger, A., and Graboys, T. B. (1978). 'Interpretation by Physicians of Clinical Laboratory Results'. *New England Journal of Medicine*, 299, 99–1001.

Chemla, Karine (1997). 'What Is at Stake in Mathematical Proofs from Third-century China?' *Science in Context*, 10, 227–51.

Chemla, Karine (2000). 'Les Problèmes comme champ d'interprétation des algorithmes dans *Les neuf chapîtres sur les procédures mathématiques* et leurs commentaires. De la résolution des systèmes d'équations linéaires'. *Oriens-Occidens*, 3, 189–234.

Cherniak, Christopher (1986). *Minimal Rationality*. Cambridge, MA: MIT Press.

Church, Alonzo (1956). *Introduction to Mathematical Logic*. Princeton, NJ: Princeton University Press.

Clack, Beverley (ed.) (1999). *Misogyny in the Western Philosophical Tradition*. London: Macmillan.

Collins, J., Hall, E., and Paul, L. (2001). *Causation and Counterfactuals*. Cambridge, MA: MIT Press.

Cope-Kasten, Vance (1989). 'A Portrait of Dominating Rationality'. *Newsletters on Computer Use, Feminism, Law, Medicine, Teaching*

(American Philosophical Association), 88(2), 29–34.

Copi, Irving and Cohen, Carl (1998). *Introduction to Logic* (10th ed.). Saddle River, NJ: Prentice-Hall.

Cosmides, Leda and Tooby, John (1996). 'Are Humans Good Intuitive Statisticians after All? Rethinking some Conclusions from the Literature on Judgment under Uncertainty'. *Cognition*, 58, 1–73.

Cresswell, Max (2001). 'Modal Logic'. In Goble, Lou (2001) (ed.). *The Blackwell Guide to Philosophical Logic*. Oxford: Blackwell.

Davidson, Donald (1974). 'On the Very Idea of a Conceptual Scheme'. In *Inquiries into Truth and Interpretation* (2001, 2nd ed.), pp.183–98. Oxford: Oxford University Press.

Davidson, Donald (1996). 'The Folly of Trying to Define Truth'. *Journal of Philosophy*, 93, 263–78.

Davidson, Donald (2004). *Problems of Rationality*. Oxford: Oxford University Press.

Devitt, M. (1981). *Designation*. New York: Columbia University Press.

Dodd, Julian (2000). *An Identity Theory of Truth*. New York: St Martin's Press.

Dodd, Julian (2002). 'Recent Work on Truth'. *Philosophical Books*, 43, 279–91.

Dougherty, M. V. (2004). 'Aristotle's Four Truth Values'. *British Journal for the History of Philosophy*, 12, 585–609.

Dudman, Vic (1991) 'Interpretations of "if" sentences'. In Jackson (ed.) (1991).

Dummett, Michael (1981). *Frege: Philosophy of Language* (2nd ed.). London: Duckworth.

Ellis, Brian (1990). *Truth and Objectivity*. Oxford: Blackwell.

Engel, Pascal (1991). *The Norm of Truth: An Introduction to the Philosophy of Logic*. Toronto: University of Toronto Press.

Engel, Pascal (2002). *Truth*. Chesham: Acumen.

Etchemendy, J. (1990). *The Concept of Logical Consequence*. Cambridge, MA: Harvard University Press.

Evans, G. (1973). 'The Causal Theory of Names'. *Proceedings of the Aristotelian Society*, suppl. vol. 47, 187–208.

Evans, G. (1982). *The Varieties of Reference*. Oxford: Oxford University Press.

Falmagne, R. Joffe and Hass, M. (eds) (2002). *Representing Reason: Feminist Theory and Formal Logic*. Lanham, MD: Rowman & Littlefield.

Feyerabend, Paul (1963). 'How to Be a Good Empiricist – a Plea for Tolerance in Matters Epistemological'. In Nidditch, P. H. (ed.) (1968). *The Philosophy of Science*, pp. 12–39. Oxford: Oxford University Press.

Freeland, Cynthia (ed.) (1998). *Feminist Interpretations of Aristotle*. Pennsylvania: Pennsylvania State University Press.

Frege, Gottlob (1879). *Begriffschrift*. Trans. as *Concept Script* by S. Bauer-Mengelberg in J. van Heijenoort (ed.) (1967). *From Frege to Gödel: A Source Book in Mathematical Logic, 1879–1931*. Cambridge, MA: Harvard University Press.

Frege, Gottlob (1892). 'On Sense and Reference'. In Geach, P. and Black,

M. (eds) (1960). *Translations from the Philosophical Writings of Gottlob Frege*. Oxford: Blackwell.

Frege, Gottlob (1918). 'The Thought: A Logical Inquiry' (repr. in Blackburn and Simmons (1999), pp.85–105).

Frege, Gottlob (1964). *The Basic Laws of Arithmetic* (trans. Furth, Montgomery). Berkeley: University of California Press. Originally published as *Grundgesetze der Arithmetik, begriffschrifftlich abgeleite*. Vol. 1 (1893); Vol. 2 (1903). Jena: Hermann Pohle.

Garfield, J. L. and Priest, S. (2003). 'Nagarjuna and the Limits of Thought'. *Philosophy East and West*, 53(1), 1–21.

Gaskin, Richard (1995). *The Sea Battle and the Master Argument: Aristotle and Diodorus Cronus on the Metaphysics of the Future*. Berlin: Walter de Gruyter.

Geach, Peter (1972). *Logic Matters*. Oxford: Basil Blackwell.

Girle, R. (2003). *Possible Worlds*. Chesham: Acumen.

Goldstein, L. (2002). 'A Wittgensteinian (not Gricean) Approach to Sustitutivity Puzzles'. In Haller, R. and Puhl, K. (eds) (2002). *Wittgenstein and the Future of Philosophy*, pp.99–111. Vienna: Holder-Pichler-Tempsky.

Grattan-Guinness, Ivor and Bornet, Gérard (eds) (1997). *George Boole: Selected Manuscripts on Logic and its Philosophy*. Basel: Birkhäuser Verlag.

Greenspan, Stanley and Shanker, Stuart (2004). *The First Idea: How Symbols, Language, and Intelligence Evolved from Our Primate Ancestors to Modern Humans*. Cambridge, MA: Da Capo Press.

Grice, H. P. (1991). 'Logic and Conversation'. In Jackson (ed.) (1991).

Grover, Dorothy (1992). *A Prosentential Theory of Truth*. Princeton, NJ: Princeton University Press.

Grover, Dorothy, Camp, Joseph and Belnap, Nuel (1975). 'A Prosentential Theory of Truth'. *Philosophical Studies*, 35, 289–97 (reprinted in Grover (1992).

Hacking, Ian (1979). 'What is Logic?' *The Journal of Philosophy*, 76, 285–319 (repr. in Hughes (1993), pp.225–58).

Harman, Gilbert (1986a). *Change in View: Principles of Reasoning*. Cambridge, MA: Bradford Books.

Harman, Gilbert (1986b). 'The Meaning of Logical Constants'. In LePore (ed.) (1986). *Truth and Interpretation*, pp.125–34. Oxford: Blackwell.

Hartshorne, Charles and Weiss, Paul (eds) (1960). *Collected Papers of Charles Sanders Peirce*, Vol.V. Cambridge, MA: The Belknap Press of Harvard University Press.

Hass, Marjorie (1990). 'Feminist Readings of Aristotelian Logic'. In Freeland (1998), pp.19–40.

Hass, Marjorie (2002). 'Fluid Thinking: Irigaray's Critique of Formal Logic'. In Falmagne and Hass (2002), pp.71–88.

Hempel, Carl G. (1935). 'On the Logical Positivist Theory of Truth'. *Analysis*, 2, 49–59.

Hilbert, D. and Ackermann, W. (1950). *Principles of Mathematical Logic*. New York: Chelsea Publishing Company.

Hofstadter, Douglas (1979). *Gödel, Escher, Bach: an Eternal Golden Braid*. New York, Basic Books.

Horwich, Paul (1998). *Truth* (2nd ed.). Oxford: Clarendon Press.

Huddlestone, R. (1984). *Introduction to the Grammar of English*. Cambridge: Cambridge University Press.

Hughes, G. E. and Cresswell, M. (1968). *An Introduction to Modal Logic*. London: Methuen.

Hughes, G. E. and Cresswell, M. (1996). *A New Introduction to Modal Logic*. London: Routledge.

Hughes, R. I. G. (ed.) (1993). *A Philosophical Companion to First-Order Logic*. Indianapolis: Hackett.

Hume, David (1748/1999). *Enquiry concerning Human Understanding*, ed. Beauchamp, T. Oxford: Oxford University Press.

Irigaray, Luce (2002). *To Speak is Never Neutral* (trans. Gail Schwab). New York: Continuum.

Jackson, Frank (ed.) (1991). *Conditionals*. Oxford: Oxford University Press.

Jackson, Frank (1998). *From Metaphysics to Ethics: A Defence of Conceptual Analysis.* New York: Oxford University Press.

James, William (1907). 'Pragmatism's Conception of Truth' (repr. in Lynch (2001), pp. 211–28 and in Schmitt (2004), pp. 59–73. Page references to the latter.)

Joachim, Harold, H. (1906). *The Nature of Truth.* Oxford: Clarendon Press.

Jones, Karen (2004). 'Gender and Rationality'. In Mele and Rawling (2004). *The Oxford Handbook of Rationality*. Oxford: Oxford University Press.

Joyce, James M. (2004). 'Bayesianism'. In Mele, Alfred and Rawling, Piers (eds). *The Oxford Handbook of Rationality*, pp. 132–55. Oxford: Oxford University Press.

Kahneman, D., Slovic, P. and Tversky, A. (1982). *Judgement under Uncertainty: Heuristics and Biases*. Cambridge: Cambridge University Press.

Kant, I. (1764/1960). *Observations on the Feelings of the Beautiful and Sublime* (trans. J. T. Goldthwait), section 3. Berkeley, CA: University of California Press.

Kirkham, Richard (1992). *Theories of Truth*. Cambridge, MA: MIT Press.

Kirwan, Christopher (trans.) (1993). Aristotle. *Metaphysics: Books Gamma, Delta and Epsilon* (2nd ed.). Oxford: Clarendon Press.

Kitcher, Patricia (1990). *Kant's Transcendental Psychology*. Oxford: Oxford University Press.

Kneale, William and Kneale, Martha (1962/1984). *The Development of Logic*. Oxford: Oxford University Press.

Koehler, J. J. (1996). 'The Base Rate Fallacy Reconsidered: Descriptive, Normative, and Methodological Challenges'. *Behavioral and Brain Sciences*, 19, 1–53.

Kölbel, Max (2002). *Truth without Objectivity*. London: Routledge.

Kripke, S. (1972/1980). *Naming and Necessity*. Cambridge, MA: Harvard University Press.

Kripke, Saul (1976). 'Is there a Problem about Substitutional Quantification?' In Evans and McDowell (eds) (1976). *Truth and Meaning*. Oxford: Oxford University Press.

Künne, Wolfgang (2004). *Conceptions of Truth*. Oxford: Clarendon Press.

Le Poidevin, R. and MacBeath, A. M. (eds) (1993). *The Philosophy of Time*. Oxford: Oxford University Press.

LePore, Ernest (2000). *Meaning and Argument: an Introduction to Logic Through Language*. Oxford: Blackwell.

Lewis, Clarence Irving (1918). *A Survey of Symbolic Logic*. Berkeley, CA: University of California Press.

Lewis, Clarence Irving and Langford, Charles H. (1932). *Symbolic Logic*. New York: The Century Company.

Lewis, David (1973). *Counterfactuals*. Oxford: Basil Blackwell.

Lewis, David K. (2001). 'Causation as Influence'. In Collins, Hall, and Paul (2001).

Linsky, Leonard (ed.) (1971). *Reference and Modality*. Oxford: Oxford University Press.

Linsky, Leonard (1977). *Names and Descriptions*. Chicago: Chicago University Press.

Lowe, E. J. (2002). *A Survey of Metaphysics*. Oxford: Oxford University Press.

Lynch, Michael (ed.) (2001). *The Nature of Truth*. Cambridge, MA: MIT Press.

Lynch, Michael (2004). *True to Life: Why Truth Matters*. Cambridge, MA: MIT Press.

McCawley, James (1993). *Everything that Linguists have Always Wanted to Know about Logic** But were Ashamed to Ask*. Chicago: Chicago University Press.

McGee, Vann (1985). 'A Counterexample to Modus Ponens'. *Journal of Philosophy*, 82, 462–71.

MacIntyre, Alistair (1999). *Dependent Rational Animals*. London: Duckworth.

Mackie, John (1973). *Truth, Probability and Paradox*. Oxford: Clarendon Press.

McLaughlin, Brian (1990). *On the Logic of Ordinary Conditionals*. Buffalo, NY: SUNY Press.

Mares, Edwin (2004). *Relevant Logic*. Cambridge, Cambridge University Press.

Martinich, A. P. (1978). 'Identity and Trinity'. *Journal of Religion*, 58, 169–81.

Melia, Joseph (2003). *Modality*. Chesham: Acumen.

Millican, Peter (2004). 'The One Fatal Flaw in Anselm's Argument'. *Mind*, 113, 437–76.

Moore, G. E. (1959). 'Four Forms of Scepticism'. In *Philosophical Papers*, pp.193–222. London: George Allen and Unwin.

Neale, S. (1990). *Descriptions*. Cambridge, MA: MIT Press.

Neurath, Otto (1931). 'Soziologie im Physikalismus'. Trans. in Neurath (1983), pp.58–90.

Neurath, Otto (1983). *Philosophical Papers*. Dordrecht: Reidel.

Nozick, Robert (1993). *The Nature of Rationality*. Princeton, NJ: Princeton University Press.

Nussbaum, Martha (1998). 'Aristotle, Feminism, and Needs for Functioning'. In Freeland (1998), pp.248–59.
Nye, Andrea (1990). *Words of Power: A Feminist Reading of the History of Logic*. London: Routledge.
O'Grady, Paul (2002). *Relativism*. Chesham: Acumen.
O'Keefe, R. and Smith, P. (1997). *Vagueness: A Reader*. Cambridge, MA: MIT Press.
Over, David (1987). 'Assumptions and the Supposed Counterexamples to *Modus Ponens*'. *Analysis*, 47, 143.
Pearl, Judea (2000). *Causality: Models, Reasoning, and Inference*. Cambridge: Cambridge University Press.
Peirce, Charles Sanders (1878). 'How to Make our Ideas Clear'. In Hartshorne and Weiss (1960), pp.248–71 (repr. in Schmitt (2004), pp.41–58).
Peirce, Charles Sanders (1905). 'What Pragmatism Is'. In Hartshorne and Weiss (1960), pp.272–92.
Peters, T. J. and Waterman, R. H. (1988). *In Search of Excellence* (reissue ed.). New York: Warner Books.
Pinto, Silvio (2001). 'The Justification of Deduction'. *Sorites*, 13, 33–47. Available online at http://www.sorites.org/Issue_13/pinto.htm
Pirie, Madsen (2006). *How to Win Every Argument: The Use and Abuse of Logic*. London: Continuum.
Plumwood, Val (1993). *Feminism and the Mastery of Nature*. London: Routledge.
Plumwood, Val (2002a). 'The Politics of Reason: Towards a Feminist Logic'. In Falmagne and Hass (2002), pp.11–44.
Plumwood, Val (2002b). 'Feminism and the Logic of Alterity'. In Falmagne & Hass (2002), pp.45–70.
Price, Huw (1990). 'Why "Not"?' *Mind*, 99, 221–38.
Priest, Graham (1987). *In Contradiction*. The Hague: Martinus Nijhoff.
Priest, Graham (2000). *Logic: A Very Short Introduction*. Oxford: Oxford University Press.
Prior, Arthur (1960). 'The Runabout Inference-Ticket'. *Analysis*, 21, 38–9. (repr. in Strawson (1967).
Prior, Arthur (1964). 'Conjunction and Contonktion Revisited'. *Analysis*, 24, 191–5.
Prior, Arthur (1971). *Objects of Thought*. Oxford: Clarendon Press.
Quine, W. V. (1960). *Word and Object*. Cambridge, MA: MIT Press.
Quine, W. V. (1961). *From a Logical Point of View*. Cambridge, MA: Harvard University Press.
Quine, W. V. (1976). *The Ways of Paradox, and Other Essays* (rev. ed.). Cambridge, MA: Harvard University Press.
Railton, Peter (2000). 'A Priori Rules: Wittgenstein on the Normativity of Logic'. In Boghossian, P. and Peacocke, C. (eds). *New Essays on the A Priori*, pp.170–96. Oxford: Clarendon Press.
Ramsey, Frank (1927). 'Facts and Propositions'. In Mellor, D. H. (ed.) (1990). *Philosophical Papers*, pp.34–51. Cambridge: Cambridge University Press.

Rea, Michael C. (2003). 'Relative Identity and the Doctrine of the Trinity'. *Philosophia Christi*, 5(2), 431–45.

Read, Stephen (1988). *Relevant Logic*. Oxford: Blackwell.

Read, Stephen (1995). *Thinking about Logic*. Oxford: Oxford University Press.

Read, Stephen (forthcoming). *The Truth-schema and the Liar*.

Rice, Hugh (2002). 'Fatalism'. In Zalta, E. (ed.). *Stanford Encyclopedia of Philosophy*. Online at http://plato. stanford.edu./entries/fatalism/#2

Rorty, Richard (1991). *Objectivity, Relativism and Truth*. Cambridge: Cambridge University Press.

Rorty, Richard (1995). 'Is Truth a Goal of Inquiry? Donald Davidson vs. Crispin Wright'. *Philosophical Quarterly*, 45, 281–300 (repr. in Lynch (2001), pp.259–86).

Rorty, Richard (1998). *Truth and Progress*. Cambridge: Cambridge University Press.

Rorty, Richard (2000). 'Universality and Truth'. In Brandom (ed.). *Rorty and his Critics*, Oxford: Blackwell, 1–30.

Rorty, Richard (2002). 'To the Sunlit Uplands' [Review of Bernard Williams (2002)]. *London Review of Books*, 24/21, 31 October. Available online at http://www.lrb.co.uk/v24/n21/rort01_.html

Routley, R., Meyer, R. K., Plumwood, V. and Brady, R. T. (1982). *Relevant Logics and their Rivals, Part 1: The Basic Philosophical and Semantical Theory*. Atascadero, CA: Ridgeview.

Russell, Bertrand (1905). 'On Denoting'. *Mind*, 14, 479–93.

Russell, Bertrand (1906–7). 'On the Nature of Truth'. *Proceedings of the Aristotelian Society*, 7, 28–49.

Russell, Bertrand (1917). 'Knowledge by Acquaintance and Knowledge by Description'. In Russell (1957). *Mysticism and Logic*. Garden City, NY: Doubleday.

Sainsbury, R. M. (1995). *Paradoxes* (2nd ed.). Cambridge: Cambridge University Press.

Sainsbury, R. M. (2001). *Logical Forms* (2nd ed.). Oxford: Blackwell.

Salmon, N. (1986). *Frege's Puzzle*. Cambridge, MA: MIT Press.

Salmon, N. (1989). 'Reference and Information Content: Names and Descriptions'. In Gabbay and Guenther (eds). *Handbook of Philosophical Logic* Vol. IV, pp.409–61. Dordrecht: Reidel.

Salmon, N. (1991). *Frege's Puzzle*. Altascadero, CA: Ridgeview.

Salmon, N. and Soames, S. (eds) (1988). *Propositions and Attitudes*. Oxford: Oxford University Press.

Samuels, R., Stich, S. and Faucher, L. (2004). 'Reason and Rationality'. In Niiniluoto, I., Sintonen, M. and Wolenski, J. (eds). *Handbook of Epistemology*, pp. 1–50. Dordrecht: Kluwer.

Sanford, David H. (1989). *If P, then Q: Conditionals and the Foundations of Reasoning*. London: Routledge.

Schmitt, Frederick (ed.) (2004). *Theories of Truth*. Oxford: Blackwell.

Searle, J. (1958). 'Proper Names'. *Mind*, 67, 166–73.

Searle, John (2001). *Rationality in Action*. Cambridge, MA: MIT Press.

Sher, Gila (2004). 'In Search of a Substantive Theory of Truth'. *The Journal of Philosophy*, 101, 5–36.

Simmons, Keith (1999). 'Deflationary Truth and the Liar'. *Journal of Philosophical Logic*, 28, 455–88.

Smiley, T. J. (1995). 'A Tale of Two Tortoises'. *Mind*, 104, 725–36.

Smiley, T. (1998). 'Consequence, Conceptions of'. In Craig, E. (ed.). *Routledge Encyclopedia of Philosophy*, pp.599–603. London: Routledge.

Smith, Peter (2003). *An Introduction to Formal Logic*. Cambridge: Cambridge University Press.

Soames, Scott (1999). *Understanding Truth*. Oxford: Oxford University Press.

Soames, Scott (2002). *Beyond Rigidity*. Oxford: Oxford University Press.

Stanovich, Keith (1999). *Who is Rational? Studies of Individual Differences in Reasoning*. Mahwah, New Jersey: Lawrence Erlbaum.

Stich, Stephen (1990). *The Fragmentation of Reason*. Cambridge, MA: MIT Press.

Strawson, P. F. (1949). 'Truth'. *Analysis*, 9, 83–97.

Strawson, P. F. (1950). 'On Referring'. *Mind*, 59, 320–44.

Strawson, P. F. (1952). *Introduction to Logical Theory*. London: Methuen & Co.

Strawson, Peter (ed.) (1967). *Philosophical Logic*. Oxford: Oxford University Press.

Stroll, Avrum (1994). *Moore and Wittgenstein on Certainty*. Oxford: Oxford University Press.

Sutherland, Stuart (1992). *Irrationality: The Enemy Within*. London: Constable.

Suzuki, D. T. (1986). *An Introduction to Zen Buddhism*. London: Rider and Company.

Tarski, Alfred (1933). 'The Concept of Truth in Formalised Languages'. In Tarski (1983), pp.152–278.

Tarski, Alfred (1969). 'Truth and Proof'. *Scientific American*, June, 63–77 (repr. in Hughes (1993), pp.101–25).

Tarski, Alfred (1983). *Logic, Semantics, Metamathematics* (2nd ed.). Indianapolis: Hackett.

Ten Classics (1963). *Suanjing shishu. Qian baocong jiaodian* (critical punctuated edition of *The Ten Classics of Mathematics*). 2 Vols. Zhonghua Shuju.

Thomson, J. F. (1960). 'What Achilles Should Have Said to the Tortoise'. *Ratio*, 3, 95–105.

Urquhart, A. (1988). Review of *Relevant Logics and their Rivals: Part 1*, *Studia Logica*, June 1988, 47(2), pp.168–71.

Vision, Gerald (2003). 'Lest We Forget "the Correspondence Theory of Truth"'. *Analysis*, 63, 136–42.

Von Wright, G. H. (1974). *Causality and Determinism*. New York: Columbia University Press.

Walker, Ralph (1975). 'Conversational Implicatures'. In Blackburn, S. (ed.). *Meaning, Reference and Necessity*. Cambridge: Cambridge University Press.

Walker, Ralph (1989). *The Coherence Theory of Truth*. London: Routledge.

Walker, Ralph (1997). 'Theories of Truth'. In Hale, Bob and Wright, Crispin (eds). *A Companion to the Philosophy of Language*, pp.309–30. Oxford: Blackwell.

Walker, Ralph (2001). 'The Coherence Theory'. In Lynch (2001), pp. 123–58.

Wertheimer, R. (1968). 'Conditions'. *Journal of Philosophy*, 65, 355–64.

Wheen, Francis (2004). *How Mumbo-Jumbo Conquered the World*. London: Fourth Estate.

Williams, Bernard (2002). *Truth and Truthfulness: An Essay in Genealogy*. Princeton, NJ: Princeton University Press.

Williamson, Timothy (1994). *Vagueness*. London: Routledge.

Wilson, Ian R. (1979). 'Explanatory and Inferential Conditionals'. *Philosophical Studies*, 35, 269–78.

Wittgenstein, Ludwig (1953). *Philosophical Investigations*. Anscombe, G. E. M. and Rhees, R. (eds) (trans. Anscombe). Oxford: Blackwell.

Wittgenstein, Ludwig (1961). *Tractatus Logico-Philosophicus*. London: Routledge.

Wittgenstein, Ludwig (1979). *Notebooks 1914–1916* (rev. 2nd ed.). Oxford: Blackwell.

Wittgenstein, Ludwig (1980). *Remarks on the Philosophy of Psychology*. Oxford: Blackwell.

Woods, M., Wiggins, D. and Edgington, D. (eds) (1997). *Conditionals*. Oxford: Clarendon Press.

INDEX

INDEX